The Counseling Practicum and Internship Manual

A Resource for Graduate Counseling Students

Shannon Hodges, PhD, LMHC, ACS is an associate professor of Clinical Mental Health Counseling and director of Clinical Training at Antioch University, New England. He has 16 years' experience counseling in community agencies and university counseling centers. He is a former director of a university counseling center and clinical director of a county mental health clinic, and has another 10 years' experience supervising collegiate living groups. In addition, he has 18 years' experience teaching school counselors, mental health counselors, and undergraduate psychology students. He has authored numerous professional publications, including books, book chapters, journal articles, and essays. He has also served on the editorial review boards of several journals including the *Journal of Counseling and Development, Journal of Counseling and Values, Journal of Mental Health Counseling,* and the *Journal of College Counseling.* He has been awarded both for his teaching and his writing. Dr. Hodges is a longtime member of the American Counseling Association (ACA), the American Mental Health Counselors Association (AMHCA), and several ACA affiliate divisions. He has also just published a mystery novel with a counselor as the main character (*City of Shadows,* Athena Press). When he is not teaching or writing, he enjoys reading, jogging, and traveling to remote areas of the globe. He and his wife, Shoshanna, live along the shores of Lake Champlain in Burlington, Vermont.

The Counseling Practicum and Internship Manual

A Resource for Graduate Counseling Students

Shannon Hodges, PhD, LMHC, ACS

SPRINGER PUBLISHING COMPANY

NEW YORK

Springer Publishing Company, LLC
11 West 42nd Street
New York, NY 10036
www.springerpub.com

Acquisitions Editor: Jennifer Perillo
Production Editor: Gayle Lee
Cover Design: Steven Pisano
Project Manager: Gil Rafanan
Composition: Absolute Service, Inc.

ISBN: 978-0-8261-1832-5
E-book ISBN: 978-0-8261-1833-2

13/ 9 8

The author and the publisher of this work have made every effort to use sources believed to be reliable to provide information that is accurate and compatible with the standards generally accepted at the time of publication. Because medical science is continually advancing, our knowledge base continues to expand. Therefore, as new information becomes available, changes in procedures become necessary. We recommend that the reader always consult current research and specific institutional policies before performing any clinical procedure. The author and publisher shall not be liable for any special, consequential, or exemplary damages resulting, in whole or in part, from the readers' use of, or reliance on, the information contained in this book. The publisher has no responsibility for the persistence or accuracy of URLs for external or third-party Internet Web sites referred to in this publication and does not guarantee that any content on such Web sites is, or will remain, accurate or appropriate.

Library of Congress Cataloging-in-Publication Data
Hodges, Shannon.
 The counseling practicum and internship manual : a resource for graduate counseling students/
 Shannon Hodges.
  p. cm.
 ISBN 978-0-8261-1832-5
 1. Counseling—Study and teaching (Internship) 2. Counseling—Vocational guidance. I. Title.
 BF636.65.H63 2010
 361'.060711—dc22
                        2010023336

Special discounts on bulk quantities of our books are available to corporations, professional associations, pharmaceutical companies, health care organization, and other qualifying groups.

If you are interested in a custom book, including chapters from more than one of our titles, we can provide that service as well.

For details, please contact:
Special Sales Department, Springer Publishing Company, LLC
11 West 42nd Street, 15th Floor, New York, NY 10036-8002
Phone: 877-687-7476 or 212-431-4370; Fax: 212-941-7842
Email: sales@springerpub.com

Printed in the United States of America by Edwards Brothers Malloy

In Memory of Michael T. "Maz" Mazurchuk
September 22, 1958–June 13, 2009

He knocked on the door of my office while poking his head inside the doorway. "Got a minute?" asked the burly, unfamiliar man, his broad face sporting a smile as wide as the Niagara Gorge. As he entered my office, I could not help but notice his exaggerated, staggering mode of locomotion. "Mike Mazurchuk," he said, thrusting forth a strong hand. Besides his clear movement disability, brought on by cerebral palsy, he was sporting the distinctive black cassock and white collar of a Roman Catholic priest. This was my first introduction to Fr. Michael T. Mazurchuk, or Maz as he was affectionately known to everyone at Niagara University. He went on to say that he was interested in enrolling in the graduate mental health counseling program. Would he have a good chance at admission? After meeting with Maz for half an hour, I decided he would indeed be a very good fit for our program.

For 3 years, Maz was my advisee and student. He was an outstanding student, one any professor would recall with fondness. Not only was he academically gifted, but he also had the rare ability to bridge cultural, religious, social, sexual, and gender chasms to create community with a diverse mosaic of people. Maz's ability to connect with wounded, angry, and grieving clients was exceptional—so exceptional that all the agencies he interned with wanted to hire him. After graduation, his order moved him to Philadelphia to counsel low-income families. "I love my work with the underprivileged," he said to me just a few months before his untimely death. "Basically, it's all about justice and the lack of it. Our job as counselors is to help make the world a little more just."

A little over a year later, I received the shocking news that he died from a viral infection that spread to his heart. As a result of cerebral palsy, Maz had long learned to "push through" a disability that would have shelved many others. This same determination to keep going ultimately contributed to his death, because he was just too busy helping others to stop for treatment. To the very end of his life, he remained dedicated to the downtrodden and dispossessed, through counseling, advocacy, and bull-headed determination in the face of overwhelming odds. Maz was a tireless advocate, a person filled with unconditional love, a priest in the very best sense of the term, and what every counselor should strive to become. Rest peacefully, Maz. One day, we will all join you.

Author's Note: A percentage of the sales of this text will be donated to the Michael T. Mazurchuk Memorial Scholarship fund at Niagara University. The scholarship will assist graduate students in counseling to continue their studies.

Contents

Preface

This text originated from my interest in and commitment to promoting the counseling profession as separate and distinct from related fields, such as social work and psychology. Many practicum and internship texts combine discussions of these noble professions in an amalgamation that blurs the numerous boundaries that exist between them. My intention is to offer a counselors practicum and internship manual to be used specifically in graduate counselor education programs.

As a professional counselor and counselor educator who has supervised numerous professional counselors in the field and graduate counseling students, I believe it is essential that our profession maintain a distinction from the related fields of psychology and social work. Having made this statement regarding distinctiveness, I wish to emphasize that I have nothing but respect for professional psychologists and social workers and the excellent work they do in the mental health field. At the same time, the counseling profession must take the lead in educating, promoting, and advocating for itself. Of the three professions, counseling is the only one that primarily trains students in the practice of counseling. Although psychology and social work programs certainly do an excellent job in educating and training future psychologists and social workers, counseling is an ancillary, as opposed to a primary, function for professionals in those fields.

I struggled to develop this book for several years, toying with various outlines and then promptly consigning them to the recycle bin. Finally, in the winter of 2009, I became more serious and developed a prospectus for publication, and the people at Springer Publishing Company were interested enough to take me up on my desire to publish this book. As a child, I recall Rev. Stanley Cooper, our minister, preaching on the topic of "Be careful what you wish for." Brother Stanley was more accurate than I could ever have imagined, as writing a book is very hard work indeed (at least it is for me!).

Naturally, your practicum and internship experience will vary greatly depending on your specialization (i.e., school versus mental health counseling), the type of placement (e.g., inpatient, outpatient, public versus private school, etc.), your particular supervisor, and the beliefs, attitudes, and experiences you bring to practicum and internship. Because the practicum/internship is the backbone of any counseling program, I encourage you to make the most of your experience by being proactive. Ask questions of your supervisor, take advantage of any training your practicum/internship site offers, and be willing to ask for assistance when you feel you need it. I also encourage my students to "make mistakes" because that suggests you are trying to stretch your skills and learn. It is crucial that you reflect on and learn from your mistakes so that you will be less likely to repeat them.

I would like to share my own practicum/internship experience in the hope that it proves illustrative. From the winter of 1986 through late spring of 1987, I had a very challenging and rewarding practicum and internship at a small college counseling center at what was then known as Western Oregon State College (now Western Oregon University). The college, then with an enrollment of some 3,000 students, was a close-knit community, where relationships were strong and virtually everyone knew everyone else. The practicum/internship provided a complete therapeutic experience involving providing individual, group, and the occasional couples counseling, career advising, psychoeducational workshops, resident advisor training, crisis intervention, guest speaking in undergraduate classes, and teaching a 2-hour course for "reentry" students. (Reentry students were those returning to college after an extended absence.) The experience was often intense and required considerable reading, viewing videos, attending meetings and providing advocacy for students.

Each week, the director, Dr. Merlin Darby, who was a very skilled and encouraging supervisor, would lead a staff meeting wherein the five interns would take turns presenting difficult cases. Everyone would critique the intern who presented the case. The director was popular, very experienced, and had a knack for coming up with key phrases that assisted my fellow interns and I in seeing angles previously hidden from view. Although we were not always comfortable in presenting cases, the director was very considerate and temperate in his critique. Each week, it seemed, that I learned something constructive that I had previously lacked. The meeting would occasionally include a representative from the medical staff providing medical consultation.

In addition to operations within the counseling center, I was frequently called on to consult with faculty, student affairs staff, and parents. Our offices, although decidedly not fancy, were spacious, with ample bookshelves, comfortable furniture, and tasteful throw rugs to accent the décor. The support staff was generally very supportive and seemed to value our work. For me, the internship placement was almost ideal. I felt myself a key component of the campus and a valued member of the counseling staff. Then one day in late spring, I completed my internship and later graduated from the Oregon State University Counselor Education program.

My entry into full-time community counseling work was an abrupt wake-up call into the baser realities of the profession. Suddenly, I was working in a residential psychiatric center, on what was a swing shift during the week with a double shift on Saturdays. I had no real office, as we operated on milieu treatment, with an entirely group focus. As the newest member of the treatment team, I felt like an outsider and although the staff was courteous, the center was not the homey, close-knit pleasant environment that the college counseling center was. Our clients, who were called *patients*, were typically of three types: adolescents placed in the center by their families for psychiatric care, those adjudicated by the juvenile court system, or children or adolescents discharged from the state psychiatric hospital. Unlike the college population, they were oppositional, often defiant—hardened by serious physical, sexual, and emotional abuse, and parental neglect—unhappy to be there, and definitely uninterested in what treatment we could provide. To top it off, the psychiatric center forced me to work with a behavioral type program when I considered myself a humanistic, client-centered counselor.

I was overwhelmed, frustrated, and unhappy with my job, and wondering if I had made a mistake in entering the field. I longed for the comfy confines of a college campus, where I could be part of a learning environment dedicated to supporting students well on their way to fulfilling their dreams, not a residential center where much of my efforts involved confronting sex offenders and violent adolescents. Needing advice, I sought out my former supervisor Dr. Darby at the college counseling center. He listened patiently, then explained that most counselors do not begin by working in college centers, but in treatment facilities like the one in which I currently worked. He encouraged me to stick the job out until I found something else and challenged me to see the potential in the tough kids I counseled.

In a short time, I found my former supervisor's counsel very wise. Soon, I began to get along better with the staff and my relationships with many of the patients improved. I also came to feel that the job was far more demanding of me emotionally, psychologically, and required far more therapeutic skills than my internship. In time, even the behavioral system began to make real sense to me as it provided needed structure in the adolescents' lives. I still preferred working with college students (who can be quite challenging themselves!), but I had learned the value of broader clinical experience. The entire experience forced me to grow and adapt in ways I could not have previously imagined.

I mention my personal story to illustrate a broader point. Namely, many graduate counseling students complete their practicum/internship in an environment where they feel secure, challenged, respected, and safe. Then the experience ends and they are released into a broader, sometimes less-certain, and perhaps "scarier" environment. In my nearly 25 years of experience in the field, I have discovered my own rocky beginnings are very common for many recent graduates of counseling programs.

A more salient point to my story is that I have come to see my former job at the psychiatric center as a critical link in my beginnings as a professional counselor. Had it not been for the intense struggles the job required, I wonder if I would have developed the resilience needed for more in-depth psychotherapeutic work. The demands of a residential psychiatric center counseling a population resistant to therapeutic intervention was likely the best thing that could have happened to my career. But at the time, because I was experiencing so many struggles, I could not have known that.

Regardless of your own professional experiences, I hope you will find this text to be helpful and illuminating regarding your path toward becoming a professional counselor. Although we have many specialties and divisions in our field, we are indeed one profession. So, welcome to the profession of counseling! I wish all of you a long, meaningful journey full of both challenge and fulfillment.

Shannon Hodges

Acknowledgments

A lot of work goes into writing a book. In my undergraduate days, I imagined writing books, articles, and so forth, to be exciting, exotic work (yes, I was *very* naïve!). The past 2 decades, however, have taught me that writing involves far more perspiration than inspiration. Still, for those of us who write—regardless of *what* we write—there is something in the process that I would call alluring. Speaking for myself, the topics of books occur to me at odd moments then take long periods of dormancy before the concept emerges into full creation.

Writing a book also takes a lot of people behind the scenes, providing opportunity, encouragement, and critique. I wish to thank my wife Shoshanna for continuing to encourage me in my writing endeavors. Also, I send a hearty thanks to the people at Springer Publishing Company, especially Jennifer Perillo, for providing me the opportunity to write and publish this book. I hope you will find your faith in me well founded.

CHAPTER 1

Introduction to the Counseling Profession and the Practicum/Internship

Congratulations! You have completed a portion of your graduate program in counseling and are preparing for practicum! The practicum and internship experience is the backbone of any counseling program. It is likely you are experiencing a variety of emotions: enthusiasm, anxiety, anticipation, uncertainty, and many others. Regardless of the amount of classroom preparation you already have, starting your initial practicum will be unlike any other academic experience.

Beginning a practicum/internship represents a major step in your development. Although previously you may have practiced in-class techniques with peers and made DVDs of mock sessions with friends, you will now begin actual counseling. In my experience, this tends to be the most stressful experience in the curriculum. Although students may have mastered the individual techniques, and performed well in mock counseling sessions, establishing a therapeutic relationship with actual clients requires a different skill set. The initial experience at the onset of practicum can leave the most resilient of students feeling overwhelmed by the nature of the counseling relationship.

The practicum and internship are important because instead of reading about, for example, depression, acting out behavior, alcoholism, and bipolar disorder, you will actually be assisting real people struggling with these and other developmental and/or mental health issues. You will also receive an education in the inner workings of your field setting—whether a school, mental health or addictions agency, or residential psychiatric center. You will encounter numerous counseling professionals, who will demonstrate various approaches to their work (e.g., Cognitive–Behavioral Therapy [CBT], client-centered, Dialectical Behavioral Therapy [DBT], etc.). Ethical and legal issues will be paramount; it is hoped that you will receive training in crisis intervention, the chain of command in the event of a trauma, and how to deal with litigation, among other issues.

You may be wondering, "How can I survive my practicum and internship?" The goal of this book is to provide orientation and guidance to help you successfully navigate your field placement. First, this chapter will discuss various general issues regarding the counseling profession itself; then it will offer a brief overview of the practicum/internship process. Future chapters will discuss many of these issues in more detail. But, as first things should come first, let us review some basics of the counseling profession.

IDENTITY

Since the origins of the counseling profession in 1952, most counselors have held membership in American Counseling Association (ACA). As an organization, the composition of ACA has been mixed, "like a ball of multicolored yarn," and sometimes within ACA there has been an emphasis within the specialties of counseling as opposed to the overall profession (Bradley & Cox, 2001, p. 39). "Other professions such as medicine have overcome the divisiveness that comes within a profession where there is more than one professional track that practitioners can follow. ACA has not been as fortunate" (Gladding, 2009, pp. 26–27).

However as the counseling profession has grown stronger, achieved licensure in all states and territories, and been more accepted by the public, ACA has begun to benefit for this progression. The recent 20/20 initiative, *Principles for Unifying and Strengthening the Profession* (2010), involving 29 counseling organizations represent a key step toward professional unity. The 20/20 initiative includes long-range planning and solidified leadership working toward common goals across all 29 counseling organizations. Though this major step toward unification has taken far longer than some would like, it provides a blueprint for future growth and continued unity. As a graduate student reading this text, you will be called on to play a major role in the development of a unified counseling profession. Although there are numerous choices and options beginning counselors can make to enhance the profession, this author recommends the following:

1. As the ACA is *the* flagship organization; all counselors, regardless of counseling specialty, should hold membership their entire professional lifetime;
2. All counselors should also hold a membership in their specialty area. For example, school counselors should maintain membership in the American School Counselor Association (ASCA), mental health counselors should join the American Mental Health Counselors Association (AMHCA), and so forth.
3. All counselors should join their respective state counseling organization. State organizations assist ACA and other national affiliate organizations with lobbying on the state and local level. This ensures a stronger counseling presence at the state level and helps strengthen ACA, ACSA, AMHCA, and other national organizations.

If beginning counselors reading this text will simply do the above, they will help the counseling profession achieve parity with their mental health colleagues in psychology and social work.

Because the counseling profession is broad—encompassing ACA, 19 affiliate organizations, and other such as the National Board for Certified Counselors (NBCC) and the Council for Accreditation of Counseling and Related Educational Programs (CACREP) and others—unity will always be a work in progress. Still, as readers are the counseling profession's future, I am optimistic the profession will be far more unified in the future.

Definition of Professional Counseling

Though it is likely most readers of this text have studied counseling in-depth, some may not have come across a precise definition of "counseling." Until recently, there was no consensus on how counseling was to be defined. While most definitions of counseling likely were more similar than different, strength tends to come in precision, especially in defining the term forming the cornerstone of our profession (i.e., counseling). Fortunately, delegates of the groundbreaking "20/20: A Vision for the Future of Counseling" arrived at the following succinct definition of counseling at the 2010 national conference of the ACA: "Counseling is a professional relationship that empowers diverse individuals, families, and groups to accomplish mental health, wellness, education and career goals" (Linde, 2010; May, 1981, p. 5).

Who we are as a profession is clearly crucial to our identity as professional counselors, and having a common definition is a very important step for the counseling profession.

Maturation of a Profession

The counseling profession has come a long way since its creation in 1952. The first state to pass counselor licensure was the state of Virginia in 1976, and now with the passage of California counselor licensure, all 50 states, Washington DC, and Puerto Rico have enacted counselor licensure. This achievement especially in the face of opposing mental health professions, represents a major accomplishment. Regardless of the feat, there are still a few goals the counseling profession is working toward.

Consensus on how counseling is defined represents a critical point for the profession; otherwise, what type of an organized profession cannot agree on how its name sake is defined? Cashwell (2010) refers to the "20/20: A Vision for the Future of Counseling" initiative as "maturation of a profession" (p. 58) from adolescence into early adulthood. Cashwell also breaks down this growth process into several recognizable benchmarks that have recently been met:

"The passage of California Senate Bill 788, resulting in California becoming the 50th U.S. state with counselor licensure.

Regulations implementing the Mental Health Parity Act and Addiction Equity Act of 2008, essentially mandating that insurance companies use the same limits and cost-sharing requirements for mental health and addiction services as used for other services.

Results of the Institute of Medicine's TRICARE study, which recommended removing physician referral and supervision requirements for counselors' services, ultimately paving the way for independent practice for professional counselors under the Department of Defense's TRICARE program.

There is *one* organization, the ACA, that serves as our professional membership organization.

There is *one* accrediting body, CACREP, that serves to promote professional counselor preparation.

There is *one* organization, the American Association of State Counseling Boards, involved in the organization of state licensure boards, which regulate the practice of counseling.

There is *one* national credentialing body, the NBCC, that monitors voluntary national certification of counselors.

Today, the number of CACREP-accredited programs is rapidly approaching 600, with CACREP now integrated into the language of many state licensure laws (Cashwell, 2010, p. 58).

He goes on further to express there are still several making points before the counseling profession reaches full adulthood. There are:

Far too few professional counselors are members of ACA. Counselor educators should encourage ACA membership among students as a commitment to lifelong learning and professional growth, not as a short-term requirement or a way to get liability insurance.

Licensure regulations, often initially written in ways necessary to glean passage of laws in the face of oppositional lobbying, should be reviewed by state boards with a focus on strengthening professional identity. In many states, it is far too easy for people with professional identities other than that of counselor to become licensed. Licensure regulations that ensure that licensees are trained and identify as professional counselors will greatly strengthen the Counseling profession" (Cashwell, 2010, p. 58).

Medicare: The Counseling Profession's Next Frontier

Probably the biggest hurdle remaining for the counseling profession is achieving the privilege of billing Medicare. Counselors currently are not approved to bill Medicare. For this to change, the U.S. Congress must pass federal legislation to be send to the president to sign such legislation into law. The counseling profession has come very close, seeing passage of a bill in both the House of Representatives and the Senate at separate times. Though efforts to gain Medicare billing privileges have not been successful, the counseling profession is consistently getting its message before the House and Senate and approval is a matter of time. To assist the counseling profession in clearing this major hurdle, graduate counseling students should join ACA (and their affiliate professional organization, e.g., ASCA, AMHCA, etc.) and inquire of their faculty as to how to lobby congress. Also, the ACA Web site has made lobbying senators and congressional representative very easy and convenient. Simply go to the ACA's Web site (www.counseling.org/), then click on the "Public Policy" link, then the link titled "Legislative Update," which will offer several options including one for lobbying congress on Medicare reimbursement for counselors. I would encourage every graduate student reading this text to use ACA's Web site to contact and lobby their senators and congressional representatives to support counselors in gaining Medicare billing privileges.

It must also be mentioned that some counseling students may be placed in a practicum or internship where they are being supervised by a mental health professional who is a social worker, psychologist, marriage and family therapist, and so forth. Your supervisor may oppose the counseling's effort to gain Medicare privileges. If they do oppose this, treat them with respect even though you will disagree with their position on this issue. Remember, you are in a vulnerable position with regard to your relationship with your field supervisor and will likely need a letter of reference when you are applying for a job. In addition, developing the ability to dialogue, or at the very least to disagree respectfully, is one of the most useful skills you can develop.

PROFESSIONAL COUNSELING ORGANIZATIONS

As a graduate student in a counseling program, it is important for you to understand that you are becoming a part of a larger profession. In addition to your graduate counseling department, there are local, state, national, and international counseling organizations that you may become involved with. Professional activity is essential for the health and well-being of the counseling profession. Many of these organizations also play an important role in the practicum and internship process.

Throughout this book, I will mention organizations such as the ACA, the ASCA, the AMHCA, the American Rehabilitation Counseling Association (ARCA), and others which represent the counseling profession. These professional organizations advocate and lobby for the profession, offer professional standards and guidance, and publish helpful journals, books, DVDs, and more. For this reason, it is my strong opinion that all professional counselors and graduate students should purchase a membership in ACA (and/or ASCA, AMHCA, ARCA, etc.). I will primarily advocate for membership because ACA is the national umbrella organization and it is my belief that all counselors should be members. In addition, I would encourage counselors (and graduate counseling students) to maintain membership in their specialty area, whether that area is in school counseling, mental health counseling, rehabilitation counseling, and so forth. Keeping an active membership with these organizations is an investment in the profession's future. Failure to maintain professional membership is akin to divesting in the professional stock of the very profession you have worked so hard to enter. So, keep your membership current; it will provide both you and the field important dividends.

Over the following sections, I will briefly describe some of the key organizations that you will likely encounter as a student or over the course of your
professional career.

American Counseling Association

The flagship organization for counseling is the ACA. ACA was founded in 1952
as the American Personnel and Guidance Association (APGA) and much later
was renamed to more accurately reflect the organization (Gladding, 2009). The
ACA has some 44,000 members, making it the world's largest counseling organization. ACA has 19 divisional affiliates including the aforementioned ASCA,
ARCA, AMHCA, and many more. For a complete list of ACA divisions, as well as
other relevant counseling associations, see Appendix A. For students in a graduate counseling program, the *ACA Code of Ethics* (ACA, 2005) is the primary ethical code; however, the ASCA has a separate ethical code, as does the AMHCA,
ARCA, and all ACA-affiliate organizations.

Although you may have studied ethical and legal issues in an ethics course,
it has been my experience as a counselor field supervisor and counselor educator that graduate students cannot read enough about ethical issues. Therefore,
throughout this book I will refer to the ACA's code of ethics (and occasionally
those of the ASCA, AMHCA, etc.). Furthermore, although other books may discuss the ethical codes of other professions (such as the American Psychological
Association or the National Association of Social Workers), it is my intent to keep
the discussion specific to counseling codes of ethics. The *ACA Code of Ethics* and
the *ASCA Code of Ethics* are reprinted in full with permission in Appendix B and
Appendix C.

One of the more challenging learning curves for student counselors
involves the integration and use of this code. As a student, you will be treated
as a professional and, as such, will be expected to apply your professional
ethics to situations involving clients in the practicum and internship setting.
My recommendation is for all counseling students to read their code of ethics
prior to beginning practicum. As a student and future professional, you will
be held responsible for maintaining practice consistent with your professional
ethical code.

Professional ethical codes are not meant to be exact roadmaps, but rather
exist as a guide to assist counseling professionals in making decisions in the best
interests of their clients (Wheeler & Bertram, 2008). For example, you have been
counseling Yvonne, a fourth-grade girl struggling with her parents' divorce. Her
teacher asks you how Yvonne is doing in counseling, expressing that she wants
to help. You feel caught between your desire to protect confidentiality and at the
same time be helpful. Based on your understanding of the ACA or *ASCA Code of
Ethics*, how would you proceed?

This is the type of situation students will face while on practicum and
internship. Students frequently are dismayed to learn that ethical codes are not

written in stone—rather, they are living documents, shaped by court decisions, legislative initiatives, and professional changes. A more thorough exploration of legal and ethical issues will be covered in chapter 3.

Council for Accreditation of Counseling and Related Educational Programs

The CACREP sets standards for many professional counseling education programs. CACREP guidelines include the required parameters for practicum and internships for counseling students in Addiction Counseling; Career Counseling; Clinical Mental Health Counseling; Marriage, Couple, and Family Counseling; School Counseling; Student Affairs and College Counseling; and Counselor Education and Supervision (CACREP Web site, 2009; for a complete list of CACREP accredited counseling programs, go to http://www.cacrep.org/directory/directory.cfm).

Some related programs are not accredited by CACREP. The Commission on Accreditation for Marriage and Family Therapy Education (COAMFTE), established by the American Association for Marriage and Family Therapy, is the accrediting agency for clinical programs in Marriage and Family Therapy, which are separate from Marriage and Family Counseling program accredited by CACREP (for a complete list of COAMFTE accredited programs, go to www.aamft.org/cgi-shl/twserver.exe?run:COALIST).

The Council on Rehabilitation Education (CORE) is the accreditation organization for rehabilitation counseling programs (for a complete list of CORE accredited programs, go to http://www.core-rehab.org/progrec.html).

CACREP has set forth practicum and internship criteria for graduate counseling programs, which will be discussed later in this chapter.

National Board for Certified Counselors

The NBCC is a voluntary organization that credentials counselors (NBCC, 2009). Most counselors who earn a credential from NBCC are National Certified Counselors (NCC) or Certified Clinical Mental Health Counselors (CCMHC; for a complete list of all NBCC certifications, go to www.nbcc.org).

Certification, unlike licensure, is an optional credential. However, students should be aware that most state licensure boards have adopted one of the NBCC's examinations as the state licensure examination. Some states use the National Counselor Examination (NCE), whereas others use the National Clinical Mental Health Counselor Examination (NCMHCE). The Certified Rehabilitation Counselor Examination (CRCE) is administered by Commission on Rehabilitation Counselor Certification (CRCC), a separate organization from NBCC.

The NBCC awards the designation of NCC or CCMHC to counseling professionals who successfully pass the examination. (Applicants from a CACREP accredited program may take the NCE or CCMHC in their final semester of their counseling program.) The NBCC also awards counseling credentials in specialty areas of counseling including career, gerontological, school, clinical mental health, and addictions counseling. These specialty area certifications require additional course work and professional experience as well as the passage of an examination. Counselors seeking certification in a counseling specialty area must first obtain the NCC certificate.

Council on Rehabilitation Education

CORE sets the standards and qualifications for becoming a Certified Rehabilitation Counselor (CRC). Applicants who have completed a CORE-accredited master's degree program are eligible to take the CRC examination upon graduation. Applicants from non-CORE–accredited programs must complete a 600-hour internship supervised by a CRC and additional employment under the supervision of a CRC. The CORE requirements for practicum and internship will be covered later in this chapter.

Because I have mentioned various national counseling organizations, I have provided a list of the 19 ACA affiliate organizations, plus an additional organization:

Divisions and Affiliates with the American Counseling Association (ACA):

American College Counseling Association (ACCA)
American Mental Health Counselors Association (AMHCA)
American Rehabilitation Counseling Association (ARCA)
American School Counselor Association (ASCA)
Association for Adult Development and Aging (AADA)
Association for Assessment in Counseling (AACE)
Association for Counselor Education and Supervision (ACES)
Association for Counselors and Educators in Government (ACEG)
Association for Creativity in Counseling (ACC)
Association for Lesbian, Gay, Bisexual, and Transgender Issues in
    Counseling (ALGBTIC)
Association for Multicultural Counseling and Development (AMCD)
Association for Specialists in Group Work (ASGW)
Association for Spiritual, Ethical, and Religious Values in Counseling
    (ASERVIC)
Counseling Association for Humanistic Education and Development
    (C-AHEAD)
Counselors for Social Justice (CSJ)
International Association of Addictions and Offender Counselors
    (IAAOC)
International Association of Marriage and Family Counselors
    (IAMFC)
National Career Development Association (NCDA)
National Employment Counseling Association (NCEA)

I will also add:

International Association for Counselling (IAC)

Be aware of your own ACA divisional affiliate and changes they may make for the future. For example, all school counselors should be aware of ASCA's National Model titled, *The Role of a Professional School Counselor* (2004), that states that appropriate activities for school counselors include "working with one student at a time in a therapeutic, clinical mode" (Kraus, Kleist, & Cashwell, 2009, p. 60). ASCA's National Model also defines a school counselor as "a certified licensed educator trained in school counseling with unique qualifications and skills to address all students' academic, personal/social and career development needs" (Kraus et al. p. 60). Now, I mention the ASCA National Model because, along with the 20/20 initiative mentioned earlier, it represents one of the more significant changes in the counseling profession. All students enrolled in school counseling programs should be aware of the ASCA National Model and how it impacts their future roles as professional school counselors. It is likely that other national affiliate organizations of ACA will, like ASCA, undertake major efforts to define their professional scope of practice. This is another reason counselors should hold professional memberships as they are then more likely to maintain an awareness of changes within their profession.

GETTING LICENSED

To protect public safety, states have established licensure for various mental health professionals, including social workers, marriage and family therapists, and, of course, counselors. Professional counselors are now licensed in all 50 states, the District of Columbia, and Puerto Rico. Licensure laws establish minimum standards for counseling and related mental health professions. Each state and territory has a licensure board responsible for issuing licenses, handling ethical complaints regarding potential counselor malpractice, and enforcing state regulations regarding the practice of counseling. In some states, one board is responsible for overseeing the practice of counseling as well as social work, marriage and family therapy, and so forth.

Licensure is the primary credential you will seek as it will be required for professional practice, billing insurance, diagnosing and treating mental disorders, and other requirements of professional practice. The basic state licensure requirements are listed in Appendix D. For a complete list of state-by-state requirements, check the *Licensure Requirements for Professional Counselors*, published and updated annually by the ACA (2010).

Within the United States, a number of different titles are used to identify licensed professional counselors. The following are among the most common:

- Licensed Professional Counselor (LPC)
- Licensed Mental Health Counselor (LMHC)
- Licensed Clinical Professional Counselor (LCPC)
- Licensed Clinical Mental Health Counselor (LCMHC)

Obtaining licensure is usually a three-step process. The first step involves completion of a master's degree in counseling. The second requires the accumulation of the state required number of post-master's clock hours while supervised by a licensed mental health professional (e.g., licensed counselor, social worker, psychologist, psychiatrist, etc.). Most states require individuals to accumulate between 2,000 and 3,000 supervised clock hours. Finally, the individual must pass the required counselor examination. Some of the examinations are the following:

- NCE—administered by the NBCC, this is the most common examination used by states for licensure.
- NCMHCE—also administered by the NBCC, this examination focuses more specifically on mental health practice and is used by a smaller number of states as the licensure examination.
- CRCE—administered by the CRCC, passage of this examination is also accepted in some states for licensure of rehabilitation counselors.
- Examination for Clinical Counselor Practice (ECCP)—also administered by NBCC, passage of the ECCP is required to obtain the CCMHC credential issued by NBCC (passage of the NCMHCE is also accepted). Currently, two states accept passage of the ECCP as their state licensure examination: Illinois and North Carolina.

Because of the many variations in counselor licensure among states, I recommend *Licensure Requirements for Professional Counselors* (ACA, 2010). This text provides licensure requirements for all 50 states and territories, including required counseling program, credit hours, licensure examination, post-master's supervision hours, whether a temporary permit is required prior to licensure, and so forth.

OCCUPATIONAL OUTLOOK FOR COUNSELORS

The counseling profession has expanded considerably in the past 50 years. Originally, counselors worked primarily in schools, college career centers, and in public and private agencies devoted to career or vocational guidance. Today, counselors work in a broad variety of settings, including schools, addiction treatment centers, residential psychiatric centers and hospitals, college and university counseling centers, rehabilitation clinics, and many more. The U.S. Bureau of Labor Statistics (BLS; 2010) estimates that in 2010, there were 665,500 professional counselors, and this will grow to an estimated 782,200 by 2018 (BLS, n.d.). Although all specialties of counseling are expected to grow, some will increase more dramatically than others (see Table 1.1).

As you can see from Table 1.1, the future of employment in the counseling profession is very promising. My recommendation is that you stay current of the

TABLE 1.1	Projections Data From the National Employment Matrix		
OCCUPATIONAL TITLE	**EMPLOYED IN 2008**	**PROJECTED EMPLOYED IN 2018**	**% CHANGE**
Counselors (all)	655,500	782,200	+18
Breakdown by specialty area:			
Substance abuse and behavioral disorder counselors	86,100	104,200	+21
Educational, vocational, and school counselors	275,800	314,400	+14
Marriage and family therapists	27,300	31,300	+14
Mental health counselors	113,300	140,400	+24
Rehabilitation counselors	129,500	154,100	+19
All other counselors	33,400	37,800	+13

Source: Data from Bureau of Labor Statistics, n.d.

always-shifting employment landscape by regularly reviewing the employment outlook in your area, state, and region. BLS updates occupational projections every 2 years (you can review their findings online at www.bls.gov and search on "counselors").

PRACTICUM VERSUS INTERNSHIP

Faculty, counseling literature, field supervisors, and counseling students will often use the terms *practicum* and *internship* interchangeably. There are, however, some important distinctions between these terms. In this text, we will consider practicum to be the first field placement for counseling students. Compared to the internship, the practicum typically requires fewer *clock hours* (the total number of hours the student is required to complete) and fewer *direct client contact hours* (hours where the student is in direct contact with clients). Practicum is, in a sense, a "pre-internship" to determine if the student is appropriate to proceed to internship.

Internship, on the other hand, begins the semester after the practicum has been completed and requires more clock hours and more direct client contact hours. Most counseling programs usually require one semester of practicum and three semesters of internship. (For counseling programs on the quarter system, internship may be spread over four to five quarters.)

Most of the guidance and information presented throughout this book will apply equally to the practicum and/or internship; thus, the term *practicum/ internship* will typically be used to refer to the field placement. When a distinction between the two is necessary, it will be made.

PRACTICUM/INTERNSHIP REQUIREMENTS

Because practicum and internship are so different from the typical classroom, students may naturally be confused regarding the requirements for successful completion.

All CACREP-accredited counseling programs must follow specific guidelines for the practicum and internship experience (CACREP, 2009 Standards).

For practicum:

- A clinical placement in a particular field setting (school, agency, treatment center, etc.)
- A minimum of 100 clock hours over a minimum 10-week academic term
- At least 40 clock hours of direct service with actual clients
- Weekly interaction that averages 1 hour per week of supervision throughout the practicum by a program faculty member, a student supervisor, or a site supervisor who is working in biweekly consultation with a program faculty member
- An average of 1.5 hours per week of group supervision that is provided on a regular schedule throughout the practicum by a program faculty member or a student supervisor
- Evaluation of the student's counseling performance throughout the practicum, including a formal evaluation after the student completes the practicum

Note: For the practicum experience, a triadic model of supervision is often encouraged. In the triadic model of supervision, three roles are specified: the supervisor, the supervisee, and the role of observer (Boylan & Scott, 2009). The supervisor's role is conducted by the field site supervisor, who directly observes the practicum student's work through cocounseling and reviewing tapes or DVDs. The supervisor then provides ongoing feedback in as 1 hour weekly setting.

The supervisees are, naturally, the practicum students, who meet in the weekly classroom setting with the university instructor assigned to the small group practicum.

The observers are one supervisee and the instructor who provide critique to the second supervisee in a triad meeting of the on-campus practicum group.

For internship:

- The same type of clinical placement as practicum
- 600 clock hours, begun after successful completion of the practicum

- At least 240 clock hours of direct service, including experience leading groups
- Weekly interaction that averages 1 hour per week of supervision throughout the internship, usually performed by the on-site supervisor
- An average of 1.5 hours per week of group supervision provided on a regular schedule throughout the internship and performed by a program faculty member
- Evaluation of the student's counseling performance throughout the internship, including a formal evaluation after the student completes the internship by a program faculty member in consultation with the site supervisor (CACREP, 2009 Standards).

Some counselor education programs will exceed CACREP standards and may require additional clock hours and contact hours. Students should confer with their faculty advisor to ensure the placements they are considering can meet CACREP standards.

As mentioned earlier in the chapter, the COAMFTE is the accrediting agency for clinical programs in Marriage and Family Therapy (separate from CACREP's accredited Marriage and Family Counseling programs). COAMFTE's standards of accreditation requires 500 direct contact hours and numerous other requirements (these can be accessed through www.aamft.org/about/coamfte/AboutCOAMFTE.asp).

Finally, Rehabilitation Counseling programs are accredited by the CORE. Their practicum and internship requirements are stated in the Accreditation Manual for Rehabilitation Counselor Education Programs (these are available at www.core-rehab.org/accrman.html).

We will now look at some of the practicum/internship requirements in more detail.

Contact Hours

For practicum, a minimum of 100 clock hours are required, but 40 of these must involve direct services to students or clients (CACREP, 2009). Direct contact hours most typically include counseling (individual, group, couples, and family), intakes, psychoeducational trainings, and presentations to classes. Your graduate program should have documentation forms available for you to document your clock and contact hours. An example of such a documentation form can be found in Figure 1.1.

For internship, counseling students need to record a minimum total of 600 clock hours and 240 hours of direct contact. Internship is typically split into two or three semesters, with the student documenting the same types of activities noted in the preceding practicum section. As a student proceeds from practicum to internship I then internship II, he or she will likely be given more responsibility.

FIGURE 1.1   Hourly Activities Log*

Weekly Practicum/Internship Hours Log
Practicum: 100 Clock Hours (40 Direct Hours/60 Indirect Hours)
Internship: 300 Clock Hours (120 Direct/180 Indirect Needed)

Date	Direct Hours*	Clock Hours**	Supervisor Signature

Total Direct Hours _____   **Total Clock Hours Completed** _____

_____   _____
Student Signature   **Date**

_____   _____
On-Site Supervisor Signature   **Date**

_____   _____
University Supervisor Signature   **Date**

* Direct Hours—Individual, group, couples, family counseling, cocounseling, intakes, assessment, phone crisis counseling, psychoeducational or support groups, and any direct contact with clients.
** Total Clock Hours—Any work activity that does not involve direct contact with clients. Practicum requires a minimum of 100 clock hours, of which 40 hours should be direct contact.
Internship requires 300 clock hours, of which 120 hours should be direct contact.

*Counseling students need to track their practicum/internship hours in a log format to be signed by their on-site clinical supervisor and the university supervisor at the conclusion of each semester. The university supervisor keeps the log in the student's files.

Practicum/Internship Class

The practicum/internship class time (called *group* in CACREP guidelines) involves a review of counseling responsibilities. Classroom activities include the following:

- Viewing and critiquing video/DVDs of counseling or actual mock counseling sessions
- Providing and receiving critique from faculty and peers
- Role-playing problematic scenarios encountered on the practicum/internship
- Discussing various therapeutic approaches and interventions
- Students sharing their experiences on the practicum/internship

Practicum/internship class will be discussed further in chapter 6.

Academic and On-Site Supervision

Counseling students are required to spend an average of 1 hour per week in individual, on-site supervision at their placement throughout the practicum. In addition, practicum students must meet weekly in a small group run by a program faculty member or counselor education doctoral student a student supervisor, or a site supervisor who is working in biweekly consultation with a program faculty member. The brief explanation of the triadic supervision model was previously mentioned. Though not all counseling practicum programs in the U.S. will be run using triadic supervision, it has become a common model for many counseling programs.

These individual meetings provide an opportunity for more in-depth exploration of counselor skill, effectiveness, and professional ethics. The clinical supervisor or professor will generally be concerned with issues such as the following:

- What strengths does the student possess?
- What struggles does the student appear to be having?
- How is the student adapting to the school/agency?
- Is the student able to write effective accurate case notes?
- Does the student display the required counseling knowledge, therapeutic skills, and professional dispositions necessary for a professional counselor in training?
- Can the student establish and facilitate the therapeutic encounter?
- Can the student develop adequate treatment plans?
- Does the student understand his or her current professional limits?
- Can the student manage the caseload he or she has been assigned?
- Can the student receive feedback without becoming defensive?
- Does the student understand how to apply the code of ethics?

- Can the student display both empathy and at the same time set appropriate boundaries with clients?
- Should a client suddenly disclose that he or she is in crisis, would the student know how to proceed?
- Does the student understand the seriousness of confidentiality?
- How well does the student understand cultural issues in counseling?

The list of potential questions is much longer than those listed here, but this should give you a good idea of the types of issues you may discuss with your supervisor. Supervision will be discussed in more detail in chapter 6.

It is hoped that you now have a brief introduction to counseling and your practicum/internship experience. In the next chapter, we will look at how to select and evaluate a potential practicum/internship placement.

CHAPTER 2

Selecting and Applying for a Practicum/Internship

The practicum and internship is the backbone of any graduate counseling program. Depending on the type of program and the particular institution you attend, you will spend anywhere from 700–1,200 clock hours on your practicum and internship experience, depending on whether your program is CACREP accredited and also your state's requirements for licensure. For many counseling students, practicum and internships offer the first opportunity to work with clinical populations. Thus, choosing an appropriate field setting and site is vitally important. In this chapter, I will discuss all aspects of selecting the appropriate practicum/internship site.

SELECTING A PRACTICUM/INTERNSHIP

Procedures for choosing a practicum and internship setting will vary depending on the counseling program. For example, in some programs, the faculty may actually select the placements, and then assign the students in particular settings. Although this method is regressive, it does lessen the burden for the students.

A more common method of selection involves students and faculty working conjointly on practicum and internship selection. In many cases, the student meets with their faculty advisor and discusses the types of placements that might match up with the student's interests and aptitude.

One of the first tasks for you as a student seeking a practicum is to meet with your faculty advisor to discuss your interests. Begin thinking and researching the types of placements (or field settings) that you are interested in. For example, if you are interested in school counseling, be aware that elementary school placements are significantly different from those in high schools. For counseling students interested in mental health, rehabilitation, or other community-based programs, you will have several variables: inpatient or outpatient; addictions (outpatient or residential), college counseling center, community college counseling center, correctional setting, and so forth. Your advisor can point you in the direction of possible placements that are within your area of interest. Your advisor will also be able to inform you whether or not your practicum aspirations are realistic. For example, some placements will not accept master's level students, and others may insist on taking only social work interns. This may be disappointing, but you need to know this information before investing too much time in the search process.

I recommend that after meeting with your advisor, you brainstorm some 8–10 possible placements that are within your areas of interest. Then, get busy with a Web search. Many local agencies, schools, and other institutions will have Web sites that you can research for more information. The following sections in this chapter will show you particular issues to watch out for as you do your research. I can tell you, from having run community and university counseling programs, students who have done their homework on a given placement are far more likely to be selected.

As you gather information about various placement settings, you may wish to keep track of the relevant details about each one, along with your impressions about their suitability for you. Figure 2.1 offers a practicum/internship site information form that you can use to keep track of each site that you evaluate.

Students should also be aware that it takes a great deal of effort on the part of the faculty to establish relationships with schools, hospitals, clinics, and college counseling centers. Because of the work involved, many counseling programs have long-standing agreements with particular schools and agencies. Such agreements ensure that the counseling program will have enough placements and the agencies will have practicum and internship students to help with their workload. Thus, the decision to seek a practicum with a given school or agency should not be taken lightly, because one bad performance by a student could jeopardize an entire placement. It is also worth mentioning that practicum and internships provide a school or agency with a trial period and occasionally, provided the student counselor has performed well and that there is an opening, a job offer from said placement is a possibility. Again, possible employment depends on the school's or agency's policies, budget, and guidelines.

Clinical Populations

A key question to consider is what type of clients you are interested in counseling. For students in school counseling programs, the issue is more basic. You will complete your practicum in an elementary, middle, or high school. Granted, there are variations on the theme, such as private schools, schools serving specialized students (e.g., schools for the visually impaired, the deaf, etc.), as well as those educating "at-risk" or exceptional learners.

Counseling students in mental health counseling, rehabilitation, marriage and family counseling, and the like, will choose between inpatient versus outpatient clinics, addictions versus mental health, or a hospital or residential addictions treatment center, working with children, adolescents, adults, couples, families, and so forth.

All students should carefully consider the population they are interested in counseling. Now, despite whatever you may have heard, completing a practicum and internship in, say, an addictions clinic, does not mean you will be required to work in addictions for the rest of your professional career. A practicum and internship spent counseling in a high school does not mean you will never get a job counseling in a middle school. Fortunately, the skills and interventions

| **FIGURE 2.1** | Practicum/Internship Site Information Form* |

Date of Contract: ____/____/____

Agency/School/College Site: _____

Address: _____

_____

_____

_____

Phone: ( ) _____ - _____   Web site: _____

Contact Name: _____

Contact's Job Title: _____

Contact's Phone Number: ( ) _____ - _____   ext. _____

Contact's E-mail: _____

Write a brief description of the site, population it serves, whether inpatient, outpatient, and anything that seems pertinent.

_____

_____

_____

_____

_____

Student's versus site's schedule: How well does your schedule match that of the site? (e.g., Do you need weekend and evening hours for practicum/internship?)

Continued

FIGURE 2.1   Practicum/Internship Site Information Form* *Continued*

Based on my contact with this site (phone conversation, e-mail, interview, etc.), does the site seem:

A. Very interested in me doing a practicum/internship with them.
B. Moderately interested in me doing a practicum/internship with them.
C. Not interested in me doing a practicum/internship with them.

Based on my understanding of this placement, I would rate my interest for this site as:

Uninterested   Low   Average   Above Average   High

I would rate my fit (e.g., values, type of population served, view of staff, supervisor, etc.) for this site as:

Poor   Average   Good   Excellent

Next Step: Do you have a formal interview set up with this site? Yes/No

If you have an interview set up, consider the following checklist:

1. Do you have an up-to-date résumé?
2. A cover letter?
3. Directions to the site?
4. Have you visited their Web site to learn about the agency and the clients they counsel?
5. If you know someone who has interned at the site, have you spoken to them regarding their experience?
6. Do you have any concerns about this site? If so, how serious are they?
7. Have you spoken with your faculty advisor about this site?
8. Have you done any mock interviewing in order to prepare for a potential interview? (Note: Not all practicum/internships will require a formal interview, although many will. Treat a practicum/internship interview as serious as a job interview.)

*This form is to assist you in gathering information regarding potential practicum and internship placements. Copy this form and use it as a worksheet when searching for a placement. Use one sheet per placement.

required can be tailored to various ages and populations. One exception: If you are enrolled in a marriage and family counseling or therapy program, you will, of necessity, be required to counsel couples and families (Gladding, 2009), so some restrictions will apply.

Naturally, your interests may not be as clearly defined at this point in your counseling career. Do not stress, because there is plenty of flexibility in the counseling field. It is not uncommon for counselors to begin their careers in one specialty area (e.g., addictions) and move to one totally different (e.g., school counseling). Some lateral moves within the profession will require more education or training (moving from an agency setting to a school, for example), whereas others will effect no change other than a focus on a different population (counseling children to counseling adults).

Here are some questions regarding client population for consideration in selecting a practicum/internship:

- What clinical populations would I like to counsel?
- Do I prefer inpatient or outpatient settings?
- What are the advantages or disadvantages to a practicum/internship in an elementary school? A middle school? A high school?
- Does the philosophy of the site match my personal values? (Note: This is particularly an issue with some private schools and agencies. What populations does the clinic's nondiscrimination statement include and exclude? Some agencies are pro-choice and others staunchly anti-abortion.)
- Would I like the challenge of a special population such as a prison, jail, or state psychiatric hospital?
- How diverse are the students and/or clients the school, college, or agency serves?

The last question addresses *multicultural competencies* as espoused by Sue, Arredondo, and McDavis (1992) and later adopted by the Association for Multicultural Counseling and Development (AMCD; Arredondo et al, 1996). The definition of *multicultural* has recently been more broadly defined to include issues of disability, socioeconomic status, religion, sexual orientation, and culture, as well as race or ethnicity. Some of the beliefs, knowledge, and skills of culturally skilled counselors are the following:

- They understand their own cultural heritage.
- They recognize the limits of their multicultural competency and expertise.
- They understand how their own cultural heritage may contribute to their biases and how racism may affect their personality and work.
- They are constantly seeking to understand themselves as racial and cultural beings and are actively seeking a nonracist identity.
- They seek consultative help, are familiar with relevant research, and are actively involved with clients outside the counseling setting. They can send and receive verbal and nonverbal communications accurately and appropriately. (Arrendondo et al., 1996)

Many counseling programs, particularly those accredited by Council for Accreditation of Counseling and Related Educational Programs (CACREP) or Council on Rehabilitation and Education (CORE), address the various multicultural competencies through their curriculum, training, portfolio requirements, and diverse practicum and internship placements. An important factor in your development is to begin to consider multicultural issues when you counsel clients. No one needs to be a cultural anthropologist to be culturally competent. Rather, when you do work with the culturally different, read up on the culture of the client and if you are unsure about something, ask your client for clarification. Most clients will appreciate that you were respectful enough to ask about their culture. Furthermore, given the literally thousands of cultures (and subcultures) in the world, no one can be an expert in all. The important consideration is to be respectful and acquire new information. Cultural issues will be discussed in more detail in chapter 7.

Level of Responsibility

It is also important to remember that as you progress from practicum through internship you will likely be given more responsibility. Your clinical supervisor's first priority is to ensure the emotional well-being and safety of the clients he or she serves. As you increase in skill and confidence levels, your supervisor is likely to give you more autonomy.

Another factor to consider is that, on your placement, you may work alongside doctoral interns from counselor education, counseling psychology, clinical psychology, social work, and other programs. Doctoral students will naturally be given more responsibility and autonomy than master's level students. This may be frustrating for graduate students in master's degree programs, but these students should bear in mind that this is not a personal criticism, but rather reflects a higher level of training. Master's level counseling students who matriculate on to doctoral programs in counselor education, counseling psychology, and the like will likely appreciate the greater degree of latitude at that point.

Your Site Supervisor

Your site supervisor will play a key role in your practicum/internship experience. In addition to clinical issues, site supervisors also serve as mentors and role models. CACREP requires the following for on-site supervisors (CACREP, 2009 Standards):

- A minimum of a master's degree in counseling or a related profession with equivalent qualifications, including appropriate certifications and/or licenses
- A minimum of 2 years of pertinent professional experience in the program area in which the student is enrolled
- Knowledge of the program's expectations, requirements, and evaluation procedures for students
- Relevant training in counseling supervision

Ideally, your on-site practicum supervisor will be a professional credentialed in counseling. It is much easier for a licensed mental health counselor to mentor a graduate student in counseling than a graduate student in a social work program. Likewise, a student in a school counseling program is best suited to have a licensed or state-certified school counselor providing supervision than a school psychologist. Because of proliferation of the various mental health professionals, however, social workers or psychologists often supervise graduate counseling students and professional counselors in the workplace. Although these related mental health professionals may do a very good job of supervising, they likely neither will be as informed about issues specific to the counseling profession, nor may they be advocates for counseling organizations (such as the American Counseling Association [ACA]) as they would for their own professional organizations. Finally, all the mental health professions have their own codes of ethics. Fortunately, these ethical codes are more similar than different (Remley & Herlihy, 2007). However, if your on-site clinical supervisor is a social worker or psychologist, he or she likely will not be familiar with the ethical code for counselors. This means your faculty advisor or practicum/internship classroom instructor becomes even more important to you.

While you are investigating a practicum site, here are some questions to ask regarding your site supervisor:

- What profession does your practicum supervisor belong to (e.g., counseling, psychology, social work, etc.)?
- What is your practicum supervisor's primary code of ethics?
- What credentials does your practicum supervisor hold (licensed counselor, licensed clinical social worker, state-licensed or state-certified school counselor, licensed psychologist, etc.)?

Although the various organizations may be initially confusing to you, the practicum provides an opportunity to begin to understand the larger mental health profession. Furthermore, you will spend your professional career working alongside psychologists, social workers, marriage and family therapists, and other professionals in mental health. Establishing a respectful, working relationship across disciplines is a must for counselors and anyone else in the mental health profession. On your practicum and internship, as well as during your future professional career, you will work in multidiscipline teams with many different mental health professionals.

An important consideration for all counseling students to be aware of involves the varying licensure standards regarding supervision during the practicum/internship. Many states simply specify that the graduate counseling student must be supervised by a mental health professional licensed in a core discipline (e.g., counseling, social work, psychology, etc.). Others, such as the state of Massachusetts, require the student to be supervised by a licensed mental health professional with 5 years counseling experience. Because I teach and supervise counseling students in New England, our program makes all students aware of this requirement, which is informally referred to as the *Massachusetts model*. Therefore, ask your faculty advisor about any licensure requirements in your state. Even better yet, check out your state's licensure requirements online (a complete list of state licensure boards and Web sites is located in Appendix D).

If asked about their theoretical orientation, many counseling supervisors would likely state they have an integrated or eclectic approach (Ivey & Ivey, 2007). Others may strongly identify with particular therapeutic approaches, such as Solution-Focused Therapy (SFT), Narrative Therapy, Dialectical Behavioral Therapy (DBT), Cognitive–Behavioral Therapy (CBT), and so forth (Gladding, 2009). In many cases, the theoretical orientation of your supervisor may not radically change your experience as a supervisee. For example, a supervisor trained in CBT may not be significantly different than one operating from an SFT. A supervisor whose theoretical orientation is psychodynamic, or one who uses Eye Movement Desensitization and Reprocessing (EMDR), will likely use a far different approach. This is not a criticism of any particular approach, but recognition that some approaches will require a different style of supervision.

Regardless of the theoretical orientation your supervisor works from, I strongly suggest that you "study up" on your supervisor's approach. For example, if your supervisor informs you that he or she uses CBT in counseling, you will want to read up on it. It would also be advisable to ask your supervisor to recommend books, journal articles, and DVDs on CBT.

Learning one particular approach is an advantage in that it narrows the scope of practice for a practicum/internship student and gives the student the opportunity to develop a clear professional identity. A disadvantage is that you may not learn enough about other viable therapeutic approaches. Furthermore, it is important to be aware of the research, which suggests that using any particular theoretical approach is less important, in terms of overall effectiveness, than therapeutic attachment (Wampold, 2001).

Accreditations and Affiliations of the Site

Practicum/internship placements are naturally going to have wide variation depending on the type of placement. A high school setting differs from a community mental health clinic, a psychiatric ward in a hospital, an inpatient addictions treatment center, or a university counseling center. Part of your continuing education in the broader mental health field lies in understanding the variations among the numerous settings, the professionals that staff them, and the various accreditations such placements hold.

In chapter 1, we discussed the importance of accreditation for graduate educational programs in counseling. Similarly, many practicum sites will hold national certifications. National agencies that accredit clinical placements include the International Association of Counseling Services (IACS), The Joint Commission and the Commission on Accreditation of Rehabilitation Facilities (CARF). These national accreditations are separate and distinct from programmatic accreditations such as CACREP.

Field settings, which hold a national certification, will likely have a stronger reputation in the mental health field and will provide a more enriching practicum or internship experience than unaccredited facilities. Having made this statement, placements in unaccredited agencies and college counseling centers should not be viewed with disdain. Accreditation, although certainly an advantage, does not guarantee a successful placement.

If you are looking at a practicum placement and you notice that it is (for example) CARF accredited, it would be wise to go to the CARF Web site and read up on the agency. The same would apply to any other listed accreditation. When you interview for a practicum or internship, you want to be able to demonstrate your knowledge of an accreditation, its mission, and how accreditation impacts patient or client care.

- CARF: www.carf.org
- IACS: www.iacs.org
- The Joint Commission: www.jointcommission.org

Professional Practices and Resources

In addition to understanding the type of setting your practicum is in (e.g., school, rehabilitation, inpatient addictions, etc.), you will need to be aware of professional and developmental issues within the setting. For starters, you want to ask about the orientation process your placement offers to new practicum and internship students. Some agencies and schools have a formalized training requiring a student to spend several days learning the agency, its operation, and rules and regulations. Others, particularly smaller organizations, will have very brief, informal trainings. In all settings, you will want to know the organization's guidelines, which hopefully will be contained in a formal document and provided to you.

THE INFORMATIONAL INTERVIEW

After you have selected a few placements, contact them to see about arranging informational interviews. I would counsel students seeking a practicum to contact the appropriate person at the desired sites directly using the phone or e-mail. Do not simply send out résumés and cover letters without first contacting the site directly. First of all, the site may not have a placement for you, in which case your résumés and cover letter will be ignored. Secondly, most clinical supervisors, or their designee (such as the personnel department) prefer to be contacted directly, even though they are busy people. Your faculty advisor and/or the practicum/internship site coordinator will likely have many contacts themselves.

Now, many schools and agencies will have established guidelines that require the student apply first, and then be called for an interview. Others, however, have very informal procedures and will be happy to arrange an informational interview. Be sure to check with your selected site to see if an informational interview is a possibility.

Whether the interview is informational or more formal, you need to practice answering questions that your interviewer is likely to ask. I suggest you work with your advisor and/or the campus career center. You may also check texts such as *What Color is Your Parachute* (Bolles, 2009), or one I coauthored with Amy Reese Connelly, *A Job Search Manual for Counselors and Counselor Educators: How to Navigate and Promote Your Counseling Career* (Hodges & Connelly, 2010). You will need to be prepared to answer questions related to the setting you are interested in. For example, if you are interviewing with a representative from an inpatient psychiatric center, be aware of what types of issues they treat, patient ages, number and training of staff, or whether they operate from a particular therapeutic orientation (e.g., CBT). because these issues may come up in their questions.

You also should have five to eight questions prepared that you can ask the interviewer. The interview is your chance to demonstrate you have done your homework on the setting. Saying "I don't have any questions," suggests either a lack of research, arrogance, or, perhaps, disinterest. Some questions, which you may wish to ask, have already been raised in previous sections of this chapter. "The Formal Interview" section later in the chapter will offer even more.

APPLYING FOR THE PRACTICUM/INTERNSHIP

Some schools, college counseling centers, and agencies will have a formal application process, which requires that you fill out an application packet, whereas others have an informal process where you are instructed simply to show up on a certain day and time for an interview. One large university where I have placed students has a very extensive application process, including a résumé or curriculum vitae (CV), cover letter, letters of recommendation, and a formal interview with several members of the counseling staff. Formality tends to be more common with doctoral students, although master's degree students will want to be prepared for all contingencies. Here are some tips to remember:

1. Is there a formal application for the practicum/internship? If so, make sure you are aware of all the application requirements.
2. If there is an application form, photocopy it and draft your answers in ink, then go back and type the answers in. (In some cases, the site may send you an electronic copy, in which case, you can type and edit freely on your computer.)
3. Make sure all words are spelled correctly. As the cliché goes, you do not get a second chance to make a first impression.
4. Know the due date for the application. You might be a strong candidate, but a late application makes a statement about your organization and follow-through.
5. If you do not understand something on the application, contact the site and ask for clarification.

6. Ask your faculty advisor to read over your application prior to submitting it.
7. Does the application process require letters of support from faculty members or others? If so, give your reference ample notice before the deadline. Ample notice would be 10–14 days. Do not drop the reference request on them 3 days before the deadline.

Your Résumé or Curriculum Vitae

When planning to apply for a practicum or internship, I suggest you operate as if you are applying for a professional counseling job. This involves having an updated and effective résumé or CV. A résumé is a one- or two-page summary of your skills, experience, and education; a CV is longer and more detailed. For master's level counselors and counselor education students, a one- to two-page résumé is a must. For doctoral students in counselor education, use the CV model.

Because this book targets practicum and internships, I will not offer detailed information about how to write an effective résumé or CV; however, some basic information (and further resources) can be found in chapter 12.

The Formal Interview

As previously mentioned, interviewing for a practicum or internships varies considerably. Some potential placement sites will request an interview with a clinical director and a few staff. In other cases, a line counselor or social worker will conduct the interview. Regardless of the possible variations, you will want to be thoroughly prepared and take a few copies of your résumé or CV to the interview.

The following are some key questions to anticipate during the interview:

- Why are you interested in applying for a practicum/internship at this site?
- What are your long-term professional goals?
- What specific skills and abilities make you suited for this placement?
- What are your strengths?
- What are your weaknesses?
- What questions do you have for me/us?

See chapter 12 for more interview questions and suggested answers, as well as certain inappropriate questions that should not be asked on an interview.

Here are some questions for you to ask during the interview:

- Who would be my primary supervisor? What are his or her training and credentials?
- Is the agency accredited? If so, by whom?
- What types of counseling-related responsibilities would I be carrying out (e.g., individual, group, couples, family counseling, psychoeducational groups, mediation, etc.)?

- What theoretical orientation do staff counselors use (e.g., Cognitive Behavioral, Solution-Focused, etc.)?
- Will there be opportunities for additional training?
- When can I expect to hear a decision regarding a placement?

Actors, musicians, athletes, and politicians prepare well in advance of their big event and you should do the same in preparing for an interview. Get with a friend, fellow student, or a career counselor and practice answering questions such as those mentioned previously. You might also have a friend or the career counselor video tape your performance and then provide critique. You do not need to be perfect, but interviewers will be impressed by thorough answers, well-groomed applicants, good posture, and appropriate eye contact.

When you have completed the interview process, always follow up with a thank-you letter. Interviewers will appreciate this simple gesture. Thank-you letters also illustrate that you know how to lay the foundation for future positive relations. Should you be accepted by this practicum/internship site, such follow-through will be important in interagency relations.

THE PRACTICUM/INTERNSHIP CONTRACT

Prior to beginning the practicum or internship, the student, the practicum/internship coordinator, and the on-site supervisor should sign a contract agreeing to the basic counseling and related responsibilities the student will be performing. Such contracts may be called a learning contract, a practicum and internship contract, and so forth. Regardless, the agreement should explicitly delineate responsibilities of the student, faculty, on-site supervisor, counseling program, and clinical setting.

At institutions where I have worked, the practicum/internship contract is developed by the faculty, and then critiqued by university legal counsel to ensure legal issues are covered. Some agencies will also have their own contract and require the student, faculty, and on-site supervisor to sign. All parties should read the contract before signing, and then they should keep a copy for their own records.

It is critical that supervisors and students develop a mutual understanding regarding the knowledge, skills, and dispositions that the placement requires. The duties, obligations, organizational guidelines, and so forth, should be made clear prior to the beginning of the placement.

Naturally, no contract can cover all eventualities, but the contractual language should be clear and easily understood by all parties. The contract should address the following:

- Weekly supervision by the on-site supervisor and the faculty advisor. CACREP and CORE guidelines require 1 hour of supervision per week carried out in an individual or group format.

- The clock hours and direct contact hours the student is required to complete each semester.
- The type of clinical duties the student will be assigned. Examples may include individual, group, couples, family counseling, addictions assessments, academic advising, whether the student will conduct testing and assessment and what types, intakes, and so forth.
- The name of the on-site supervisor.
- How conflicts are to be addressed.
- The right to terminate on behalf of both the counselor education program and the organization if either party feels the relationship is not working. This termination agreement protects the student, program, and placement.
- Duration of the internship. Some contract specify that the placement will last for the duration of the student's practicum/internship (anywhere from 600–1,000 clock hours depending on the program), although others spell out an expectation of one academic year.

An example of a practicum/internship contract is offered in Appendix E.

FINAL ISSUES TO CONSIDER

Figure 2.2 offers a checklist of issues to consider and tasks to complete as you begin your search for a practicum/internship placement. In addition, here are a few final points to bear in mind:

- Have you purchased student liability insurance? ACA and the American Mental Health Counselors Association (AMHCA) now include student liability insurance in the cost of student membership, so purchasing a student membership in ACA or AMHCA is recommended as opposed to simply purchasing student liability coverage. Some counseling programs will of course, require students to maintain membership in ACA, AMHCA, ASCA, or another professional affiliate.
- Have all parties agreed that the student is a good fit for the placement?
- Have all parties agreed to and signed the Practicum and Internship Contract?
- Have all parties met to finalize the agreed-upon supervision, beginning and ending dates of the practicum/internship, and how to work out potential student counselor–supervisor conflicts?
- It would be wise for you to read up on the school's or agency's policies and procedures manual. (If they lack a manual, this is a red flag!) Then give yourself adequate time to adjust to the real-life setting.

It is hoped that what you have read so far has helped you choose and achieve your desired practicum/internship placement. In chapter 3, I will give a brief overview of common legal and ethical issues you may encounter.

FIGURE 2.2 Practicum and Internship Checklist*

■ **Get a working résumé** (if you lack one): Examine your work background for skills, experiences, and interests related to the type of placement you desire. Make sure your résumé is accurate and up to date.

■ **Examining your résumé, what types of experiences do you have that would assist you in doing counseling work?** (e.g., have you been a BA/BS chemical dependency counselor, case manager, special education teacher or aide, staffed a collegiate living group as either a resident director [RD] or resident advisor [RA], worked as a camp counselor, etc.?) Related experience usually helps when looking for a practicum as it implies you understand the demands of human services work.

■ **Coursework:** Be prepared to explain specific courses and additional training you have had that could bolster the case for the school or agency to select you. Have you been trained in diagnosis, treatment planning, assessment, or couples and family counseling? Have you had additional training in creative arts therapy (e.g., dance therapy, art therapy, music therapy, etc.), trauma counseling, mediation, and so forth?

■ **Interests and orientation:** What type of setting do you prefer? Inpatient? Outpatient? Elementary, middle, or high school? Would you want a setting that provides familiar work or one that offers something new? (For example, if you have been a middle school teacher, would you want to be placed in a middle school counseling office, or would you prefer a different setting?)

■ **Scheduling:** Because most graduate students in counseling programs also work, perhaps have families and numerous other demands, what type of placement would best fit your schedule? For example, if you work day shifts during the week, you may need a placement that offers evening and weekend work. Be realistic regarding time commitments, travel to your placement, academic requirements, and such.

■ **Types of clients:** What types of clients are you interested in working with? Examples include age, cultural background, special populations, and so forth. If you are unsure about what types of clients you would like to counsel, you may wish to speak with your academic advisor to clarify your interests.

■ **Ongoing training opportunities:** When examining potential placements, does the school, agency, university counseling center offer in-service training? If so, what types (some placements will provide training on various topics such as Dialectical Behavioral Therapy [DBT], mediation, play therapy, etc.)? Some placements will offer training free of charge or at a discount to practicum and internship students.

Continued

| FIGURE 2.2 | Practicum and Internship Checklist* *Continued* |

■ **Theoretical orientation:** Do any of the placements you are considering operate on one theoretical approach (e.g., Cognitive–Behavioral Therapy [CBT], Eye Movement and Desensitization and Reprocessing [EMDR], psychodynamic, a particular spiritual approach, etc.)? Consider this issue carefully, as some agencies may not fit well with your values. Is there a potential conflict regarding theoretical approach, spirituality, or something else?

■ **The supervisor:** Have you met with or are you familiar with the supervisor? Checking with your faculty advisor and students who have been supervised at a particular school, agency, or college counseling center is a good idea. Also, what type of qualities would you want a supervisor to possess? What type of supervisor would you work best with?

■ **Do you have concerns regarding the placement (or placements) you are considering?** Any issues of safety, supervision style, professional fit, and so forth (e.g., Does counseling in a prison, psychiatric hospital, or other residential setting with higher-risk clients intimidate you?).

■ **Career issues:** What are your career goals (e.g., I want to run an addictions treatment clinic)? How well does the placement you are considering fit with your career goal(s)? What types of placements would be most beneficial to your future career plans? (Be aware that your plans may change.)

■ **Additional considerations:** What other issues or concerns do you have regarding practicum and internship?

*This checklist is designed to assist you in planning for the types of field placements that will best fit your background, interests, and orientation.

CHAPTER 3

Ethical and Legal Issues

Ethical codes have been a part of the medical and healthcare professions for some 3,000 years. The first professional ethical code was codified by Hippocrates, a Greek physician; his *Hippocratic Oath* is still taken by medical school graduates (Remley & Herlihy, 2007). To protect the public, ethical codes have been established in many other professions, such as law, psychiatry, and certainly counseling.

For counseling students, reading and understanding the *ACA Code of Ethics* (see Appendix B) is a vital requirement. The basic core of the *ACA Code of Ethics* involves a concept known as *beneficence*, or doing what is in the best interest of the client (Wheeler & Bertram, 2008). Functioning in the client's best interests includes protecting confidentiality, practicing within your scope of competence, avoiding harm, avoiding conflicts of interests regarding your clients, and refraining from sexual and business relationships with clients, to mention a few. All of these will be discussed in this chapter. Counselors practicing in various specialty areas must also be familiar with the ethics of their particular specialty (e.g., American School Counselor Association, American Rehabilitation Counseling Association, American Mental Health Counselors Association [AMHCA], etc.)

Beyond the codes of ethics, counselors must also comply with existing federal and state laws. In fact, an important part of ethical practice is awareness of state and federal law with regard to professional practice (Wheeler & Bertram, 2008). Like ethical codes, state and federal laws are in a constant state of flux, influenced by legislative action and court decisions. The landmark *Tarasoff* case and the HIPAA federal legislative action, both of which will be discussed in this chapter, highlight important examples of how legal decisions impact the counseling profession. Counselors who do not follow state and federal laws may be prosecuted in criminal courts. Furthermore, civil litigation against a counselor may result when said counselor has breached ethical guidelines.

COMPETENT ETHICAL PRACTICE FOR COUNSELORS

The mere reading of ethical standards is not the last word in ethical practice, but rather, a commencement. Students in counselor education programs, as well as professional counselors, need ongoing training and consultation regarding competent ethical practice. The most basic ethical requirement is that counselors "practice only within the boundaries of their competence" (American Counseling Association [ACA], 2005, Section C.2.a). How can a counselor exactly determine his or her parameters of competence? It is difficult to answer this question because counseling is a very broad profession. However, just as attorneys could never be competent in every area of law (no matter what large billboard ads might suggest), counselors could never be competent to offer services in all therapeutic areas. A counselor who is skilled in treating individuals may not be as competent in counseling families. Counselors who are very skilled in counseling clients with severe mental disorders may not be competent in counseling middle-school children.

Competence is a legal issue because society expects professionals to be competent and asserts this standard through state licensing boards and the legal system. Counselor competence is the second most frequently reported area of ethical complaint after sexual misconduct (Neukrug, Milliken, & Walden, 2001).

HEALTH INSURANCE PORTABILITY AND ACCOUNTABILITY ACT

One of the most far reaching and influential congressional legislative actions with regard to the mental health field is the Health Insurance Portability and Accountability Act (HIPAA). Congress passed this sweeping legislation in 1996 to ensure people would be able to maintain insurance coverage when changing jobs and in response to concerns of privacy regarding the electronic transfer of records (Remley & Herlihy, 2007). Counselors' and other mental health professionals' billing insurance must comply with HIPAA standards.

Given that most nonschool practicum and internship sites will be subject to HIPAA regulations, it is very important that you understand it. Naturally, your supervisors will likely provide both training and oversight regarding HIPAA and other federal policies impacting professional practice. Still, it is a good professional practice to be proactive and read the HIPAA requirements. You may visit the HIPAA Web site (http://www.hhs.gov/ocr/hipaa). In addition, professional counseling organizations, such as ACA, AMHCA, and others, periodically offer trainings in HIPAA compliance.

INFORMED CONSENT

Informed consent means that clients must know and understand basic issues about the process of counseling: their rights, counselor responsibilities, fees charged, counselor training, access to records, and limits to confidentiality, for example. Most clients (or students) are not experts in the mental health arena and must, of necessity, rely on their counselors to provide them with the information necessary to make informed choices (Handelsman, 2001).

During informed consent, counselors must provide the client with information pertinent to the counseling relationship. As stated earlier, this includes fees, counselor training, and such, but also outlines the client's rights and responsibilities, including provisions for mandated clients, the client's right to terminate counseling, expectations (e.g., client and counselor are both punctual, fees are paid on time, etc.), emergency plans for after-hours coverage, and so forth. Written documentation of these issues is strongly advised, given possible liability issues; in fact, HIPAA requires written documentation of informed consent (Madden, 1998).

The *ACA Code of Ethics* (ACA, 2005, Section A.2.b) outlines the information that should be discussed with the client when obtaining informed consent:

- The purpose, goals, techniques, procedures, limitations, potential risks, and benefits of counseling services;
- The counselor's qualifications, including relevant degrees held, licenses and certifications, areas of specialization, and relevant experience;
- Arrangements for continuation of services should the counselor become unable to continue counseling;
- The implications of *Diagnostic and Statistical Manual of Mental Disorders*, fourth edition text revision (*DSM-IV-TR*), diagnosis, use of assessments, and reports;
- Fees and billing information (generally not applicable in schools and most college or university counseling centers);
- Confidentiality and its limits;
- The client's right to inspect his or her record and to participate in counseling treatment; and
- The client's right to refuse any recommended services or modality change and be advised of the consequences of refusal.

In addition to those issues suggested by the ethical code, numerous counseling professionals have recommended that additional information be included:

- A description of the counselor's theoretical orientation (written in language the client can understand) or a brief statement regarding the counselor's philosophy (Corey, Corey, & Callanan, 2007);
- Information regarding the logistics of counseling, such as length and frequency of sessions, procedures for making and canceling appointments, policies regarding phone contact between sessions, and how to contact the counselor in the event of an emergency;
- Information regarding insurance reimbursement, including the fact that any diagnosis assigned will likely become part of the client's permanent health record and the risks inherent with this (Welfel, 2006);
- Information alternatives to counseling, such as 12–step groups, support groups, self-help books, medication, and other services;
- When applicable, a statement regarding video or audio taping, along with a statement that the client's case may be discussed with the clinical supervisor or a consultant (Corey et al., 2007); and
- The client's recourse if dissatisfied with counseling services, including names and contact information for supervisors and addresses and phone numbers of licensing boards and professional organizations (Welfel, 2006; Remley & Herlihy, 2007)

Figure 3.1 offers a sample informed consent form that a client might sign.

FIGURE 3.1   Informed Consent for Clients

Jane Doe, MS, LMHC, NCC
1719 Freud Lane
Therapy, NY 10017
jane.doe@aol.com
Phone: (123) 456-7890

My Qualifications

My practice includes counseling with children, adolescents, and couples. I am also a New York State Certified Mediator. I hold a master's degree in Mental Health Counseling, am a Licensed Mental Health Counselor (LMHC), and a Nationally Certified Counselor (NCC). I have postgraduate training in Cognitive–Behavioral Therapy from the Beck Institute in Philadelphia. My postgraduate experience includes 10 years as a community mental health counselor.

The clinic's fees are set by your insurance carrier, so you want to consult your carrier for any questions. For uninsured clients, we offer a sliding fee scale with minimum fees set equal to the lowest billable insurance carrier ($60.00 per session). Most insurance carriers will allow 8–10 sessions.

The General Course of Counseling

I appreciate that you have come to our clinic and I want to be thorough and specific in helping you achieve the goals you have set. My job is to provide assessment and counseling and work conjointly with you to set treatment goals. It is true that in counseling success depends on the client actively wanting to change. Counseling is not an exact science, and at times the counselor, in consultation with you, may need to revise the goals of treatment. Some assessment will be carried out at the intake time and other assessments may be added later for further clarification. Unless otherwise stated, all counseling sessions are 50 minutes long.

If you have been mandated for treatment to this agency, you will be required to sign a Release of Information Form so this counselor and the agency can provide necessary information to the agency, parole officer, court, or other official that mandated your treatment.

Anytime you have questions regarding your treatment, please feel free to ask.

Record Keeping and Confidentiality

Ethically and legally, I am required to keep records of all our contacts. Legally, you have the right to see all information generated between us. You must provide explicit permission for information to be revealed, unless the law specifies otherwise (see exceptions to confidentiality). Thus, with your written consent, I will provide information to anyone with a legitimate need. You are also entitled to a copy of any records generated in this office. This clinic keeps records for 10 years past the last date of contact. Then, because of space and privacy concerns, records are destroyed in compliance with state law and professional ethics.

Continued

FIGURE 3.1	Informed Consent for Clients *Continued*

Exceptions to Confidentiality

The following are legal/ethical exceptions to confidentiality in this state:

- When child abuse/neglect is suspected.
- When elder abuse is suspected.
- In the case of imminent danger of suicide.
- In the event of a clear and specified threat to a third party.
- If a life threatening contagious threatens a third party (e.g., AIDS, HIV+).
- When a client provides written permission (Release of Information Form).
- If a judge mandates a release of information.
- If a client sues a counselor or makes false charges against a counselor.

Client as Consumer

As a client in counseling, you are encouraged to participate actively and fully in your own treatment. Many counselors will assign homework activities, reading, and so forth. You are encouraged to follow through with as many homework assignments as possible. In addition, keep your counselor apprised when you cannot complete out-of-session assignments so that the two of you can make a new plan. Also, if you feel you do not fully understand something, ask your counselor for clarification. Clients who take an active approach to their treatment are likely to make more therapeutic progress than those who are passive.

Your Rights as a Client

Although you are encouraged to discuss the issues with your counselor first, if for any reason you believe your rights have been violated, you have a right to file a grievance.

For Ethical Issues

American Counseling Association (ACA)
5999 Stevenson Ave.
Alexandria, VA 22304
1-800-347-6647

New York State Board for Mental Health Counselors
State Education Department
Office of the Professions
89 Washington Ave.
Albany, NY 12234-1000
www.op.nysed.gov

I have read and understand all information presented here in the informed consent document.

_____   _____

Name   Date

CONFIDENTIALITY AND PRIVILEGED COMMUNICATION

Confidentiality is arguably the most important concept in the delivery of counseling services. Without confidentiality, clients would be less likely to disclose personal or sensitive information, and many would refrain from seeking counseling services entirely (Miller & Thelan, 1986). Within the mental health field, confidentiality is viewed as essential to the counseling relationship. Clients need to know that their counselors will respect their privacy, whereas counselors know that an effective counseling relationship is built on a foundation of trust. Clients involved in a deeply personal relationship like counseling have the right to expect that what they divulge in sessions will be kept private (Corey et al., 2007). Naturally, concerns regarding the ability to protect the right of confidentiality frequently emerge. However, complaints against counselors for breach of confidentiality are actually quite rare. Various studies have shown that less than 5% of complaints to ethics boards involve a breach of confidentiality (Garcia, Salo, & Hamilton, 1995; Pope & Vasquez, 1998).

On the other hand, in one study, 62% of psychologists surveyed reported that they had unintentionally violated their clients' confidentiality (Pope, Tabachnick, & Keith-Spiegel, 1987). Some of the risks to unintentional violations of confidentiality are listed here:

- Sending confidential information through the Internet: Web-based counseling presents serious challenges to privacy.
- Violations through e-mail exchanges: Counselors should always assume e-mail is not a confidential method of information delivery and should refrain from disclosing names, personal information, and other data, in e-mail.
- Violations over the telephone: Telephone transmission of information may not be secure.
- Violations via fax: Client information is frequently faxed from one organization to another; given how busy most offices are, confidential information can easily be passed on.
- Confidential information left on answering machines: Counselors in private practice should use an answering service, and refrain from leaving any details on an answering machine.
- Discussing cases in insecure locations: Remley and Herlihy (2007) relate a story of two counselors discussing a client in a crowded elevator, only to discover that the client was standing behind them!

Clearly, there are many ways counselors can unintentionally violate a client's confidentiality. Graduate students in counseling programs must be very diligent in maintaining client privacy. Although it is natural for students to want to debrief with one another, bear in mind your ethical obligations are the same as those of professional counselors (ACA, 2005, Section F.8.a). Your communications must not reveal any sensitive information that would allow third parties to readily identify a client. Case notes, assessments, DVDs, and audiotapes of sessions must be stored in secure locations with access limited to faculty and on-site clinical supervisors.

Privileged Communication

The legal concept of *privileged communication* refers to any conversation that takes places within a protected relationship, such as that between an attorney and client. The law often protects against forced disclosure of such conversations, although there are exceptions.

The application of privileged communication to the mental health field arose in the groundbreaking legal case, *Jaffee v. Redmond* (1996). In that case, the Supreme Court determined that a social worker could not be compelled to reveal the private records of a client. The case was the first to uphold the concept of psychotherapist–patient privilege.

Exceptions to Confidentiality

Confidentiality is not an absolute or static concept, as courts and legislative actions are constantly reshaping its parameters (Wheeler & Bertram, 2008). Federal guidelines such as HIPAA also proscribe permissible exceptions to confidentiality. As was stated previously, clients should be made aware at the beginning of the counseling relationship the legal limits of confidentiality (Wheeler & Bertram). It is important to discuss the occasions in which confidentiality may be breached, because clients may not be aware that confidentiality is not absolute. Counseling students may fear that enumerating the limits of confidentiality could inhibit a client's disclosure, although this does not appear to be a realistic concern (Baird & Rupert, 1987).

There are several general and common exceptions to confidentiality (Remley & Herlihy, 2007; Wheeler & Bertram, 2008):

- In cases of suspected abuse (child abuse, elder abuse, vulnerable populations)
- When the client is a danger to self
- When the client is a danger to others
- Clients planning future crimes
- Legal proceedings when counseling records may be subpoenaed (this would include a former client suing a former counselor)
- When a client has signed a release of information
- When the client is a minor
- Clients with serious communicable diseases
- When counseling clients who are terminally ill

Suspected Abuse

In most states, laws have been enacted for the teachers, healthcare workers, and mental health professionals regarding *mandated reporting* of suspected abuse (Remley & Herlihy, 2007). This law generally applies in cases of child abuse, although in some states it also applied to other vulnerable populations such as the older persons or the disabled (Wheeler & Bertram, 2008). Under mandated reporting statutes, if a child tells a counselor he or she is being physically or sexually abused, if the child has bruises or other injuries indicative of abuse, or if the counselor has other reasons to believe the child is being physically, sexually, or emotionally abused, the counselor is required to notify the appropriate authorities (typically a department for child welfare or children's services). Under the law, counselors cannot be sued for good faith reporting of suspected child abuse (Wheeler & Bertram, 2008).

After the report is made, a caseworker will be assigned to investigate. If the caseworker determines probable cause for abuse or neglect, he or she will refer the case to local law enforcement authorities. If, after an investigation, the authorities determine that abuse is occurring, the next step may be legal action for criminal prosecution of the abuser(s) or civil action to determine the best placement for the child's welfare. In many cases, the child will be removed from the home for a period (and in some cases, permanently). Child abuse and neglect will be discussed further in chapter 9.

Danger to Self and Others

Probably the most common situation in which a counselor will be required to breach confidentiality arises when a client makes direct and specific threats of suicide or of harm to a third party. The legal and ethical issues that arise in these situations are discussed in the *Tarasoff* case (*Tarasoff v. The University of California*, 1976). The case began when a psychologist at the university counseling center received a viable threat from a student that he intended to kill his former girlfriend (Tatiana Tarasoff). The psychologist reported the student to the university police, who briefly detained him for questioning but then released him when he promised to have no contact with Tarasoff. Tragically, when Ms. Tarasoff returned to campus, the student murdered her. The Tarasoff family sued, claiming no one from Berkeley notified them of the danger. The federal court ultimately ruled that when a "patient presents a serious danger or violence to others, the therapist incurs an obligation to use reasonably care to protect the foreseeable victim from such danger" (McClarren, 1987, p. 273).

Not all threats of violence may be serious ones; however, if a client makes an explicit threat and has a plan to achieve it, then the *Tarasoff* case would definitely apply. If a client discloses thoughts, feelings, or intentions that place the client or an identifiable third party at risk, you must document the threat, the appropriate action taken, as well as notify the proper authorities. Competent documentation is essential in crisis situations, as they may ultimately involve the legal system. Should a case proceed to court for an involuntary commitment to a psychiatric center or even a correctional facility, the case record will be carefully scrutinized. You want to demonstrate you were thorough in your counseling, assessment, and decision making, and that you did everything possible to ensure the client's safety. (Working with potentially violent or suicidal clients will be discussed in more detail in chapter 9.)

Some state courts have issued decisions that limit or contradict the *Tarasoff* ruling. In Florida, counselors may breach confidentiality to prevent imminent harm, but they are not mandated by law to do so (Wheeler & Bertram, 2008). In 1999, the Texas Supreme Court held in *Thapar v. Zezulka* (1999) that counselors have no common law duty to warn readily identifiable third parties of a threat against them. By statute, Texas counselors are permitted to make disclosures to law enforcement or medical personnel in situations where there is an identifiable risk of imminent injury. However, "there is no specific grant of immunity built into the statute, which could create a decision-making challenge for the counselor" (Wheeler & Bertram, p. 82). The bottom line, of course, is for counselors to know and operate within the laws of their respective state or territory and seek clarification from supervisors or legal counsel.

Clients Planning Future Crimes

If a client discloses that he or she is planning to commit future crimes, the counselor is required to disclose this information in 17 states when the client is under investigation by law enforcement officials (Glosoff, Herlihy, & Spence, 2000). These states are Alaska, Arizona, District of Columbia, Idaho, Illinois, Indiana, Kansas, Louisiana, Massachusetts, Montana, New Mexico, Oklahoma, Oregon, South Carolina, South Dakota, Tennessee, and Washington. Types of criminal activity included in this exception are the distribution of controlled substances, selling stolen goods, and fraudulent schemes (Welfel, 2010). Counselors confronted by such circumstances should confer with their supervisor and legal representative to ensure they are in compliance with the law and their professional ethics.

Legal Proceedings

Typical legal proceedings in which counselors may encounter forced disclosure involve cases of suspected child abuse, child custody, and civil litigation against counselors (Remley & Herlihy, 2007). In such cases, the counselor may be subpoenaed by an attorney to provide information from counseling sessions with a client.

When a former client brings case against a former counselor, the client's records no longer fall under the protection of "privileged" as discussed previously (Wheeler & Bertram, 2008). In such cases, the counseling records are considered to be evidence that is necessary to establish the legal facts. If a client decides to file an ethical complaint against a counselor or sue a counselor for any reason, the client must waive the right to confidentiality. This provides the counselor the opportunity to defend himself or herself against the client's claims.

In any case of forced disclosure, counselors must seek legal advice from competent counsel. Schools, agencies, hospitals, and other institutions all have attorneys who will be able to deal with the subpoena. If you receive a subpoena (which is unlikely, but could happen), report it immediately to your supervisor. Given the possibility that counseling records could be subpoenaed, however, it behooves counselors to be judicious in what they write in the records. Should any counselor or graduate counseling student be subpoenaed, his or her written record (e.g., case notes) are likely what will be called into question. Chapter 5 discusses ways to take effective and comprehensive case notes.

Client Release of Information

This exception is based on the client's right to release information. The *ACA Code of Ethics* states, "unless exceptions to confidentiality exist, counselors obtain written information from clients to disclose or transfer records to legitimate third parties. Steps are taken to ensure that receivers of counseling records are sensitive to their confidential nature" (ACA, 2005, Section B.6.f). Many clients in counseling will waive this right, especially when insurance reimbursement is concerned.

A release from confidentiality does not give a counselor approval to release client information to anyone but to specified third parties who would have a legitimate need to know. Additionally, the counselor must establish whether that third party will be able to respect the client's sensitive information. If the counselor has any hesitation about the wisdom of releasing the client's information to a particular person, the counselor should discuss his or her concerns with the client.

Minor Clients

Issues of confidentiality and privileged communication become much more complicated when minor clients are involved. Counselors must balance the rights of minor clients with their parents' or guardians' need to know (Remley & Herlihy, 2007). The issues can be particularly problematic in school settings, where the counselor also has the added responsibility of working within the framework of school district policies.

There are also significant legal variations across states and territories. For example, the definition of *minor* varies; in many states, adulthood begins at 18 years of age, but in some it is 19 or 21 years (Wheeler & Bertram, 2008). Furthermore, some states provide that 16-year-olds can withhold certain information from their parents, such as the use of birth control. The variations among state laws certainly make for challenging and confusing situations for counselors. Because of the complexities involved, Gustafson and McNamara (1987) recommended that therapists should create a written protocol that explicitly states the conditions of and limits to confidentiality in counseling minor clients. This protocol would be reviewed with each minor client involved, signed, and kept in the record. Providing a written record reduces the potential for confusion and protects the counselor, school, agency, or other party that may be involved should legal issues arise.

It is also worth mentioning that legal issues involving minors usually also involve their parents or legal guardians. Parents and guardians should also be aware of the parameters of confidentiality with regard to their children's therapy.

Clients with Serious Communicable Diseases

Counseling clients with serious communicable illnesses raises several ethical and legal issues. "The biggest concerns for counselors involve confidentiality of client disclosures, the risk of discrimination against clients if their health status is not protected, and, the welfare of third parties at risk for infection because of their contact with the client" (Welfel, 2010, p. 133).

Mandated disclosure regarding communicable diseases is one of the more recent ethical and legal issues the mental health profession has faced and perhaps the most controversial, because legal scholars continue to debate the merits of disclosure in this arena (Anderson & Barret, 2001; Harding, Gray, & Neal, 1993). The *ACA Code of Ethics* outlines guidelines for counselors regarding disclosure in cases of communicable diseases.

> When clients disclose that they have a disease commonly known to be both communicable and life threatening, counselors may be justified in disclosing information to identifiable third parties, if they are known to be at demonstrable and high risk of contracting the disease. Prior to making a disclosure, counselors confirm that there is such a diagnosis and assess the intent of clients to inform third parties about their disease or to engage in any behaviors that may be harmful to an identifiable third party. (ACA, 2005, Section B.2.b)

A gray area in most state laws covering communicable diseases refers to mandated disclosure by physicians and other healthcare providers and is often vague on the responsibilities of mental health professionals (Welfel, 2010). Furthermore, state laws on mandated disclosure of serious communicable illnesses vary widely. Most states allow or demand disclosure in cases of serious communicable illnesses, although some states mandate privacy for the client. In states that mandate privacy, a counselor could potentially be sued for disclosure to third parties (Welfel, 2010). Given such complexities and varying laws regarding disclosure in this arena, counselors must seek legal advice about the regulations that govern mandated disclosure and privacy.

Counseling Terminally Ill Clients

Counselors working with terminally ill clients may face several ethical, legal, moral, and spiritual issues. Terminally ill clients whose pain and suffering is intense may wish to examine the option of euthanasia during counseling sessions. The topic of "rational suicide" raises many complex issues: Are counselors under the same obligation to prevent terminally ill clients from committing suicide as they would other suicides? Does a terminal diagnosis actually change the counselor's duty to warn and protect? Does a client have a right to die? Are clients who wish to hasten their own death considered rational, or should they be considered mentally ill? The *ACA Code of Ethics* discusses the matter at length.

> *Counselor Competence, Choice and Referral.* Recognizing the personal, moral, and competence issues related to end-of-life decisions, counselors may choose to work or not work with terminally ill clients who wish to explore their end-of-life options. Counselors provide appropriate referral information to ensure that clients receive the necessary help.

> *Confidentiality.* Counselors who provide services to terminally ill individuals who are considering their own deaths have the option of breaking or not breaking confidentiality, depending on the specific circumstances of the situation and after seeking consultation or supervision. (ACA, 2005, Section A.9)

Counselors who work with terminally ill clients should now be familiar with these ethical statements, but also must be aware of state laws. Naturally, when working with end-of-life issues ands decisions, counselors must consult a legal professional for guidance.

The Case of Harriet

Harriet is a 70-year-old former advertising executive who has lived a full and active life. An all-conference cross country runner in college, she completed numerous marathons, half-marathons, and other athletic events. She was married and raised three children, and has eight grandchildren. Harriet, a widow, was diagnosed with liver cancer and given 6 months to live. She seeks counseling services from Malcolm. After a couple of sessions, Harriet states that she will discontinue debilitating radiation and chemotherapy treatments; she goes on to say that if the pain becomes too unbearable, she will take her life. After consulting with a colleague, Malcolm agrees to continue with counseling, provided Harriet does not disclose when she plans to end her life.

1. What do you think about Malcolm's decision? Do you agree? Disagree? Why?
2. Are Malcolm's actions defendable on ethical, legal, and moral grounds?
3. What are the moral issues and implications to this case?
4. If you were consulting with Malcolm, what concerns would you have?

Recommendations for Practicum/Internship

Here are some recommendations to consider if you are faced with an issue of confidentiality during your practicum/internship:

■ Know your school's or agency's policies on breaching confidentiality. Keep a copy of the written policy at your disposal.

- As soon as possible, consult with your on-site supervisor.
- Keep your practicum/internship advisor apprised regarding crisis situations.
- Make sure that you have properly documented a clear rationale for breaching confidentiality in the case notes. You never know when a file may be subpoenaed and a general guideline is "If it's not written in a file it didn't happen."
- In the event you are subpoenaed, do not immediately comply with the order; this could mean you have violated confidentiality. Go immediately to your supervisor, who will notify the school or agency attorney.

TECHNOLOGY AND CLIENT RECORDS

Many counseling agencies, schools, treatment centers, and private practitioners now maintain client records, schedules, and financial information on computer software. New technology, however, brings about new risks. Hackers may compromise the system and have access to sensitive client information; thus, security is paramount. Records must also be backed up in the event that data are lost. There are numerous software programs on the market specifically designed for counseling professionals. These programs can assist counselors in the creation and management of client records, including scheduling, billing, treatment planning, progress notes, reports to outside professionals (e.g., judges, child welfare, parole and probation, etc.), and client termination summaries, to cite a few.

Three such programs are TheraScribe (www.therascribe.com), Therapist Helper (www.helper.com), and Notes 444 (www.notes444.com), among many others.

Counselors must also maintain records for the minimum period set forth by federal or state law. Some states mandate 7 years, others 10 years (Wheeler & Bertram, 2008). Counselors may also wish to keep client records for years after treatment has ended because former clients have been known to request copies of case notes or counselors may need client records to protect themselves against litigation (Wheeler & Bertram, 2008). If there is no set minimum period for retention of records, a general practice is to keep records for 7 years (Remley & Herlihy, 2007; Wheeler & Bertram).

Counseling agencies, schools, and other treatment centers would be wise to adopt an official record retention policy. Records should be kept and transmitted in accordance with HIPAA requirements and state law. The record retention policy should specify how records will be stored, where they will be stored (the location must be secure), and how and when they will be destroyed (Wheeler & Bertram, 2008).

BOUNDARY ISSUES: DUAL RELATIONSHIPS IN COUNSELING

Boundary issues in counseling typically involve *dual* or *multiple relationships*. According to Herlihy and Corey (1997), dual or multiple relationships occur when counselors take on roles outside the therapeutic encounter. Dual relationships can involve combining the role of counselor with that of minister, teacher, colleague, committee member, friend, relative, and so forth. A sexual relationship between a counselor and a client represents a dual relationship; sexual relations with clients are explicitly forbidden under the *ACA Code of Ethics*. For other dual relationships, however, the issue is less clear. The most recent revision of the *ACA Code of Ethics* recognizes that dual relationships are not necessarily unethical. Under A.5 ("Roles and Relationships with Clients"), the standard states:

> Counselor–client nonprofessional relationships with clients, former clients, their romantic partners, or their family members should be avoided, except when the interaction is potentially beneficial to the client. (ACA, 2005, Section A.5.c)

Thus, the code of ethics no longer prohibits all nonprofessional relationships per se. Naturally, determining what is beneficial to the client is not always easy. The critical factor in dual relationships is for the counselor to refrain from involvement in counselor–client relationships that could compromise the therapeutic encounter. Herlihy and Corey (1997) identified four characteristics of dual relationships that make them problematic:

First, potential dual relationships can be *difficult to recognize*. They can evolve in subtle ways. For example, a counselor may accept an invitation from a client to go out for coffee. This may lead to more social encounters until the relationship has progressed into a sexual one.

A second characteristic of dual relationships is their *potential for harm ranges along a wide continuum*—from extremely harmful to benign or even beneficial.

But because the onus of responsibility is on the counselor and not on the client, counselors must discern through consultation whether the potential benefit of crossing boundaries with a client outweighs the risks and harm.

The Case of Alice

> Alice, age 28, seeks counseling from Steve, a licensed mental health counselor in an employee assistance program her employer contracts with. Alice's goal is to resolve issues of sexual abuse from her father that she endured when she was a teenager. After 3 months of counseling, Steve initiates a sexual relationship with Alice. He rationalizes his behavior by convincing himself that she is benefitting from a healthy sexual relationship with a positive adult concerned about her sexual well-being. Alice, on the other hand, feels somewhat confused. She feels in love with Steve but wonders about the nature of their relationship and whether Steve has done this before. She is also aware that Steve is in violation of his professional ethics, if not of the state law. She wants to discuss her concerns with Steve, but also does not want to lose him either as a romantic partner or a counselor.

The Case of Hector

Hector has been coming to see Tomasina, his counselor, for nearly 6 months. Through counseling, Hector has gained the self-confidence to complete his college degree. Hector requests Tomasina attend his graduation and graduation party because he credits the counseling with Tomasina for making it possible for him to achieve his goal. After giving the matter some thought and consulting with a colleague, Tomasina agrees to attend Hector's graduation.

1. What are the differences between Steve's and Tomasina's motivations to enter a dual relationship with a client?
2. What potential for harm could result from Tomasina's attending Hector's graduation and graduation party?
3. What potential harm could come from Steve's affair with Alice?
4. If you were a counseling supervisor, how would you advise Tomasina?
5. If Alice came to you for counseling regarding her relationship with Steve, how would you advise her?

   The examples illustrate the extremes of dual relationships and counseling. Steve's motivations are suspect and a clear ethical violation, regardless of whether or not the relationship is mutually desired. Even if the client pursues the relationship and wants it to continue, the counselor has committed a serious ethical violation. Tomasina's decision to attend graduation and the party has a low probability of harming the client. The *ACA Code of Ethics* specifically states that an example of a potentially beneficial interaction is "attending a formal ceremony" (e.g., wedding or commitment ceremony, graduation, etc.; ACA, 2005, Section A.5.d).

A third characteristic is, with the exception of sexual dual relationships, *there is very little consensus among mental health professionals regarding the propriety of dual relationships.* Some, such as Lazarus and Zur (2002), have taken the position that it can be very beneficial for a counselor to engage in dual relationships with some clients. Others have taken an opposing stance. St. Germaine (1993) suggests that the power differential between the counselor and the client makes it impossible for them to have a truly healthy relationship. It is also possible that counselors can knowingly or unknowingly exploit a client when dual roles are in play. Tomm (1993) points out that the dual role itself is not problematic; rather, it is the counselor's tendency to exploit clients or misuse power.

Unfortunately, there is a paucity of research regarding the impact of dual roles and the effectiveness of counseling (Remley & Herlihy, 2007). There also is no clear consensus among counseling professionals on this issue. The recommendation here is that at this point in your student counseling career, limit dual relationships as much as possible.

The fourth characteristic that makes boundary issues so complex is that *some dual relationships are unavoidable*. For example, counselors practicing in rural, isolated communities may find it impossible to avoid dual roles with clients. Having spent almost 16 years practicing in rural communities, I would frequently discover a current or former client working on my car at the dealership, ringing up my grocery bill at the supermarket, or serving with me on a community agency. In some rural communities, there may be only one counselor for a 100-mi. area. This would make referrals nearly impossible. For school counselors, dual relationships are simply a fact of the school environment. Counselors in the military also face many of the same challenges (Johnson, Ralph, & Johnson, 2005) as do members of particular subcultures (Lazarus & Zur, 2002). People's political affiliations, ethnic identities, religious values, and so forth, can often lead to dual relationships as clients often seek counselors with similar values (Johnson et al.).

The Case of Ginger and Kimber

Kimber has been a client of Ginger's for several weeks. They both live in a small and remote community of 2,000 people in the western United States, nearly 70 mi. from the nearest town. Kimber's husband and Ginger's partner serve on the advisory board for a local charitable organization. The husband and partner develop a friendship and want to begin a social relationship that includes all four parties.

1. How should Ginger respond when her partner suggests this social contact?
2. Do you think Kimber should inform her husband that Ginger is her counselor and that she would not be comfortable in such a social relationship?
3. What potential risks are posed for Ginger and Kimber should a social relationship develop?
4. Does the fact that they live in such an isolated community change the issue?

Sexual Intimacy with Clients

The most destructive and egregious form of dual relationships with clients is that involving sexual intimacy. The prohibition regarding sexual relationships is designed to protect clients from sexual and emotional exploitation. The ethical codes of all major helping professions specifically prohibit sexual relationships with clients (Wheeler & Bertram, 2008). Ignoring this ethical standard has led to client abuse and has been the downfall of otherwise capable counselors (Remley & Herlihy, 2007). Lamb and Catanzaro (1998) found that 8% of clinicians surveyed admitted to sexual violations with clients. It is likely that this statistic is low because of underreporting among various therapists surveyed.

In addition to ethical standards, many states have laws against counselor–client sexual relationships (Wheeler & Bertram, 2008). This makes counselor–client sexual relationship not only an ethical matter but also a criminal one. Moreover, it is important to note that sexual relationships are considered a crime even if the client is a willing participant and of legal age (Wheeler & Bertram). Prison sentences and fines are both possibilities in such scenarios, and counselors who have been convicted of sexual impropriety may lose their license.

Along with criminal laws, all states have laws that carry civil suits and damages for sexual intimacies with clients (Wheeler & Bertram, 2008). The *ACA Code of Ethics* latest update expands this prohibition to include "sexual or romantic client interactions or relationships with former clients, their romantic partners, or family members . . . for a period of 5 years following the last professional contact" (ACA, 2005, Section A.5.b). The language also expands on the ethical responsibilities of a counselor who might wish to become involved in a romantic relationship after 5 years by cautioning that the counselor must demonstrate forethought and document (in written form) whether the interactions or relationship can be viewed as exploitative in some way and whether there is still potential for harm to the former client. Basically, the onus is always on the counselor to demonstrate they have *done no harm* to the client.

Maintaining Professional Boundaries

Clearly, counselors involved in sexual impropriety with the clients they serve risk doing long-term and severe emotional damage to the clients. This is to say nothing of the professional damage to the counselor, his or her colleagues, employer, family, and the profession in general. Simply put, counselors should not have sex with their clients, period.

Corey et al. (2007) emphasize several points that are especially relevant for students in graduate programs. It is common, and human, to experience an attraction to clients. Therefore, the matter of counselor–client attraction must be recognized, processed, and dealt with. A fundamental aspect of such training recognizes the distinction between attraction and acting on that attraction. Students must feel it is safe to discuss feelings of attraction with their professors and clinical supervisors without the fear of being judged or criticized. If need be, graduate students should seek out professional counseling to help them clarify and separate personal and professional issues related to attraction

Unfortunately, some research suggests that despite ethical training and education, students who disclosed client attraction to their supervisor did not develop an appropriate understanding of the ethical boundaries regarding that attraction (Housman & Stake, 1999). A small percentage (7%) even thought that sex with a client might be ethical and therapeutic. On the other hand, 47% thought that any sexual feelings for clients were unacceptable. The former group could run into serious ethical and legal problems, whereas the latter may have difficulty because they may be unable to address feelings of attraction.

Recognizing that attraction is natural is the most realistic approach to take. There are some warning signs for counselors to pay attention to when they feel an attraction for a client:

- Giving the client extra time beyond the session
- Dressing up on the days you see that client
- Revealing inappropriate personal information to the client, such as your relationship status, type of person you are attracted to, and so forth
- Daydreaming about romantic escapades with the client
- Agreeing to meet with the client outside the treatment center, school, and so forth
- Encouraging the client to call you after hours even if it is not an emergency
- Initiating physical contact with the client
- Offering or accepting gifts from the client

Other Boundary Issues of Concern

Besides sexual relationships with clients, counselors should be cautious and judicious about entering into other dual relationships. Bartering with a client for goods and services is not prohibited by the *ACA Code of Ethics*, although a counselor should be very cautious about the practice. A common form of bartering involves the exchange of services. For example, a client might be a self-employed contractor having difficulty paying for counseling. He may offer renovation work in return for counseling services. This agreement raises many questions: Is it a fair exchange of services? Also, what if the counselor is unhappy with the renovation work? Conversely, what if the client is unhappy with the counseling? What happens if the client decides to leave counseling but has not finished the renovation work?

The *ACA Code of Ethics* offers guidelines for counselors to help them determine whether a potential bartering arrangement might be acceptable. The code states that counselors may participate in bartering only if three criteria are met: the relationship is not exploitive or harmful and does not place the counselor in an unfair advantage, if the client requests it, and if such arrangements are an accepted practice among professionals in the community (ACA, 2005, Section A.10.d).

Social relationships were discussed previously. Essentially, counselors should limit social relationships to special occasions (e.g., funerals, weddings, etc.) as much as possible. When counselors blend the roles of counselor and friend, they create a conflict of interest that compromises the objectivity needed for good professional judgment (Pope & Vasquez, 1998). Counselors will meet clients in outside social contexts without prior planning on either's part. Therefore, counselors should discuss with their clients how they might be affected by encountering the counselor outside the office and how such chance encounters should best be handled.

At times, clients will offer gifts to their counselors. As a counselor who has had his or her fair share of gifts offered, I can attest to the discomfort a counselor feels in choosing to maintain clear boundaries and a desire to not hurt the client's feelings. One agency I worked in had a written policy of not accepting gifts from clients. This policy was written into the informed consent form they signed at the onset of counseling. Naturally, even if advised of such prohibitions, some clients will forget or will try to present a gift anyway. Whether to accept or not to accept a gift may also depend on its monetary value. Few counselors would accept a costly work of art from a client, though most would likely accept a crayon drawing from a child. Evidently, many mental health professionals would express the monetary value of the gift was the critical aspect. Borys (1988) discovered that 84% thought that it is ethically permissible to accept a gift worth less than $10, but only 18% thought that it is ethical to accept a gift worth $50 or more.

It may also be prudent to consider the client's motivation. A client may be offering a gift as a small token of sincere gratitude. This would be considerably different from a client offering a gift as a means of manipulation. Remley and Herlihy (2007) recount an example of the client who was an excellent baker; the counselor accepted the first two baked offerings. When the client came with the third treat, the counselor used the situation as a means of exploring the client's motivation.

Counselors should also be aware of cultural considerations. Giving and accepting gifts is a common practice in many cultures as a means of showing gratitude and respect (Sue & Sue, 1998). Counselors need to ensure as much as possible that their own discomfort at being presented with a gift does not overshadow their sensitivity to what the gift means to the client (Remley & Herlihy, 2007). When counselors do choose to accept a gift, they should notify their supervisor. It might also be a good idea to document the gift in the case notes, its relative monetary value, and why the counselor accepted it.

The Case of Jim

Jim is an addictions counselor working on a tribal reservation in the American Southwest. As a member of the tribe, Jim is acutely aware that he must balance a fine boundary between cultural expectations and professional ethics. Because he works in a traditional healing community, he is occasionally expected to visit clients in their homes, have meals with the client's family, and participate in spiritual purification ceremonies with them.

1. What types of ethical and boundary difficulties would you expect Jim to face in this scenario?
2. How does Jim's culture change his professional situation?
3. How might Jim manage both ethical responsibilities and cultural expectations? Or, what would be realistic regarding the balance between maintaining ethical boundaries and cultural norms?

Continued

There are many counselors in a similar situation to Jim. An interesting aside to note is that I have noticed that legal discussions regarding situations such as Jim's tend to be quite different from those regarding mainstream, dominant, white culture. It would be interesting to hear from Jim's tribal legal counsel regarding any ethical and legal risks of Jim's situation.

LIABILITY INSURANCE

For counselors practicing in the United States, professional liability insurance is an absolute necessity. Although graduate counseling students on practicums and internships are far less likely to be sued than professional counselors, they are not immune to litigation (Wheeler & Bertram, 2008). Counseling students in Council for Accreditation of Counseling and Related Educational Programs (CACREP)-accredited programs are required to carry student liability insurance, and many non-CACREP programs now require coverage as well. Fortunately, students who purchase a membership with the ACA or the AMHCA receive student liability insurance as part of their membership. Students may also purchase student liability insurance through many independent carriers.

For a client plaintiff to prevail in a malpractice lawsuit against a counselor, the plaintiff must prove the following elements (Prosser, Wade, & Schwartz, 1988):

1. The counselor had a duty to warn the client to use reasonable care regarding providing counseling services.
2. The counselor failed to conform to the required duty of care.
3. The client was injured.
4. There was a reasonably close casual connection between the conduct of the counselor and the resulting injury (known as *proximate cause*).
5. The client suffered an actual loss or was damaged.

The good news regarding litigation against counselors and other mental health professionals is that proving all of these elements of malpractice is difficult (Remley & Herlihy, 2007). Roughly 20% of cases filed against mental health professionals result in a judgment against the therapist (Conte & Karasu, 1990). Still, even an unsuccessful lawsuit could potentially end a counselor's practice (Remley & Herlihy), and being sued is stressful, expensive, and time-consuming (Remley & Herlihy). Naturally, the best way to deal with lawsuits is to lessen the risk of litigation by practicing within the boundaries laid out in the *ACA Code of Ethics*, be meticulous in writing case notes, limit dual relationships as much as possible, refrain from romantic relationships with clients, receive ongoing supervision, and continue upgrading your education through your professional life. These simple recommendations are no guarantee against being sued, but they lower a counselor's window of vulnerability to lawsuits.

CHAPTER 4

Clinical Issues in Practicum/Internship

In this chapter, I will offer a brief overview of common clinical issues you may encounter at the practicum/internship site, along with suggestions and examples to assist you in counseling and assessment. Students beginning the practicum may find the experience difficult at first, because they are actually encountering real people with real issues instead of theoretic scenarios in a textbook or on a DVD. Compounding the issue is the amount of information and data that accompanies counseling. The type of method, the information gathered, and how records are managed and stored vary from setting to setting. Perhaps the most important concept for graduate counseling students to keep in mind when they are providing counseling is that the therapeutic relationship is likely more important than particular technique or theoretical approach (Miller, Hubble, & Duncan, 1996; Wampold, 2001).

Although no one chapter could possibly cover all the clinical issues and skills you need, this chapter will outline some of the basic skills that you should be aware of: building the therapeutic alliance, handling intake and basic assessments, understanding counseling techniques, and other basics. The next chapter will discuss clinical writing skills that you will need to document your sessions.

BUILDING THE THERAPEUTIC ALLIANCE

The most critical factor in establishing the counseling relationship is creating an attachment with the client or clients (Beck & Weishaar, 2008; Rogers, 1951). Creating this alliance involves a process of establishing trust, respect, openness, and the willingness to take emotional risks (Ellis, 2001). Once an alliance is established, the client can begin to disclose to the counselor the reasons he or she has sought out counseling. The initial interview is your first and best opportunity to begin establishing such an alliance. Ivey and Ivey (2007) suggest a structured model for the initial interview:

- Building rapport and structuring a process that has as its purpose the building of a working relationship with the client
- Gathering information, defining the problem, and identifying client assets to determine why the client has sought out counseling and how he or she views the issue

■ Determining outcomes, which enables the counselor to plan therapy based on what the client is seeking, the client's viewpoint, and what life would be like without the existing problems
■ Exploring alternatives and confronting incongruities, which is a critical task for the counselor to assist the client in resolving his or her problems
■ Generalization and transfer of learning, which is the process whereby changes in the client's thoughts, feelings, and behaviors are carried out in his or her everyday life

Weinrach (1989) advocates that counselors address issues most frequently raised by clients when beginning therapy. This may include some of the following questions:

■ How often can I expect to have an appointment?
■ How might I reach you in an emergency?
■ What happens if I forget an appointment?
■ How confidential are counseling sessions?
■ What do I do in an emergency?
■ When is it time to end treatment?
■ What are my financial responsibilities?
■ How often do I obtain reimbursement from insurance?

Beginning counselors should be aware that the counseling process may be new as well as intimidating to clients beginning therapy. Because clients come to counseling feeling burdened, overwhelmed, depressed, anxious, frustrated, and so forth, they may not be well attuned to the process. Questions like those just mentioned can help clarify the counseling relationship and address basic concerns of the client.

It is also worth noting that not all clients enter the counseling relationship voluntarily. *Mandated clients* (those who are required to enter counseling by a spouse, boss, probation officer, judge, principal, or other person) are a reality in all clinical settings, and mandated clients are likely to show less investment in the counseling process (Cox & Klinger, 2004). Regardless of whether the client has come voluntarily or is mandated, the process of initiating therapy begins with acknowledging the issues listed previously.

INITIAL INTAKE FORM

The intake form is a common information gathering form. Many counseling settings will use some variation of this form to gather basic information about a new client. Intake sheets typically include name, address, family history, previous counseling and psychiatric treatment, medications, and other information. The intake is usually common in mental health settings, although many schools use a similar form (sometimes called a developmental history form; Sommers-Flanagan & Sommers-Flanagan, 1999).

Figure 4.1 offers an example of an intake form.

FIGURE 4.1   Initial Intake Form

Name: _____   Date: ____/____/____

Address: _____   City: _____   State: ____

Zip Code: _____   Phone: _____ (H) _____ (W/C)

Identifying Information

Age: _____   Date of Birth: ____/____/____   Place: _____

Sex: Female ____   Male ____   Height: ____ Ft. ____ In.   Weight: ____ Lbs.

Occupation: _____

Marital Status: M ____   S ____   D ____   Sep. ____   Other: ____

Spouses/Partner's Name: _____   Age: _____

Occupation: _____   Employer: _____

Name(s)/Ages of Children: (If applicable):

_____

_____

_____

_____

Referral Source: _____

Address of Referral Source: _____

Treatment History

Are you currently taking medication?   Yes: ____   No: ____

If yes, name of medication(s): _____

Provider of medication(s): _____

Continued

FIGURE 4.1　　Initial Intake Form *Continued*

Have you received previous psychiatric/psychological treatment?

Yes: _____　No: _____

If yes, name the provider: _____

Dates of Counseling/Psychiatric Treatment: _____

_____

Has any close relative ever had psychiatric treatment or been committed to a psychiatric hospital?　Yes: _____　No: _____

If yes, please explain:

_____

_____

_____

What factor(s) led you to seek counseling services: _____

_____

_____

Symptoms:_____

_____

Treatment Outlook: If you were to feel better, what would be different?

_____

_____

What personal strengths do you possess that can help with your treatment?

_____

_____

Continued

FIGURE 4.1   Initial Intake Form *Continued*

Family History

Mother's Name: _____   Living: _____   Deceased: _____

Father's Name: _____   Living: _____   Deceased: _____

Brother(s)/Sister(s):

Name: _____   Age: _____   Living: _____   Deceased: _____

Name: _____   Age: _____   Living: _____   Deceased: _____

Name: _____   Age: _____   Living: _____   Deceased: _____

Educational History

High School: _____

    Location: _____

    Dates Attended: _____   Degree: _____

College/University: _____

    Location: _____

    Dates Attended: _____   Degree: _____

Technical School: _____

    Location: _____

    Dates Attended: _____   Degree: _____

Graduate/Professional: _____

    Location: _____

    Dates Attended: _____   Degree: _____

INITIAL ASSESSMENT

The types of assessment you conduct with clients will vary greatly depending on your setting and client population. An educational placement, such as a middle school, will require considerably different data than a residential psychiatric center. Proper assessment is influenced by the following considerations (Hood & Johnson, 2007, pp. 14–15):

- Where is the assessment taking place? In a high school counseling office? In a correctional setting?
- When is the assessment occurring? Junior year in anticipation of preparing for college or technical school? Or, prior to beginning graduate school?
- Why is the assessment being undertaken? Has the client been referred for counseling and assessment because of concerns about his mood?
- How is the assessment conducted? By computer? Pen and paper?

In mental health settings, some variations of the Mental Status Examination (MSE) is likely to be conducted as part of the intake process (Seligman, 2004). School counselors, however, are unlikely to use the MSE, although they may use some type of developmental questionnaire. The MSE is designed to provide the counselor with baseline information regarding the client's appearance, affect, cognitive functioning, orientation, judgment, short- and long-term memory, insight, and more (Polanski & Hinkle, 2000).

Although not a standardized psychological instrument, the MSE is frequently used in mental health settings for the purposes of assessment, diagnoses, and treatment of mental disorders. Typically conducted during the initial intake interview, the MSE can provide counselors with helpful categorized information for formalizing objective and subjective client data. Although numerous formats of the MSE exist, the two versions provided here offer examples of the MSE. Figure 4.2 shows a brief version of the MSE, and Figure 4.3 offers an MSE for older children, adolescents, and adults.

COUNSELING TECHNIQUES

Most counseling programs offer graduate training from various theoretic approaches (Gladding, 2009). In your program, you may study theoretic approaches such as psychodynamic, client-centered, cognitive behavioral, solution focused, and existential—just to name a few. Because they explore so many counseling theories, students often put together an integrative approach, meshing techniques from this list of various theories. The proliferation of approaches and techniques can definitely be confusing for students regarding what technique to use with which particular client.

| FIGURE 4.2 | Mental Status Examination (Brief Version)* |

Now, I am going to ask you a series of questions to test your concentration and memory. Answer to the best of your ability. Okay, any questions before we begin?

Orientation to Time:

What year is this? (1 point)
What season is this? (1 point)
What is the month and date? (1 point)
What day of the week is it? (1 point)
(Maximum of 4 points)

Orientation to Place:

What is the name of this institution/school/agency? (1 point)
What floor are we on? (1 point)
What city and state are we in? (1 point)
What county is this? (1 point)
(Maximum of 4 points)

Immediate Recall:

I am going to say three objects. After I say them I want you to repeat them. They are "ball," "flag," and "tree." Now say them. Remember them because I will ask you to repeat them later. (Interviewer: 1 point for each; maximum of 3 points)

Attention:

(Serial 7s. Choose from either item below but not both)

Subtract 7 from 100 and continue until I tell you to stop. (Interviewer: Continue until subject makes an error. 1 point for each correct answer up to a maximum score of 5 points)

Spell the word "world" backwards. (1 point for each correct letter; maximum of 5 points)

Delayed Recall:

What are the three words I asked you to remember? (1 point for each; maximum of 3 points)

Naming:

Show subject a pen and wrist watch and ask to name them. (1 point for each; maximum of 2 points)

Continued

FIGURE 4.2   Mental Status Examination (Brief Version)* *Continued*

Repetition:

Repeat the following sentence exactly as I say it. "No ifs, ands, or buts." (I point for each word; maximum of 3 points)

Stage Command:

"Now I want to see how well you can follow instructions. I'm going to give you a piece of paper. Take it in you right hand, use both hands to fold it in half, and then put it on the floor." (I point for each command; maximum of 3 points)

Reading:

Show the subject a headline written on the following page and ask him or her to read what it says silently and then to do what it says. (I point; Note: You may write anything. The point is to see if the client understands it.)

Copying:

Give subject a clean sheet of paper and ask him or her to copy the geometric design printed on the next page. (I point)

Writing:

On the same sheet of paper, ask the subject to write a complete sentence. (I point)

Scoring Procedures:

Total (Maximum Score) = 30

Note:

Scores of 23–30 indicate expected or *normal functioning*. Scores lower than 23 suggest the presence of *cognitive impairment*.
23–30 = *no cognitive impairment*
18–23 = *mild cognitive impairment*
 0–17 = *significant cognitive impairment*

MSE scores may be invalid if the subject has less than a ninth-grade education, is intoxicated, or is under the influence of other drugs.

Source: Adapted from Polanski & Hinkle, 2000; Folstein, Folstein, & McHugh, 1975.

*A Mental Status Examination (MSE) is a common subjective form of assessment that typically accompanies a clinical intake. This MSE is a common example of a brief or short version. Short versions are often used in clinical settings to regularly assess change in a client.

FIGURE 4.3   Mental Status Examination for Older Children, Adolescents, and Adults*

The areas to be covered for the written Mental Status Examination report:

Prior to beginning, explain:

1. Who you are. (counselor)
2. Who you represent. (school, clinic, prison, etc.)
3. Why the MSE is taking place. (request, standard procedure, etc.)
4. Informed Consent. (confidentiality, training or education, fees—if applicable)
5. Always ask, "Do you have any questions?"

When interviewing a client, always remain calm and in control. Exaggerated verbal and non-verbal responses may invalidate the interview.

A. Heading

Name

Age

Date of Birth

Gender

Interview Site

Date of Interview and Report

Reason for Referral

B. Appearance and Behavior

1. How did the client present himself or herself?
2. How did the interviewee look (Note: grooming, height, weight, facial appearance, special adornments, jewelry)?
3. How did the interviewee act during the interview (Note: bizarre gestures, postures, repetitive movements, poor eye contact, slow movements, excessive movements, etc.)?
4. Was the interviewee's behavior appropriate for his or her age, education, and vocational status?
5. How did the interviewee relate to the interviewer (e.g., was he or she wary, friendly, manipulative, approval seeking, hostile, superficial, etc.)?

Continued

FIGURE 4.3   Mental Status Examination for Older Children, Adolescents, and Adults* *Continued*

C. Speech and Communication

1. How was the general flow of the interviewee's speech? (e.g., Was it rapid, controlled, hesitant, slow, pressured?)
2. Does the interviewee have speech impediments?
3. How was the general tone and content of the interviewee's speech? (Note: for example, over or under productivity of speech, flight of ideas, paucity of ideas, loose associations, rambling, tangentially, neologisms, bizarre use of words, incoherence, etc.)
4. What was the relationship between verbal and nonverbal communication?
5. Was there the relationship between tone and content of the communications?
6. How interested was the interviewee in communicating?

D. Thought Content

1. What did the interviewee discuss? (Note: for example content that he or she brought up spontaneously)
2. What were the problem areas?
3. Were there any recurring themes?
4. Were there any signs of psychopathology, such as obsessions, delusions, hallucinations, phobias, or compulsions?

E. Sensory and Motor Functioning

1. How intact were the interviewee's senses—hearing, sight, touch, and smell?
2. How adequate was the interviewee's gross motor coordination?
3. How adequate was the interviewee's fine motor coordination?
4. Were there signs of motor difficulties such as exaggerated movements, repetitive movements (tics, twitches, tremors, bizarre postures, slow movements, or rituals?)

F. Cognitive Functioning

1. What was the general mood of the interviewee? (e.g., Was he or she sad, elated, anxious, tense, suspicious, or irritable?)
2. Did the interviewee's mood fluctuate or change during the interview?
3. How did the interviewee react to the interview? (e.g., Was he or she cold, friendly, cooperative, suspicious, or cautious?)
4. Was the interviewee's affect appropriate for the speech and content of the communications?
5. What did the interviewee say about his or her mood and feelings?
6. Was the self-report congruent with the interviewee's behavior during the interview?

Continued

FIGURE 4.3   Mental Status Examination for Older Children, Adolescents, and Adults* *Continued*

G. Insight and Judgment

1. What is the interviewee's belief about why he or she was coming to the interview?
2. Is the belief appropriate and realistic?
3. Is the interviewee aware of his or her problem and the concerns of others?
4. Does the interviewee have ideas about what caused the problem?
5. Does the interviewee have any idea about how the problem could be alleviated?
6. How good is the interviewee's judgment in carrying out everyday activities?
7. How does the interviewee solve problems of living? (e.g., impulsively, independently, responsibly, trial and error, etc.)
8. Does the interviewee make appropriate use of advice or assistance?
9. How much does the interviewee desire help for his or her problems?

H. Questions to Ask the Interviewee: (Note: This section is geared for older children, adolescents, and adults. For preschool and K–2, many of these questions may be inappropriate.)

Key: Questions 1–4 and 8–10 test general orientation to time, place, and person respectively; 11–16 test recent memory; 17–20 test remote memory; 21–23 test immediate memory; 24–25 test insight and judgment; and 26–28 test oral reading and spelling skills.

1. What is today's date?
2. What day is it?
3. What month is it?
4. What year is it?
5. Where are you?
6. What is the name of this city?
7. What is the name of this clinic? (or school, etc.)
8. What is your name?
9. How old are you?
10. What do you do?
11. Who is the president of the United States?
12. Who was the president before him?
13. Who is the governor of this state?
14. How did you get to this clinic (or school counseling center)?
15. What is your father's name?
16. What is your mother's name?
17. When is your birthday?
18. Where were you born?
19. Did you finish elementary school? (if appropriate)
20. When did you finish high school? (if appropriate)

Continued

FIGURE 4.3   Mental Status Examination for Older Children, Adolescents, and Adults* *Continued*

21. Repeat these numbers back after me: 6-9-5, 4-3-8-1, 2-9-8-5-7.
22. Say these numbers backwards: 8-3-7, 9-4-6-1, 7-3-2-5-8.
23. Say these words after me: ball, flag, tree.
24. What does this saying mean; "A stitch in time saves nine."
25. What does this saying mean: "Too many cooks spoil the broth?"
26. Read back the three words I gave to you earlier. (ball, flag, tree)
27. Write the words given previously. (ball, flag, tree)
28. Spell these words: spoon, cover, attitude, procedure.

I. Conclusion

At the conclusion of the Mental Status Examination report, write your name, and credentials:

Source: Adapted from Niagara University Mental Health Counseling Manual.

*Longer versions of the MSE are more typically used when a client is beginning counseling. The format above represents one example of an MSE.

The reality is that counseling is a trial-and-error and retrial process between the counselor and client. There is no-one-size-fits-all approach that faculty and clinical supervisors can give to students. Student counselors in a practicum/internship simply need to try different techniques. The more you use various techniques, the more you can learn and build on your existing skill set. Here are some basic counseling techniques and interventions practicum you will likely use:

- Open-ended questioning: "What brought you in today?"
- Reflection of feeling: "How did you feel when your spouse left?"
- Paraphrasing: "So, it sounds like you were upset at your roommate."
- Summarizing: "It sounds like you believe that you are beginning to feel a sense of confidence regarding recovering from your divorce. You are reaching out to friends, attending a weekly support group, even contemplating dating again. That sound about right?"
- Scaling question: "On a scale of 1 to 10, with 1 meaning you feel *very depressed* and 10 meaning you feel *great*, where would you put yourself?"
- Gestalt empty chair technique: "Ok, let's say your father was sitting in that empty chair beside you. What would you want to say to him regarding his verbal abuse?" Also, the empty chair technique can be conducted using a psychodrama approach, where the client will sit in the empty chair and play the role of the absent person (e.g., father, mother, spouse, etc.). The client will also play themselves.
- Reframing: "You mentioned 'I always fail.' But earlier I heard you say you just completed a college degree. It seems to me it might be more accurate to say, 'I have my failures, but I'm also successful.'"
- Homework: "Ok, here's what I'd like you to do between now and next week's session. You have talked about a desire to make friends. So, I'd like you to speak with three new people in the next week. Then, we'll discuss how that goes in next week's session."
- Artwork (with younger clients): "Ok Ellen, I have some paper and crayons. I'd like you to draw your family on this large sheet."
- Role plays: Like the empty chair technique discussed previously. Clients, especially couples and families are primed for role plays. Individual counseling also should involve role plays from time to time. Role plays are often used for issues involving confrontation, asking for a date, assertiveness with a roommate, setting limits with a parent, and so forth.

Now, this is a brief list of several techniques that students will use on their practicum. Do not let yourself get too overwhelmed by techniques, because they take time to learn. Also, keep in mind that techniques may not be the most important aspect of counseling success (Miller et al., 1996; Wampold, 2001).

When you do use techniques, give the client time to answer before moving on to the next intervention. Present yourself as calm and engaged; suggest to the client that he or she is your only point of focus. Clients will likely be encouraged that you are attending to them so intently. In fact, it is unlikely that anyone else will attend to clients the way that their counselors do. After all, counseling, unlike friendship, is a one-sided relationship. It is also very important to be genuine when you are counseling clients. Although there is no exact formula on authenticity, it starts with understanding your own beliefs, attitudes, and values.

One of the most critical aspects of the practicum experience is learning to trust your own instincts (Gladding, 2009). Some counselor educators might call this process learning to listen to your "inner voice." A supervisor of mine was once fond of saying, "When you have spent time counseling, you develop an inner counselor as your guide. This guide is honed through education, experience, and self-reflection. Learn to heed this voice." To become a successful counselor, each student in training must learn to recognize his or her own voice and to put the suggestions of that inner voice into action. Listening to our inner voice is likely another path to becoming the genuine practitioner, which Carl Rogers (1942, 1951) wrote about decades ago. In addition, understand that the inner voice will not be perfect regarding what technique or intervention to use with a client, because counseling is an inexact science. Still, awareness of your own inner voice is likely the most reliable path to take in the counseling experience.

THE CLINICAL RECORD

Keeping accurate client records is vital to effective counseling and ethical practice. Remley and Herlihy (2007) suggest client records contain the following information:

- Intake information. This category includes personal demographic data about the client, such as name, address and phone number, date of birth, gender, ethnicity, education, marital status, and previous psychiatric and counseling history.
- Assessment/testing information. Assessment provides specific information the counselor might otherwise not have on areas such as current drug use, depression, suicidal ideation, hopefulness, and so forth.
- Psychological assessment. The Beck Depression Inventory-II, Minnesota Multiphasic Inventory-2 (MMPI-2), and so forth.
- Psychosocial family assessment. Assesses client's current level of functioning in his or her family and/or his or her community.
- Vocational and educational assessment. How stable is the client's employment status? What is his or her level of education or desired education?
- Drug and alcohol assessment. Assesses past and current use of chemical substances through interviewing and testing with the Michigan Alcohol Screening

Test (MAST), Substance Abuse Subtle Screening Inventory-3 (SASSI-3), and other tests related to drug and alcohol.

■ Health assessment. Assessment of recent health issues, surgeries, procedures, and current use of medications.

■ Treatment plan. The treatment plan identifies and sets the parameters for how counseling is to be carried out, including statement of the problem, treatment goals, and steps to reach the goals.

■ Case notes. Documentation of progress, clinical impressions, evaluation of each session, and homework assigned to the client (see chapter 5 for more on how to write effective case notes).

■ Termination record. A summarization of treatment, success, lack of success, and so forth (see chapter 11 for more on client termination).

CLOSING THE SESSION

Standard counseling sessions are typically 50 minutes (there may be some variation). Counselors, especially new ones, should try to begin and end sessions on time, because this illustrates to clients the importance of set beginnings and endings. Counselors who allow sessions to begin late and extend beyond the parameters are modeling poor boundaries to the client. Such "loose" behavior on the part of the counselor may ultimately be unhealthy for the client in jobs, relationships, and in other social encounters. Of course, this statement is culture specific. Western cultures tend to value more rigid timelines, whereas some eastern and indigenous cultures have more flexibility regarding time (Lee, 2003, 2006). Still, counselors must be cognizant of timely schedules, because clients and colleagues will likely expect you to be prompt.

Many beginning counselors do have difficulty closing sessions with clients who insist on pushing the session beyond its limits. There is the old adage of the client who says nothing of note for 49 minutes, then drops a bombshell ("I'm pregnant," "My home's being foreclosed," "I've just flunked out of college," etc.). I have experienced many such incidents myself. If a client truly is in crisis—that is, a danger to himself or herself or others—then do not let the client leave (see chapter 9 for more information on clients in crisis). In the absence of such a risk, it is important that you stay as close to the set parameters as possible.

Benjamin (1987) emphasizes two important concerns in closing a counseling session. First, both the counselor and the client should be aware that the session is ending. This means the counselor has covered time limits in the intake session. Counselors would also be wise to make some statement during closing time like, "Ok, it looks like our time is about up . . ." Secondly, no new material should be presented during the closing. If the client "drops" something on you at the very end of the session, you might say, "That's an excellent starting point for next time" (if it is not a crisis).

When it comes to ending sessions, be brief and simple. Remind the client of time limits by saying, "We have just 5 minutes left." This can help the client refocus and also serves to keep the session on track. You might also say something like, "Time is almost up. Could you summarize what you learned today?" Gladding (2009) emphasizes that it is helpful to have the client summarize what happened in the session. This emphasizes the client's responsibility by forcing the client to reflect back on the salient points and recap them. This is also a tacit way of illustrating that the counselor values what the client sees as the important points of the session. The counselor certainly can provide the summarization, but it prevents the client from achieving momentum. Some counselors use nonverbal gestures such as standing up or pointing to their watch. There are many ways to end the session. The best guideline is to be clear, low key (so as not to hurt the client's feelings), and firm. Then, the final aspect of session termination is setting an appointment for the next session.

FINAL SUGGESTIONS

Here are some suggestions for your transition to the practicum/internship experience:

■ Remember, in the beginning, everyone was a rookie. Give yourself time to make the transition. When you feel stressed and overwhelmed, check in with your supervisor. Also, get to know your fellow practicum students. You can be good supports for one another. In fact, some graduate students have even begun practicum support groups.
■ As you begin practicum, be aware that you will be critiqued. The important aspect here is to be open to critical feedback. Naturally, even with the most benign and constructive type of feedback, it is natural to experience some degree of defensiveness. Be open to the feedback from your on-site clinical supervisor and your faculty practicum supervisor. But, do not be afraid to ask clarifying questions (see chapter 6 for more information on critique and feedback).
■ Take initiative. Clinical supervisors are generally impressed with practicum students who read and ask questions regarding agency, school, or university counseling center policies. If there are written policies and procedures manuals at your site (and there should be!), read and refer back to it.
■ Make a point of showing up on time for all your shifts. Interestingly, in all my years as a counselor educator, one of the most common complaints is tardy practicum/internship students.
■ Complete all responsibilities in a timely manner. Make sure all case notes are written and filed after each session (or certainly before you leave the practicum site).

■ Make sure you take care of yourself. Counselors cannot begin to help people in need unless they are emotionally healthy themselves. Make time for stress-reducing activities that you enjoy, such as physical fitness (jogging, cycling, swimming, power walking, yoga, aerobics, etc.), centering activities such as meditation, prayer (for those so inclined), reading, and so forth.

■ Understand that counseling actual people can be a complex endeavor. Give yourself time to adjust as counseling is unlike any experience you have previously had.

Finally, I tell all my students not to be afraid of making mistakes. In fact, I instruct them they *should* make mistakes, because making mistakes indicates they are stretching their skill set. One of the worst mistakes student counselors can make is being inert because of "fear of saying something wrong." It is unlikely you will tell the client something that will be permanently damaging. Now, you will commit verbal errors occasionally, because every counselor does. If you believe you have offended the client, honesty is the best policy ("I apologize. I may have offended you by that question/comment. Let me try and rephrase . . ."). Very few clients will expect perfection from their counselor (and should a client expect perfection, that would be an issue for the two of you to explore!). The critical factor is that you are able to learn from your mistakes. Be proactive and solicit advice from your on-site supervisor and university supervisor.

CHAPTER 5

Clinical Writing Skills

Writing clear and descriptive case notes is very different from most other types of writing. By now, you have likely had lots of experience in writing, for example, through American Psychological Association (APA) style research papers in your counseling classes. You may also have written poetry, short stories, journal articles, and maybe even blogs. In these cases, the objective is to entertain, persuade, or inform. Unlike those other types of writing, your objective in writing case notes is merely to create an accurate and informative record of treatment and client progress (or lack thereof). Although it is likely that training in counseling skills receives the most attention in graduate programs, clarity in clinical writing may be even more important (Seligman, 2004), especially should a client's file be subpoenaed. This chapter is designed to provide an overview on writing clear, concise, and effective case notes. Also, students should remember that like all other counseling training, developing good, clear, and concise clinical writing skills takes time and comes through experience.

Remember, when writing case notes, you are not writing for a wide audience—in fact, in most cases, you actually hope your case notes never see the light of day! However, you must remember that your notes are not simply for yourself but serve as treatment history for future clinicians, human service professionals, law enforcement personnel, the client, and, shudder, even the courts. An ineffective writer who makes numerous grammatical errors or leaves out pertinent information will lose his or her professional credibility at minimum, and, at maximum, could be on the short end of a lawsuit. Should that unlikely event come to pass, you want your written record to support you.

Unfortunately, many graduate counseling programs seem to put little emphasis on training students in writing clinical case notes (Cottone & Tarvydas, 2003). This is of great concern when one considers that what is (and is not) recorded in case notes can be the difference between liability and sound legal standing (Wheeler & Bertram, 2008). Many professions, such as medicine, train students with the notion that their notes will be read by various professionals and that they must always be ready to defend whatever is in the record (Remley & Herlihy, 2007). In my opinion, counselors must be trained with the same emphasis in mind.

Most writers are made, not born. As a college professor and a writer myself, I can verify that writing does not come easy to most people. Most of us struggle to transform our thoughts into coherent sentences and paragraphs. The best teacher for writing case notes is some combination of instruction, reading an experienced clinician's case notes, perusing appropriate reference texts on writing case notes, and practice, practice, practice writing your own. During your practicum or internship, ask for the case notes of veteran counselors to see their style. Notice how they have learned to write—what they put in the notes and what they left out. The specific style and content will vary from one counselor to another and one client to another. However, the professionalism will likely be consistent. This is also an area where your field supervisor should be your coach. Your field supervisor may critique your case notes and, if not, feel free to ask him or her to do so.

CLIENT RECORDS AND THE STANDARD OF CARE

In the distant past, it was common for counselors and other mental health professionals to intentionally refrain from keeping client records (Wheeler & Bertram, 2008). This unfortunate (and now unethical) practice is passé. Over the past two decades, the standards regarding information, storage, and transmission of client records have all been raised. "In fact, failure to maintain adequate client records could form the basis of a claim of professional malpractice because it breaches the standard of care expected of a practicing mental health professional" (Wheeler & Bertram, 2008, p. 115).

These standards impact nearly all counselors, regardless of the setting. However, it should also be acknowledged that record-keeping requirements for K–12 school counselors are not as clear as for counselors in mental health settings (Bertram & Wheeler, 2008). The U.S. Department of Education, state agencies, school systems, administrative districts, and individual schools often develop record-keeping policies that may or may not coincide with standards for mental health regulations and policies (Wheeler & Bertram). Regardless of the setting you ultimately work in, you will need to become competent and skilled in writing clear case notes, because you may still be compelled to testify in a court of law. Should you find yourself in this unfortunate and sometimes traumatic experience, your case notes will become the focus of the attorney's cross-examination. On this matter I can speak from experience. As a director of a county clinic early in my career, I was compelled to go to court regularly. In every case, the attorneys focused most of their attention on the written records. After all, although a client's or counselor's memory may fade, the written records will remain the same.

Standard of Care: Clinical Management

Well-written case notes clearly assist in the clinical case history and provide a rationale for past and current treatment. Because the nature of counseling implies continuous growth and change, case notes should reflect how the client is progressing in his or her treatment. Case records provide documentation of quality care, including what has worked, what has not worked, and why. Case records also ensure some degree of protection from legal liability by demonstrating and documenting the strategic planning on the part of the counselor and treatment team. Case notes also establish that the counselor conducted himself or herself as a competent professional. After all, written records are the only concrete proof the counselor has regarding client treatment and therapeutic progress. As it is often said in the mental health field, "If it ain't written down, it don't exist."

One of the more distressing issues that can arise in counseling is when a client discloses the intent to harm himself or herself or other parties. When clients disclose thoughts, feelings, or intentions that place himself or herself or an identifiable third party at risk, the counselor must document the threat, and the appropriate action taken, as well as notify the proper authorities. Competent documentation is essential in crisis situations, as such are likely to involve the legal system. Should a case proceed to court for an involuntary commitment to a psychiatric center or even a correctional facility, the case record will be carefully scrutinized.

Quality documentation also facilitates continuity of care from one counselor to another (Wheeler & Bertram, 2008). Whether the transfer is temporary (for example, the counselor is on vacation or out of the office) or permanent, the case record provides continuity of care. In such cases, well-written, up-to-date case notes are a means of communicating important information to a new clinician or court official.

Standard of Care: Legal Implications

Counseling records sometimes become legal documents in court cases—such as when clients are involved in custody battles, litigation, workers' compensation, probation hearings, charges of abuse, and so forth. Case notes should reflect that the counselor made the client aware of his or her rights through informed consent (see chapter 3). Clients must understand that confidentiality is not absolute, and that a counselor will need to break confidentiality under certain required circumstances (e.g., danger to self or others, legally mandated court testimony, child abuse, etc.). Fortunately, most cases will not evolve into a judicial hearing, but the counselor must prepare each case record with the understanding that the case could proceed to court. Also, always remember that with a legally mandated client, a court official (or probation officer) will be viewing the file, and your report could make a big difference in a client's life.

So, assume that the client record you are creating will wind up being scrutinized in a courtroom. This foundation will assist you in carefully creating a well-documented file that will accurately reflect the client's progress. Because records can become public records (as in court proceedings), counselors should not include identifying information about third parties (such as family members, extramarital lovers, etc.) unless that information has a direct bearing on the client's treatment.

Clearly, client records do not always reflect a favorable impression on the client and may be detrimental in a legal hearing. Nevertheless, the case file should accurately reflect what has occurred in counseling, including a client's noncompliance with treatment, should such be the case. Although a counselor may be tempted to artificially inflate a client's compliance and progress in counseling, this could be construed both as malpractice and as falsifying a legal document, both of which could jeopardize a counselor's career (Wheeler & Bertram, 2008).

Standard of Care: HIPAA Compliance

As discussed in chapter 3, counselors who practice in public and private settings, where insurance is billed, fall under the Health Insurance Portability and Accountability Act (HIPAA) of 1996. The major intent of HIPAA was to address electronic transmission of client care information through mediums such as the Internet. State laws have been crafted to ensure further HIPAA compliance, especially with regard to client privacy (Wheeler & Bertram, 2008). Some counselors, such as school counselors and counselors working in college and university counseling centers, may be exempt from HIPAA, although many of the latter may attempt to operate in compliance with HIPAA regardless.

HIPAA will primarily impact the counselor with regard to progress notes, or what I call case notes. Case notes are given an added level of protection if they are maintained in a separate physical or electronic location. This means that disclosure of case notes requires a separately executed client authorization if the case notes are maintained in a separate file (Remley & Herlihy, 2007). Naturally, counselors can easily integrate case notes within a single file; this is common practice, and in such practices, case notes would fall under the general guidelines governing disclosure (see chapter 3).

Although HIPAA provides a definition of psychotherapy notes, important questions remain unanswered. For example, would standard SOAP notes (to be discussed later in this chapter) be considered *psychotherapy notes*? In my experience, many agencies assume they are. What about the family or group counselor, who considers the couple, family, or group as the client? How would this approach be affected by HIPAA? Or, what about the counselor who has ethical concerns regarding the legitimacy of *Diagnostic and Statistical Manual of Mental Disorders* (*DSM*) diagnoses, based on past and present discrimination (Schwartz & Feisthamel, 2009) and refuses to use the system? These and other relevant questions regarding HIPAA remain unanswered (Bertram & Wheeler, 2008).

Standard of Care: Risk Management Strategy

The final reason for keeping records is very simple. Well-documented case files provide effective defense for counselors responding to lawsuits or ethical complaints (Wheeler & Bertram, 2008). Should questions arise about what the counselor did or, as in legal and ethical cases, failed to do, well-documented records provide protection. If you are accused of something and what you did was not noted in the record, you have no defense. Case notes and well-organized files are legal documents and provide a rationale for treatment. Case files are also typically read by colleagues and supervisors in the same agency, school, and hospital, and this collateral support strengthens the counselor's case.

Wheeler and Bertram (2008) refer to high-risk cases, such as those involving potentially suicidal clients, clients who express homicidal intent, HIV-positive clients with multiple sexual partners, and cases of suspected abuse. From a risk management standpoint, they recommend such cases to be fully documented through the following steps:

- **At-risk situation:** Document what the client did or said that suggested he or she was considering engaging in or was actively engaging in a high-risk activity.
- **Assessment:** Based on your clinical experience and knowledge of the client, document the severity level of this threat.
- **Options:** List the options you consider as appropriate responses based on your assessment. Listing options demonstrates that you were thinking broadly and that you considered a range of alternatives before reaching a decision.
- **Rule out:** Describe what options you ruled out and why each was determined to be inappropriate. These descriptions clarify your clinical decision making and make the case that you acted appropriately.
- **Consultation and/or supervision:** If there is time, obtain and document any colleague consultation or supervision you received to evaluate and clarify a course of action.
- **Actions taken:** Describe the options you chose, including what you said or did. This helps clarify how you implemented the options you determined to be appropriate.
- **Follow-up:** Document what happened, what you did, and how things progressed until there was resolution. (Wheeler & Bertram, 2008, pp. 122–123)

My experience has taught me the great value of one additional step: Consult your supervisor. Anytime that you encounter a high-risk case, consult with your supervisor as soon as possible and document that you consulted him or her and note any suggestions. From experience, I can tell you that a supervisor's worst nightmare is to be caught unaware because a counselor did not apprise them of a high-risk case.

Now, as a counselor in training, you must understand that no amount of protection is absolute. However, should you maintain an up-to-date case file, write clear case notes and treatment plans, and follow the above suggestions in high-risk cases, you will have the odds on your side. But, regardless of how thorough you are regarding case notes, proper documentation, and consultation with your supervisor, the risk remains, albeit very small. Therefore, keep your professional liability insurance current.

RECOMMENDATIONS FOR RECORD KEEPING

As discussed in chapter 3, agencies and settings differ in terms of how they take, maintain, and store records. Many are moving to electronic-based notes systems. Whether your school or agency uses paper or electronic records, Mitchell (2007) offers the following advice regarding record keeping:

- Service providers need timely, accurate, and comprehensive information. Lack of information can impede quality of care because the decision-making process is placed at risk.
- An organization must comply with its own written policy related to record keeping and confidentiality. In the event of litigation or allegations of unethical conduct, "failure to comply" can be used against the service provider.
- One way to avoid misuse of information is to have trained employees who are committed to protecting the privacy of each client. (p. 45)

Mitchell (2007) also offers eight assumptions counselors should make regarding electronic records:

1. The counseling record will be subpoenaed and the court must understand what went on in counseling.
2. The counselor may or may not be with the agency when it happens. Someone else will have to read and understand what the counselor wrote.
3. Legislation that opens a record to the client exists now or will be passed. In fact, the *Code* (*ACA Code of Ethics*) already provides the client with reasonable access to records.
4. The counselor's notes will not be accurate if he or she takes days or weeks to write a note, so they should be written as soon as possible. (Practicum and internship students will not be retained if such delays occur!)
5. The note will be the best possible reflection of the counselor's professional abilities.
6. No contact is considered a professional service until the counselor's entry is in the record.
7. The notes will be used by the Division of Audits to verify a legally reimbursable service as defined by the funding source.
8. The service documentation and personnel file will be requested by the Board of Inquiry in the event of allegations of unethical conduct. The *ACA Ethical Code* also requires that counselors cooperate with investigations. (p. 460)

Counselors never know who might be called on to inspect a record. Therefore, always write case notes with the assumption that what is written will be read and evaluated at some point in the future. Keeping this possibility in mind should not overly inhibit you, but should help you keep close to the facts. It is important to remember the following:

- Your clients have a legal right to review their record and obtain a copy.
- Your clients have a right to demand that you provide copies of case notes to their physician, other mental health professionals, and attorney.
- Your clients have a right to subpoena your case notes.
- Third parties can also subpoena case notes when involved in legal cases involving the client, even over the client's or counselor's objections.
- The legal representatives of deceased clients, in most states, have a right to inspect the deceased client's case notes.
- In cases of litigation, case notes may well become public.

Understand that you may be compelled to testify regarding why you wrote what you wrote in the case notes. Essentially, once you write something in a case file, you are responsible for defending what you wrote.

GENERAL RECOMMENDATIONS FOR WRITING CASE NOTES

There are three key points to keep in mind with regard to case notes. One, case notes provide a tracking recording of the client's treatment, progress, or lack of progress. Two, case notes provide clear documentation of decisions and actions the counselor has made during treatment. Three, case notes provide a rationale and defense for the counselor should the case become a legal one. Case notes also provide evidence that the counselor is following best practices—in other words, what any sound, ethical counselor would do in similar circumstances.

One important element is the ability to distinguish objective information (who said what, or what you directly witnessed during a session) from subjective impressions (conclusions you developed as a result of counseling the client). Quite often, because of the large volume of clients you will see and because of the passage of time, you may confuse the objective with the subjective. It is very important that you are able to separate what was actually observed or documented from what you believe to be the case. Objective documentation is what you will be held accountable for in a court case should you be unfortunate enough to be the object of such. For example, do not write "The client seems to be a drug addict." The client may not be an addict and recording of such libelous information could significantly harm the client and be grounds for a lawsuit (Wheeler & Bertram, 2008). On the other hand, if the client is being treated for chemical dependency, noting that would be accurate record keeping.

Because a client may be verbose, client quotations should be kept to a minimum and only the most significant should be included, otherwise counselor accuracy may be called into question (Cameron & turtle-song, 2002). Hart, Berndt, and Caramazza (1985) suggest that an individual is able to accurately recall only vestigial bits of verbatim information. This suggests that after a 50-minute counseling session, a counselor's ability to recall specific information with any accuracy is questionable (unless of course the session has been recorded). So, keep quotations to a minimum; note only key words or a brief phrase. Key words or phrases might include plans for suicide, homicide, comments suggesting a dramatic change in life circumstances, a major change in the client's well-being, and so forth. Quotations may be cited to document inappropriate or abusive language toward the counselor or others. Comments suggesting significant denial should be documented. For example, a father accused of abusing his son with a whip might say, "I only beat him when he cries." Because the child's physical and emotional health may be at stake, his comments should be recorded. The counselor might note, "States, 'I only whip him when he cries.'"

It is also important to document statements that suggest the client may be confused regarding time, place, and person is experiencing an abrupt change in his or her mental status. For example, if the client becomes disoriented and is confused as to who he or she is, or the circumstances regarding being in counseling, the counselor should record this. To assess the client's mental status, a mental status examination or a mini-mental status examination should be administered (see chapter 4).

A client's change in attitude, either positive or negative, should be recorded because it serves as evidence for counseling effectiveness or ineffectiveness. A statement such as, "Counseling has helped me get sober and put my life back together," might be written as "Reports 'counseling is really helping.'" This information is especially important if the client was mandated to counseling and presented to the first session as oppositional. The goal is not to provide a verbatim account of what the client said, but to reflect current areas of client concern and to support or validate the counselor's interpretations and interventions.

Because case notes may be read by insurance officials, court officials, other mental health professionals, and so forth, the counselor should be judicious about the type of information included in the case record. Political, religious, and racial views should not be included in the case notes unless they directly relate to the focus of treatment (Eggland, 1988). The counselor also should not repeat inflammatory statements that are critical of other mental health providers, because such comments could antagonize clinicians and compromise care. Instead of using the actual names of client's object of animus, the counselor might substitute terms such as "other staff" or "mental health professional." It is of further importance to remember that the names a client mentions during counseling sessions should not be included in the record unless they have a direct relationship to treatment.

Another guideline to follow is to be constructive (Baird, 2005). Remember, your clients have a right to inspect the file and you do not want to record anything that might incite additional animus, assign blame, or be personally demeaning.

Brevity is the operative word when writing case notes. Counselors should express essential ideas, but keep notations brief because of space and time constraints. Instead of writing, "the client states," use shorthand terms such as "reports," "states," "describes," "indicates," "complaints of," and so forth (Cameron & turtle-song, 2002). Instead of writing, "Today the client says I'm having lots of conflict with coworkers since the last counseling session where we met," the counselor might write, "Client reports increased conflict at work since last sessions." Furthermore, because it is obvious that the counselor is the scribe, it is not necessary for the counselor to refer to himself or herself.

Students often ask me, "How long should it take me to write case notes?" My suggestion is a 10-minute time frame, because this is about the maximum time you can expect between sessions. (Sometimes you have less, of course.)

SOAP FORMAT

There are several different formats used for writing case notes. All were developed to provide a continuity and consistency to a generally subjective exercise on the part of the counselor. Because of its popularity among mental health professionals, I recommend the SOAP (subjective, objective, assessment, plan) format. Figure 5.1 shows a sample SOAP write-up form, which uses *DSM* categories.

Subjective

This section should provide a narrative of the client's feelings, concerns, problems expressed, goals, thoughts expressed, the intensity of problems expressed, and the problems' impact on significant relationships. Relevant comments provided by close family members, court officers, and other officials should also be noted in this section. The client's perception of the issues should be clear to an outside reader of the record. Counselors should be thorough although be brief in their summarizations.

Objective

The objective section is made up of what can be "seen, heard, smelled, counted, or measured" (Cameron & turtle-song, 2002, p. 288). Generally, there are two types of objective information: outside documented reports and the counselor's own observations. The latter, the counselor's observations, are composed of any psychological, interpersonal, or physical findings relevant to treatment. Objective information could consist of the client's appearance, behavior, and affect; compliance with treatment; oppositional nature; and client's strengths. This section may also refer to the client's mental status and competence to continue treatment. Supportive outside written reports such as psychological or psychiatric reports, assessments, medical records, prison records, school records, and so forth would be included in the objective section.

FIGURE 5.1   *DSM-IV* and SOAP Client Case Notes Format

Page 1 of 2

Name(s) and age(s) of client(s): _____
_____
_____

Date: ____/____/____   Code(s): _____   Session #: _____

Presenting Problem: _____
_____
_____
_____

Medications:

Cite Criteria for Axis I Diagnosis:

_____
_____
_____
_____

DSM-IV Preliminary Diagnostic Impressions (For educational and training purposes only. Not intended as a final diagnosis):

Axis I:

Axis II:

Axis III:

Axis IV:

Axis V: GAF/CGAS/FGAF =

Continued

FIGURE 5.1   *DSM-IV* and SOAP Client Case Notes Format *Continued*

(Range 0–100)
Prescriptive. Not intended as a final diagnosis.

Subjective (S): _____

_____

_____

_____

_____

_____

_____

Objective (O): _____

_____

_____

_____

_____

_____

_____

_____

Assessment (A): _____

_____

_____

_____

_____

_____

_____

Plan (P): _____

_____

_____

_____

_____

_____

_____

Code: psy. = psychiatric referral; a = acute; cr = chronic; R/x = meds; Tx = treatment;
         pr = parental access restricted; wc = ward of court; npr = no previous records

Counselor's Signature _____

The counselor's choice of language in this section should reflect accuracy in content. Terms that seem less precise such as "appeared," "seemed," "possibly," and so forth should be avoided. Naturally, because counseling is not an exact science, some degree of latitude is expected. Terms such as "evidenced by" is a descriptive term that implies direct observation. For example, let us say the client arrived 15 minutes late for session, was unkempt, and had difficulty maintaining his or her focus in session. This behavior is inconsistent with previous sessions where the client was on time and engaged with the process. When writing this in the case notes, the counselor might say, "Appeared depressed as evidenced by tardiness, less involvement in the counseling process, and poorly groomed."

When writing the objective section of the report, the counselor should refrain from using pejorative language ("slob"), stating opinion not supported by facts ("lazy"), and personal judgments ("He's a loser"). Terms that have a negative connotation and subject to speculation such as "dysfunctional," "rude," "obnoxious," "normal," "abnormal," and the like should be avoided. For example, a counselor should not write, "Client arrived stoned to the session and proceeded to be uncooperative and unprofessional." The counselor might instead record, "Client smelled of pot, struggled to maintain focus, and had difficulty sitting in the chair."

Assessment

The assessment section is a summarization of the counselor's clinical impressions regarding the client's problem or problems (Cameron & turtle-song, 2002). The assessment section serves to synthesize and analyze the information expressed in the subjective and objective sections. The assessment section includes a psychiatric diagnoses based on the *Diagnostic and Statistical Manual of Mental Disorders, Text Revision* (*DSM-IV-TR*; American Psychiatric Association, 2000). Although there is much controversy regarding use of the *DSM*, and certain diagnoses in particular, *DSM* diagnoses are considered a standard part of treatment (Remley & Herlihy, 2007; Wheeler & Bertram, 2008), and required for financial reimbursement. Diagnoses are simply a reality of professional practice. Ginter and Glauser's (2001) opinion is that the assessment section of the SOAP format includes clinical impressions. Sometimes clinical impressions will be recorded in the form of "rule out" or "rule in" when the counselor is not entirely confident in assigning a diagnosis. Clinical impressions can assist other clinicians in reaching a final diagnosis because they provide guidance on previous assessment. When reporting clinical impressions in the SOAP notes, counselors should clearly identify them as such. Counselors should also identify the evidence for the prospective diagnosis because this documents the clinical process the counselor followed and that the counselor operated regarding standard procedures.

Clinical Impressions

Appropriate use of clinical impressions is vital both for writing good case notes and for effective counseling practice. Consider the following example: A counselor working in an outpatient mental health clinic is conducting an intake and assessment for a 6-year-old boy referred by his school counselor for possible attention deficit/ hyperactivity disorder (ADHD). The school counselor's report describes the child as having difficulty maintaining his focus for even brief time periods (i.e., 5 minutes), being frequently out of his seat, frequently interrupting his teacher and peers, and having a tendency to self-injury caused by constantly hurrying (e.g., running into chairs, tables, tripping, etc.). When the child's history is being taken, the mother discloses that she often consumed alcohol throughout her pregnancy. Although there is not enough evidence for a diagnosis of fetal alcohol syndrome, the counselor's clinical impression is to "rule out fetal alcohol syndrome" and to refer the child for a neurological evaluation. The neurologist can examine the counselor's report and take the information into account as she makes a diagnosis.

The assessment portion of the SOAP format is the most likely portion to be read by outside reviewers such as counselors, psychologists, social workers, court officers, child welfare case workers, and such (Cameron & turtle-song, 2002). Consequently, counselors should take pains to ensure that the assessment section is supported by the subjective and objective sections, as these portions lay the foundation for a diagnosis or diagnostic impressions. When considering a diagnosis, the counselor should ask the following questions: "Is there sufficient data to support a particular client diagnosis?" (Cameron & turtle-song, 2002), and "Am I prepared to defend my diagnosis?"

The counselor must be prepared to defend that diagnosis to parents, colleagues, supervisors, and, if necessary, in a courtroom. Naturally, considering the full ramifications of a diagnosis can be intimidating, although declining to provide a diagnosis based on the fear of the consequences is also unappealing and possibly unethical. The best advice for counselors is to make the most informed decision possible, and to be able to demonstrate the steps you took to arrive at your diagnosis.

Plan

The final section of the SOAP format is the plan. The plan is built on the information within the subjective, objective, and assessment sections. This section generally consists of two parts: the action plan and the treatment prognosis. The information to be noted in this section includes the date of the next appointment (or, if it is the final session, to note that this is the final session and include aftercare), interventions used during the session, treatment progress, and homework assigned (if any).

The counselor should note client progress, or lack thereof, in the plan section, because this will have a direct bearing on further treatment. Typically, progress assessments are described in terms such as "good," "fair," "excellent," "guarded," or "poor," accompanied by an explanation supporting the progress assessment. The plan section of the SOAP format completes the case notes section.

Table 5.1 summarizes each SOAP section and the type of information that should be recorded.

TABLE 5.1 SOAP Case Notes Examples

SECTION	DEFINITION	EXAMPLE
Subjective (S)	What the client tells you, what pertinent others tell you about the client, how the client experiences the world	Client's feelings, concerns, and problems; comments by clinicians and pertinent others; client's orientation to time, place, and person; client's verbalized attitudes toward helping
Objective (O)	Factual information, what the counselor personally witnessed, what was measured through testing or assessment, documentation from other parties	The client's appearance, affect, behavior, test results, and so forth; materials from other agencies to be noted and be attached
Assessment (A)	Summarizes the counselor's clinical thinking regarding the patient's diagnosis	Include clinical diagnosis and impressions; may include *DSM* diagnosis (or possible diagnoses)
Plan (P)	Describes the parameters of treatment, consists of an action plan and prognosis	Action plan: include interventions used, treatment progress, and direction; include date of next appointment; prognosis: include the anticipated gains from the intervention

Source: Adapted from Cameron & turtle-song, 2002, p. 290.

The Case of Alexander

Alexander is a 28-year-old, Caucasian male, court-mandated client. He was arrested following a domestic dispute involving his female partner. Alexander presents for the first session agitated and oppositional to treatment. He discloses to his counselor, Steve, "I didn't do anything wrong . . . everybody uses a little force . . . I was just manning up!"

Throughout most of the initial session, Alexander remains defiant. He outlines his struggles in the relationship, explaining how he works 60 hours per week to support his partner and two kids, and never misses work. He says with much animus, "My damn girlfriend can do anything she wants, but I'm the one that gets arrested!" He demands that the counselor write the judge a letter explaining that he has no problems.

Later in the session, Steve learns that he grew up in a physically and verbally abusive home. At age 17, he ran away to live with his maternal grandparents, who seemed to provide the only stability in his life. He was arrested twice for driving while intoxicated, and once for a fight at a party. He reports that he feels more aggressive when he has been drinking. Alexander admits to consuming "a couple of drinks a night . . . no big deal, you know." He also reports that when he gets angry, he feels like exploding and sometimes becomes violent, punching walls, kicking the trash can, throwing chairs, and occasionally, hitting his partner. He also admits that he has "been physical" with his kids on at least two occasions, but maintains that he gets physical only "when they need to be controlled." Before the session ends, he opines, "This counseling is sissy stuff. How the hell are you going to help me with the judge, huh?" Then, he angrily leaves the office.

SOAP Write-Up for Alexander

S: Alexander admitted previous use of violence "when they [family] need to be controlled." He reports experience of domestic violence in family of origin. He ran away from home at age 17 to live with grandparents to escape family violence. Recent history is he was arrested for domestic assault on his female partner and mandated to counseling by the judge. Today was his initial session.

O: Alexander was guarded throughout most the session. At session's conclusion, he became agitated when informed he would need to attend treatment for 16 weeks, angrily stating, "Counseling is for sissies!" Then, he stormed from the office, slamming the door.

A: *DSM* Diagnosis: Physical Abuse of Adult [V61.1]. Clinical impressions: Rule out Abuse of Children [V.61.21].

P: Rescheduled for following week (6/12/09) at 3 P.M. Prognosis is guarded because of lack of insight into behavior and mandated client apparently because of a lack motivation for behavioral change. Will refer to batterers' intervention group in addition to continuing individual cognitive behavioral counseling. Next session plan is to introduce recognizing and stopping anger before it explodes.

6-5-09
Steve Washington, LMHC, NCC
Counselor, Jackson County Mental Health

Sample SOAP Notes

S: Client reports counseling has helped reduce her depressive episodes. She states she is "Feeling much lighter since coming for counseling." Client also reported her husband has noticed her mood improvement. She also noted less difficulty in getting up for work in the morning.

O: Generally compliant throughout the session. She maintained steady eye contact and participated throughout the session. Unlike the previous session, she eagerly participated in a role play focused on setting limits with her father, who has been verbally abusive with her in the past.

A: To check decrease in depression and elevation in mood, readministered the Beck Depression Inventory-2 and client's score dropped from 32 to 18, supporting client's self-statement of feeling less depressed.

P: Scheduled the next session for 6/12/12 at 3 P.M. Progress is good with her motivation, her mood improvement. Continue cognitive therapy. Next session, check on her homework of continuing to set limits with her father. She will set guidelines for their weekly phone conversation including educating father on his inappropriate abusive language. She will hang up the phone if he does not comply.

Final Thoughts on SOAP Format

Case notes and client files are legal documents and must be legible (preferably typed), accurate, and concise (Sommers-Flanigan & Sommers-Flanigan, 1999). A good general guideline to follow is to write your notes immediately after the session, because your memory is freshest at that point. Also, good case notes should be reviewed prior to the following session to facilitate continuity from the previous session to the current one. Furthermore, you may have to transfer the client to another counselor or official; in that case, readable, legible, and coherent case notes will enhance treatment effectiveness and reduce liability. Refrain from technical jargon because it is not descriptive and can be misunderstood should another professional read the file.

For consistency purposes, all client contact, including phone messages, e-mail (although use of e-mail should be discouraged because of security concerns), letters, and so forth should be recorded using the SOAP format. If an error is made in the record, never erase or use correction fluid. Note the error by either crossing out the error in pen or writing "error" and then record your initials. Some agencies even have correction sheet reports for such contingencies, with the counselor explaining the error and signing the document. The mistake and correction should be clearly identified by the counselor.

Document all client-related contacts, for example, any client information provided from a case manager, parole officer, school counselor, and so forth.

At the conclusion of the SOAP format, the counselor should date and sign his or her legal name and include job title and credentials. The counselor should also sign his or her name immediately below the last line of the *Plan* section of the SOAP notes.

RECOMMENDED READING

Jongsma, A. E., & Berghius, D. J. (2006). *The adult psychotherapy progress notes planner.* New York: John Wiley & Sons.

Jongsma, A. E., Peterson, L. M., McInnis, W. P., & Berghius, D. J. (2006). *The adolescent psychotherapy progress notes planner.* New York: John Wiley & Sons.

McInnis, W. P., Bughius, D. J. (2006). *The child psychotherapy progress notes planner.* New York: John Wiley & Sons.

Mitchell, R. W. (2007). *Documentation in counseling records: An overview of ethical, legal, and clinical issues* (3rd ed.). Alexandria, VA: American Counseling Association.

Patterson, T., & McClanahan, T. M. (1999). *The couple and family clinical documentation sourcebook: A comprehensive collection of mental health practice, forms, and records.* New York: John Wiley & Sons.

Wheeler, A., & Bertram, B. (2008).*The counselor and the law: A guide to legal and ethical practice* (4th ed.). Alexandria, VA: American Counseling Association.

Wiger, D. E. (2005). *The clinicians documentation sourcebook: The complete paperwork resource for your mental health practice.* New York: John Wiley & Sons.

Zuckerman, E. L. (2000). *The Clinician's thesaurus: The guide for writing psychological reports* (5th ed.). New York: Guilford.

CHAPTER 6

Classroom and Site Supervision

The practicum/internship experience involves not only the on-site clinical experience but also the intense supervision, both in an individual and in a classroom setting. As mentioned in chapter 1, graduate counseling students in Council for Accreditation of Counseling and Related Educational Programs (CACREP)-accredited programs (practicum and internship) are expected to spend an average of 1 hour per week of supervision with a faculty and on-site supervisor, and for practicum an additional average of 1.5 hours per week of group supervision. In this chapter, I will provide guidance to help you and your fellow students make the most of your supervision experience, both in the classroom and with your on-site supervisor.

PRACTICUM/INTERNSHIP CLASS

This class is very different from other courses you will take, for example, Counseling Theories. Typically, students discuss pertinent aspects of their placement, including challenges, what they are enjoying, what they are learning, issues on the site, and so forth. The practicum class will discuss (and perhaps view DVDs of) confidential counseling sessions. Thus, as a graduate student, you must treat the experience as if it were a supervision meeting. Like a supervision meeting in an agency or school, a large part of the experience will involve presenting clinical cases and then receiving critique from your peers and the professor. Although the practicum class can initially be anxiety provoking, it may eventually develop into a very rewarding and enriching experience. A sample syllabus of the course is provided in Figure 6.1.

When possible, practicum and internship students are expected to make recordings of actual counseling sessions. Video recordings are preferable because they allow students to observe nonverbal components of the session, as well as give everyone in the class a concrete picture of how the counselor-in-training conducted the session.

There are several procedures to follow when recording client sessions. The *ACA Code of Ethics* (American Counseling Association, 2005, Section B.6.b) states that clients must be informed when recordings are being made and must give their consent to the process prior to recording the session. Although no legal or ethical requirement stipulates the permission be given in writing, standard practice generally includes written forms of consent (Remley & Herlihy, 2007). Figure 6.2 shows a sample permission to record form.

FIGURE 6.1   Sample Syllabus

Public State University Spring 2011
Graduate Mental Health Counseling program
Department of Educational Leadership and Counseling

Professor: John Doe, PhD, LMHC, ACS   **Phone:** (123) 456-7890 (office)

Office: 328 D Academic Complex   (123) 456-7890 (home)

E-mail: professor@counseling.edu

Office Hours: M 1:00–3:00 P.M.
                          W 2:00–4:00 P.M.
                          Th. 1:00–3:00 P.M.
                          Or by appointment

Course Number and Title
      EDU 679: Mental Health Practicum
      Wednesday 4:20–7:05 P.M.
      Office # 112

Catalog Description
This course is designed to provide graduate counseling students with an introduction to professional issues in mental health practice (counseling, critiquing peers, consultation, professional issues, ethics, etc.) and in preparation for the subsequent counseling internships (EDU 685, EDU 686, and EDU 678). Students will be placed in a counseling setting for a minimum of 100 clock hours and will have weekly group seminars. This course also incorporates the ethical standards of the American Counseling Association ([ACA] www.counseling.org) and those of the American Mental Health Counselors Association ([AMHCA] www.amhca.org). Canadian students may wish to consult the Canadian Counseling Association ([CCA] www.cca.org). Students are also expected to gain relative skills, especially in the realm of consultation with other mental health professionals.

Textbooks
Remley, T. P., & Herlihy, B. (2007). *Ethical, legal and professional issues in counseling,* (2nd ed.). Upper Saddle River, NJ: Merrill-Prentice Hall.
Jiminez, H. (2008). *The mental health counseling handbook* (3rd ed.). Public State University, NY: College of Education.

Educational Philosophy
The Constructivist framework of the graduate Mental Health Counseling program forms the basis for all courses. EDU 679 (Mental Health Counseling Practicum) serves as a foundational class for mental health counselors, including professional roles and identity, a focus on the American Counseling Association's (ACA) *Code of Ethics and*

Continued

FIGURE 6.1   Sample Syllabus *Continued*

Standards of Practice. The University Mental Health Counseling program also follows the requirements of the Council for the Accreditation for Counseling and Related Educational Programs (CACREP). The eight CACREP core areas are listed as follows:

Professional Identity: *Addressed in EDU 679.*
Social and Cultural Diversity: *Addressed in EDU 679.*
Human Growth and Development: *Addressed in EDU 679.*
Career Development: Not addressed in EDU 679.
Helping Relationships: *Addressed in EDU 679.*
Group Work: May be addressed for the individual student depending on the
    practicum site.
Assessment: *Addressed in EDU 679.*
Research and Program Evaluation: *Not addressed in EDU 679.*

Course Objectives and Requirements

- Demonstrate skills in individual/group/relationship counseling using appropriate theoretical and practical perspectives.
- Demonstrate knowledge of professional ethical standards as defined by the ACA and the American Mental Health Counselors Association (AMHCA). Apply knowledge of ethical and legal perspectives to relevant counseling situations.
- Recognize and respond appropriately to professional limitations.
- Become familiar with community resources and know when and where to refer clients.
- Learn the value of providing and receiving professional consultation regarding counseling individuals, couples, families, and groups.
- Learn to give and receive feedback in the seminar format.
- Follow established professional and ethical guidelines regarding counseling multicultural and diverse client populations.
- Weekly attendance in seminar. *More than two absences will result in an unsatisfactory (U) grade. An unsatisfactory grade requires the student to wait until the following year to repeat EDU 679.*
- Read assigned chapters in text and be ready to discuss in the seminar format.
- *A score of 70% or higher on the final Ethics examination is also required before a student may progress to EDU 685. The final is based on ethical and legal issues through readings in the text and in-class discussion.*
- *Students must also receive a satisfactory evaluation in their practicum placement to move to Internship I (EDU 685).*
- *Video of a taped 30-minute session with a classroom partner or a client in a professional setting.* Students may counsel from a person-centered, cognitive-behavioral, solution-focused, integrative, and so on framework. In addition, each video will be preceded using the SOAP/DSM-IV and intake form in your *Mental Health Counseling (MGC) Handbook*. In practicum, the mock video sessions will not be graded. Next semester in Internship I (EDU 685), mock sessions will be graded.

Continued

FIGURE 6.1 Sample Syllabus *Continued*

- Learn the nuances of consultation with counselors, other mental health professionals, human services agencies, and law enforcement.
- *All students must provide proof of student liability insurance prior to beginning practicum.* Additionally, students must maintain student liability insurance throughout internship.

Methods of Instruction

Weekly sessions will be organized using a seminar approach. It is expected that students will have read and are prepared to discuss previously assigned material (i.e., text). Students will be expected to communicate their experiences in the practicum setting to other students and faculty. Feedback from others in the practicum will enhance students' perceptions and facilitate learning new approaches to counseling. Students will also present a videotape of a role-played counseling session to others in the practicum for feedback on the use of counseling skills. The professor will use the session rating form on p. 27 of the *MHC Handbook.*

Outline of Course

CLASS MEETING DATE	ACTIVITIES
Week 1	Introduction to practicum. Schedule videotape presentations. Textbook information.
Week 2	Read chapters 1, 2, and 3. Video: Ethical and Legal Issues.
Week 3	Read chapter 4: Client welfare.
Week 4	View professional video and critique.
Week 5	Student videotape presentation. Read chapters 5 and 6: Confidentiality, and Records and Subpoenas.
Week 6	Student videotape presentation. Read chapter 7: Competence and Malpractice.
Week 7	Student videotape presentation. Read chapter 8: Boundary Issues.
Week 8	Student videotape presentation. Read chapters 9 and 10: Families and Groups.
Week 9	Student videotape presentation. Read chapter 11: Evaluation, Testing, and Diagnosis.
Week 10	Student videotape presentation. Read chapter 12: Private Practice.

Continued

FIGURE 6.1 Sample Syllabus *Continued*

Week 11	Student videotape presentation. Read chapter 13: Technology and Health Care.
Week 12	Student videotape presentation. Read chapter 15: Supervision and Consultation.
Week 13	View/critique professional counseling video tape. Read chapter 17: Resolving Ethical and Legal Issues.
Week 14	Last class. Ethics examination.

Grading

The final grade (S, U, or I) will be determined by class attendance (less than three absences); a passing score on the Ethics examination (70 and above is passing); satisfactory performance on video tapes; and feedback from the students, on-site supervisor evaluation, and the university professor. Satisfactory performance in all the aforementioned areas will result in a grade of satisfactory (S). A deficient mark in any of the previously mentioned areas will result in a grade of unsatisfactory (U). A U grade would result in the student retaking EDU 679 the following year.

Checklist

- Satisfactory evaluation by site supervisor and evaluation of supervisor (turn in by final class, Dec. 3)
- Passing the Ethics examination (grade of 70 or higher).
- No more than two classroom absences.
- Satisfactory performance on videotape—not graded, but demonstrating a basic ability to create a therapeutic environment.
- Must turn in practicum timesheet (see p. 35–36 in MHC Handbook). Turn in by final class.

Bibliography

Baird, B. N. (1999). *The internship, practicum, and field placement handbook: A guide for the helping professionals* (2nd ed.). Upper Saddle River, NJ: Prentice Hall.

Corey, C. (2009). *Theory and practice of counseling and psychotherapy* (8th ed.). Belmont, CA: Thomson.

Cottone, R. R., & Tarvydas, V. M. (1998). *Ethical and professional issues in counseling.* Upper Saddle River, NJ: Prentice Hall.

Moline, M. E., Williams, G. T., & Austin, K. M. (1998). *Documenting psychotherapy: Essentials for mental health practitioners.* Thousand Oaks, CA: Sage Publications.

Sommers-Flanagan, R., & Sommers-Flanagan, J. (1999). *Clinical interviewing* (2nd ed.). New York: John Wiley & Sons, Inc.

FIGURE 6.2   Client Permission to Record Counseling Session for
Supervision Purposes

I/We, _____, hereby grant permission for
our counselor to videotape/audiotape (circle appropriate recording choice) our counseling
session on the following date(s): _____.

I/We understand that the purpose of this recording is for the clinical supervision of my/
our counselor's work. I/we provide for the following people to view the recording:

_____ (Supervisor)

_____ (Practicum/Internship Group)

The above named persons will also hold the information on the recording confidential.
The recording will be erased after the supervisor has reviewed it.

_____   Date: _____
Client Signature

_____
Client Signature

_____
Client Signature

Parental/Guardian Permission to Record Session Form
The graduate counseling program at Northern State University conducts a practicum
and internship course for the purpose of training future professional counselors. The
practicum/internship class is an advanced course requirement of all degree candidates
in Northern State University's graduate counseling program. Graduate students in
the counseling program are required to record counseling sessions as part of their
professional training and development and to be of more assistance to the clients
they counsel. The counseling sessions conducted with your child will be reviewed by
the student counselor's faculty supervisor (or, in some cases, the supervisor at this
site) and a small group of graduate students in the practicum/internship. The faculty
supervisor, on-site supervisor and graduate counseling students are all held to confidentiality and the contents of this recording will not be revealed beyond the course.
Once the recording has been played, it will be erased. By signing this form, you give
permission for your child to be recorded.
Thank you for your cooperation in this important matter.

Parent's/Guardian's name _____

Student Counselor's Signature _____

Date: _____ / _____ / _____

Students must also understand that information stored on a DVD, VHS, or any other device must be kept in a secure setting then erased after it has been reviewed by the clinical supervisor and/or the practicum/internship class (Wheeler & Bertram, 2008).

Because of liability concerns, some sites do not allow student counselors to record sessions. In that event, students are generally required to record mock counseling sessions with peers.

You should review your recording prior to presenting it in class. You should also complete an intake form, diagnostic form, and SOAP (subjective, objective, assessment, plan) case note form regarding the session (see chapters 4 and 5 for examples of these forms). These materials will provide you with a format for tying the case together, and will give the rest of the class an organized context of the client's presenting issues, ongoing struggles, counselor observations, and prognosis for treatment.

MODELS OF CRITIQUE

There are numerous models of counselor education and supervision (Benshoff, 1993; Borders, 1991). Borders advocated an instructional model involving goal setting, reading, and discussion of journal articles, case presentations, and review and critique of counseling sessions by peers and faculty. In this approach, students specify questions they would like addressed and the types of feedback they are seeking. Then, each student presents a DVD or video, which is critiqued by the rest of the class. (In this approach, all members of the class will critique the student presenting the case.) Naturally, different students will have different reactions: one student may focus on the nonverbal behavior of the client, whereas another will attend to the content. Some will focus more on specific techniques used, and others will be more concerned with whether the counselor paid enough attention to the affective domain. Students might approach the presentation from various orientations: humanistic, cognitive behavioral, or client centered, for example.

During the critique, the supervisor monitors the discussion to clarify the student's comments and to ensure that the feedback is constructive. The student being critiqued can also ask questions to enhance his or her understanding of the intention of the comments and to seek clarification. The supervisor also sets the stage by explaining the approach, appropriate feedback style, as well as modeling how to receive feedback. Another variation is the structured group supervision model (SGSM) developed by Wilbur, Roberts-Wilbur, Morris, Betz, and Hart (1991). The SGSM uses five phases:

1. **The request for assistance statement:** In this phase, students may seek support for personal growth, technical skills, and better understanding of the therapeutic process.
2. **The questioning period and identification of focus:** Students take turns questioning the student presenter.

3. The feedback statements: In this phase, group members may offer feedback related to the session with the intent of assisting the student counselor's continued development. Wilbur et al. (1991) suggest that during this phase, the student remains silent and focuses entirely on receiving the feedback. Wilbur et al. also point out that the "silence" reduces the possibility of a defensive response. Group members are instructed to offer critique in the form of statements such as "If this were my client . . ." or "What I might do . . ."
4. A pause period: Perhaps the most innovative aspect of the SGSM is the pause phase. Following the feedback, there is period of 10–15 minutes (5–10 minutes may be a more realistic time frame in some classes) during which the supervisee is encouraged to reflect on the critique while the class takes a short break.
5. An optional discussion period: After the break, the group reassembles and the supervisee responds to the feedback. These reflections may involve comments on the feedback, insights gained from the critique, how the comments were helpful, and what they might do differently the next time they see the client.

Other practicum supervisors may be more informal and use a less-structured approach to assessment. Many will use a round-robin format where each peer in the class will critique the student counselor. The student being critiqued is not held to silence as in the SGSM, and may ask clarifying questions. The faculty supervisor is generally the last to provide feedback, so as not to unduly influence the student critique.

With any feedback approach used, the instructor would be prudent to explain the nature of feedback at the onset of the semester, and then models appropriate styles of critique (e.g., commenting on the counseling approach and effectiveness versus making a personal criticism). The instructor should also avoid interrupting the feedback to empower students providing feedback. The goal of feedback is twofold: to provide an opportunity for the student counselor to stretch his or her counseling skills and to enhance the student's development in providing critique.

WRITTEN FEEDBACK

After the class discussion, a session rating scale or critique form may be used by students and/or the faculty supervisor to rate your effectiveness.

Naturally, the critique form cannot address all areas of the therapeutic encounter, but provides a brief analysis of the relative effectiveness of the student counselor. Figure 6.3 shows a sample session rating form. Many schools and agencies serving as practicum and internship settings will have their own critique form.

OFFERING FEEDBACK TO PEERS

As part of practicum/internship (and throughout your counseling career) you will be involved in critiquing counseling sessions and offering suggestions for improvement. Until now, you may not have had much opportunity to hone your critiquing skills and will likely need coaching from your instructor. Student critiques often run

FIGURE 6.3   Student Counseling Session Rating Form

Date: ____/____/____

Student: _____   Evaluator: _____

Audiotape: _____   DVD/Videotape: _____   In-Class Role Play: _____

Brief Summary of Session Content: _____

_____

_____

_____

Specific Criteria: Rating (1 = *Least*; 5 = *Best*)

1. Opening: 1   2   3   4   5

Was Informed Consent thorough and professional? Was confidentiality covered?

2. Rapport: 1   2   3   4   5

Did the counselor establish a good therapeutic alliance? (e.g., voice tone, appropriate eye contact, paraphrasing, summarizing, etc.)

3. Attending Skill: 1   2   3   4   5

Did the counselor use minimal encouragers and refrain from unnecessary interruptions? (Additionally, was counselor skilled in using therapeutic silence?)

4. Open-Ended Questioning: 1   2   3   4   5

Did the counselor make appropriate use of open-ended questions?

5. Affective Domain: 1   2   3   4   5

Did the counselor demonstrate appropriate empathy?

6. Challenging/Confrontation: 1   2   3   4   5

Did the counselor confront the client (if the situation warranted it)?

7. Solution Skills: 1   2   3   4   5

Did the counselor offer appropriate solution-seeking input? (Through techniques such as the Empty Chair, Miracle Question, Role Plays, etc.)

Continued

FIGURE 6.3   Student Counseling Session Rating Form *Continued*

8. Cultural Issues: 1   2   3   4   5
Did the counselor appear to understand and respect cultural issues?

9. Goal Setting: 1   2   3   4   5
Did the counselor set effective goals for a follow-up session?

10. Closing: 1   2   3   4   5
Was closing well orchestrated? (Or, was it too abrupt?)

11. On the following 1–10 scale, how effective was the student counselor in facilitating the counseling session? (1 = *least effective*, 10 = *most effective*) Circle the appropriate number below:

          1   2   3   4   5   6   7   8   9   10

12. What the student did best during this session was:

_____

_____

_____

13. Regarding this session, what the student most needs to improve on is:

_____

_____

_____

14. Constructive comments for the student counselor's continued development:

_____

_____

_____

_____
Signature of Evaluator

the gamut from overly critical to vague to overly positive. Overly negative feedback can impinge on a student counselor's confidence, whereas uncritical positive comments provide little educational value. An instructor must strive to create an environment where honest and critical comments are given and received.

Kadushin (1985) offered guidelines for supervisors to follow when critiquing students. These guidelines stress the importance of giving feedback that is specific, timely, focused on concrete behaviors, descriptive rather than judgmental, focused on the behaviors of the student rather than his or her personal characteristics, phrased in the form of tentative statements rather than authoritative conclusions, focused on positive issues, and, finally, selective rather than a laundry list. Consider the following example:

> **Unhelpful feedback:** "Hector, I think you need to engage the client more." (Too vague. How could Hector "engage" the client? Be specific.)
>
> **Helpful feedback:** "Hector, I think a specific way you could engage the client in the session might be to ask more open-ended questions such as, 'How could you begin to create healthy friendships?'" (The feedback in this example was targeted and specific.)

ON-SITE SUPERVISION

Students in a practicum or internship also receive weekly clinical supervision at their placement. These supervision meetings are designed to target specific issues related to the student counselor's performance at the agency or school. The supervisor's critique will generally focus on the following questions:

- Is the student counselor able to establish the therapeutic relationship?
- Is the student counselor able to set realistic goals with the client?
- What struggles does the student counselor appear to be having?
- How well does the student counselor facilitate therapeutic change during sessions?

Supervisory Style

There are various supervisory methods to use with practicum/internship students. The type of supervision provided will mostly depend on the orientation of the on-site clinical supervisor. Although numerous studies have been conducted on the effectiveness of supervision on counselor development, no evidence supports one methodology being superior to another (Granello & Granello, 2007). Interestingly, only once in my entire counseling career has anyone ever asked me, "What is your theoretical supervision style?" (This question was asked of me at an interview for a faculty position in counselor education, not in a treatment facility. But, when you become a supervisor, be able to articulate a supervision style.) In fact, my belief is that most supervisors in the field would likely be stumped at such a question. Probably, your field supervisor has developed his or her own style after several years of experience both in being supervised and in providing supervision. Most supervisors are likely influenced most by the person who supervised them.

You will probably discover that your supervisor may have a radically different style than one supervising your classmate. Some on-site supervisors are quite formal and require a student to tape an entire session. Others will listen to a brief segment of a tape, or none at all. Some supervisors will ask students to work on a particular skill, such as delivering confrontation or using a particular intervention. Others may not.

It is clear that in the supervisor–student relationship, the power differential rests with the on-site supervisor. Thus, students must become facile in negotiating a delicate balance of appearing open to critique and at the same time developing appropriate assertiveness. Openness to critique would involve listening to feedback that may be critical. The assertiveness aspect of the student role would be to ask for clarification if the he or she were unclear of the message. Consider this example:

> **Supervisor:** I need you to work on the treatment plan more, ok?
> **Practicum student:** I would like to do that. What specifically could I do to improve my performance in this area?

If you do not know what your supervisor is suggesting, or if he or she seems vague (such as in the given situation), seek clarity by asking questions. Good supervisors will appreciate your initiative. Granted, there are poor supervisors out there and some of you will have the misfortune of working under them. Having a poor supervisor provides you the opportunity to learn to deal effectively with such professionals. When you do get a supervisor who seems to be a poor communicator, is overly critical, sloppy, or seems burned out, you need to find a "safe" area to debrief this. Safe areas could include other practicum or internship students and fellow graduate students in your counseling program.

If you believe your supervisor is incompetent or unethical (as opposed to merely ineffective), your first step would be to talk with your faculty advisor or the coordinator of practicum/internship placement (ethical issues are discussed in chapter 3). Your advisor would then need to dialogue with your on-site supervisor or the director of the setting in which you have been placed. In many cases, a healthier relationship can be established, although, in some, you will likely be assigned a new supervisor. It is also possible that you may need a new placement, although that should be a last resort. It has also been my experience that in most cases (although not all), addressing conflicts with your supervisor paves the way for a more trusting and respectful relationship.

Site Supervisor as Mentor

You need to develop a strong rapport with your on-site supervisor, as he or she will not only be writing an evaluation of your performance, but will also serve as the natural contact for clinical advice. The following statement is one you need to remember when faced with ethical, legal, moral, or other dilemmas that occur at your placement site: When in doubt, always contact your supervisor at the soonest possible time. This will save both you and your supervisor much anxiety.

Now, not all questions or concerns are ethical ones. In fact, it is likely most of your questions will turn out to be operational in nature. Operational concerns relate to the ways the placement site carries out treatment, its rules, chain of command, professional orientation of its staff (psychologist, counselor, etc.), whether the setting holds one of the various accreditations, and so forth. In my more than 20-year experience with practicum and internship placements, most student concerns and conflicts fell into this latter category. Besides paying careful attention to whatever orientation your site provides, you will want to develop your own checklist of questions to ask your on-site supervisor:

- What types of training and professional development are provided to practicum/internship students (many practicum/internship sites will train or send students to trainings in various techniques, treatment models, etc.)?
- What types of resources are available to practicum/internship students (computers, access to a library, research opportunities, etc.)?
- How are client or patient records kept (online, written, and locked in a secure file, etc.)?
- What are the policies regarding taping client sessions (some organizations tape all clients and require them to sign a waiver as consent to treatment)?
- What are the emergency procedures in the event of a crisis (e.g., hostage situation; an assault at the setting; death of a client, patient, or staff member; suicide attempt; etc.)?
- Although you are a counselor-in-training, your supervisor (or most staff) may be a psychologist. Which code of ethics will you need to know?
- Has your placement informed you of how to address an allegation of sexual harassment, child abuse or endangerment, communicable disease, or any mandated reporting issue?

These questions represent a beginning point; as you proceed through your practicum and internship, you will likely come up with many more questions. Keep a notebook handy so when you have questions and concerns you can write them down. It is also worth mentioning that no policy manual, no matter how thick and comprehensive, can possibly address all contingencies. So, be smart and proactive by keeping notes and asking pertinent questions. You supervisor will likely be impressed at your initiative. If he or she is not, you may wish to consider whether the setting is the right one for you.

CHAPTER 7

Multicultural Issues and Considerations

In the early years of its existence, the counseling profession mirrored the society that encapsulated it: largely Caucasian, male dominated, and middle class (McIntosh, 1998). In 1962, the pioneering counselor C. Gilbert Wrenn suggested that "culturally encapsulated" counselors define reality according to one's set of cultural standards and fail to take into account other cultural frameworks (Remley & Herlihy, 2007). Culturally encapsulated counselors tend to judge other cultural practices through the lenses of their own culture and tend to ignore evidence at odds with their own thinking. Consequently, cultural encapsulation tends to lead to stereotyping and biased thinking against other cultures.

Wrenn's (1962) writings dovetailed with other societal movements that hastened the recognition of multicultural viewpoints, including the Vietnam War and the resulting protests, the civil rights era, the beginning of the gay rights movement, and the women's movement. These movements changed the political and social landscape of the United States, and the counseling profession as well (Wehrly, 1991). Counseling professionals finally, although slowly, began to offer multicultural viewpoints in counseling curricula, journal articles, and textbooks. In 1972, the Association of Non-White Concerns in Personnel and Guidance (now known as the Association for Multicultural Counseling and Development [AMCD]) was chartered by the American Counseling Association (ACA). It was in the mid-1990s that the AMCD and the Association for Counselor Education and Supervision created the *Multicultural Counseling Competencies and Standards* (Arredondo et al., 1996) for purposes of inclusion in counselor education programs. AMCD's standards provide a format for counselors and counselor education programs to incorporate multicultural training into professional practice and the curriculum of graduate counseling programs.

The very definition of culture has also expanded; for purposes of this chapter, *culture* is broadly defined and includes race, ethnicity, nationality, gender, sexual orientation, socioeconomic class, age, disability, and other factors that may not be readily apparent (Pedersen, 1994).

Despite the profession's best efforts, however, discrimination remains very active as even many well-intentioned counselors may have internalized issues of bias and practice discrimination without any awareness on their part (Kiselica, 1999; McIntosh, 1998). White, mainstream counselors are often reluctant to admit to harboring biased attitudes regarding race (Lee, 2003). Ridley (1989) offered several examples of unintentional racism as manifested by counselors:

- Avoiding the issue of cultural differences by claiming to be "color blind"
- Being too color conscious, thus attributing all problems to a client's cultural background
- Failing to recognize one's own issues of bias
- Facilitating codependent relationships with ethnic clients out of a need to be needed
- Misunderstanding a client's defensive reactions to the counselor's stereotypical thinking
- Misunderstanding a client's culturally learned patterns of communication or behavior

Lee (2006) suggests that "culturally responsive counseling should be based on three premises: first, diversity is real and should not be ignored; second, differences are just that—differences—and not necessarily deficiencies or indicators of pathology; and third, counselors working with diverse clients must avoid stereotypes and monolithic thinking" (in Remley & Herlihy, 2007, p. 56). A multicultural perspective asserts that diverse clients may hold values and beliefs that are different from those of the counselor. Multicultural counselor education seeks to establish a foundation for cultural pluralism in the counseling session. In this chapter, I will provide an overview of some of the issues related to becoming a culturally competent counselor.

SELF-AWARENESS: THE FIRST STEP

The beginning place for developing cultural competence is to acknowledge how your own cultural identity impacts your beliefs, values, and attitudes regarding people in society. For example, you might ask yourself, "What is my culture?" This question may be more complicated than it appears. It involves not only your race but also your nationality, region, religion, political views, gender, socioeconomic status, sexual identity, and even more. All these variations on culture play a large role in our daily actions and meditations (Sue & Sue, 1998) not to mention our interactions with clients. Counselors would be well advised to understand how their view of culture impacts counseling individuals, groups, couples, or families (Association for Specialists in Group Work, 1998; Sue & Sue, 1998). Consider the case example that follows.

The Case of Stacy

Stacy, a white female counselor in a college counseling center is counseling Jin-Lin, a freshman Chinese American student. Jin-Lin is majoring in computer engineering, although he confesses he would prefer to become a high school teacher. He maintains, however, that his parents would disapprove of him changing his major. Stacy's approach is to explore with Jin-Lin what he wants. She asks Jin-Lin if he could confront his parents and explain his own career aspirations.

- How effective do you think Stacy's approach will be? Why?
- What would Stacy need to know about Jin-Lin's family and culture to be helpful?

In Stacy's case, it might help her to understand that many Asian people are uncomfortable with confrontation, and, culturally, family wishes tend to be valued over individual desires. Stacy's apparent approach of *treating the client as she would to anyone else* could be a serious cultural error. It could also prove a serious stumbling block to further counseling with Jin-Lin.

MULTICULTURAL COMPETENCIES

Pedersen, Draguns, Lonner, and Trimble (2002) and Arredondo et al. (1996) have outlined multicultural competencies for multicultural self-awareness:

- Ability to recognize direct and indirect communication styles
- Sensitivity to nonverbal cues
- Ability to recognize cultural and linguistic differences
- Interest in cultures other than your own
- Sensitivity to the stereotypes and myths of other cultures
- Ability to describe elements of your own culture
- Ability to recognize relationships between and among cultural groups
- Acknowledgement of your own racist attitudes

The final suggestion on this list is the one likely to cause the most discomfort among students and faculty in counselor education programs. Sue (1996) and Arredondo et al. (1996) have discussed how racist attitudes and practices are deeply embedded in dominant culture. Some students and faculty are likely to argue that faulty assumptions may not necessarily be a reflection of racist attitudes. In the example of Stacy and Jin-Lin, Stacy was very well-intentioned regarding her approach, and likely meant no disrespect. Her assumption that clients do what is best for themselves is well-grounded in Western thinking. However, because she is counseling an Asian client, she would have been wise to have asked Jin-Lin what he saw as his options. A counselor's failure to dialogue with his or her client around culturally sensitive issues is likely to be interpreted as cultural arrogance or cultural ignorance. In the case of Stacy and Jin-Lin, Stacy would be well-advised to reflect on the differences in values between a Western and individualist culture, and an Eastern and collectivist one.

Having said that, it is worthwhile to remember that clients are individuals; they may not necessarily share or even agree with the values commonly associated with their culture, religion, ethnicity, and other commonly cited cultural preferences. Clearly, assisting clients to examine their own wishes and goals versus those of society and their own culture is a critical aspect of the counseling process. In such instances, however, counselors must take care to provide the client the courtesy of inquiring how his or her options might be influenced by cultural norms. Counselors must also prepare clients to anticipate and address the consequences of going against cultural, family, and other norms.

In addition to developing cultural competence, counselors need to continually educate themselves when counseling culturally different clients. Ways of developing cultural awareness involve reading and studying various cultures. Naturally, it would be impossible for a counselor of any culture to be an expert on all others. What is reasonable is for counselors to be open to learning basic information on cultures they encounter in counseling. Instruments such as the Multicultural Counseling Inventory (MCI; Sodowsky, Taffe, Gutkin, & Wise, 1994) can also be used by counselors to assess their own cultural competence and awareness.

The Case of Steve

Steve, a school counseling intern, is working in a public, inner-city high school. Steve is conducting a group information session on preparation for college. The 10-person group is made up mostly of African American and Latino students, and is mostly female. The discussion gravitates to the advantages and disadvantages of attending private versus public colleges. Steve notices Juanita, a good student, has remained silent. Hoping to draw her into the discussion, Steve asks her, "Juanita, wouldn't you feel more comfortable at a Catholic college instead of a public state university?"

- How appropriate or inappropriate was the question Steve posed to Juanita?
- What are some other strategies Steve could have used to invite Juanita into the conversation?
- If you had been in Steve's situation, what approach might you have used with Juanita?

In the case of Steve, we see once again a counselor who may have good intentions, yet may be practicing in a culturally inappropriate manner. We do not know if Juanita is of a particular religious tradition, or if she would be more comfortable at a Catholic institution. Now, it could well be that Juanita is Catholic and that she might prefer a Catholic college, but Steve does not know this to be the case.

The following list outlines cultural competencies that are recommended for counselors (Arredondo et al., 1996; Pedersen et al., 2002):

- Knowledge about the histories of cultures other than your own
- Understanding of the implications and ongoing problems of racism, oppression, and stereotyping, and their impact on diverse clients
- Knowledge of the language and slang of other cultures, and of the effect of your own communication style on diverse clients
- Knowledge of resources available for teaching and learning in other cultures
- Knowledge of aspects of traditional counseling approaches that may be inappropriate for counseling clients from diverse cultures
- Understanding of how your own culture is perceived by members of other cultures
- Knowledge of institutional barriers that impede access to counseling services for many clients from diverse cultures
- Professional expertise that is relevant to people in other cultures
- Repertoire of information that people in other cultures will find useful

There are many ways counselors can increase their multicultural competence. There are numerous texts, journal articles (in *Journal of Counseling and Development, Journal of Multicultural Counseling*, etc.), DVDs, courses, and workshops. Lee (2001), Sue and Sue (1998), and others have opined that it is of critical importance for most counselors to experience the isolation, which members of minority groups have historically experienced. They suggest working in a diverse setting, attending diverse religious and cultural events, and attending social functions for international students. One of the most important resources for your continued development is your clients. Working with people from diverse backgrounds illustrates the importance of culture, spirituality, and customs.

DEVELOPING CULTURALLY APPROPRIATE SKILLS

Another goal of multicultural education and practice is developing culturally appropriate skills and intervention strategies for counseling diverse clients (Sue, 1996). Becoming culturally skilled as a counselor requires that you go beyond your basic training in counseling techniques (Sue). Culturally skilled counselors recognize the need to serve as advocates, consultants, and liaisons to community-based organizations representing culturally different people (Lee, 2001). Furthermore, many of the traditional approaches to counseling focus on the needs of the individual, which may not be appropriate in counseling clients dealing with social oppression and discrimination (Remley & Herlihy, 2007). To be an effective counselor, you must develop an array of helping skills that account for not only the individual client, but also the broader society in which your clients reside.

Advocates for multicultural counseling have challenged the profession to embrace a sense of social activism (Lee, 2006). This involves confronting the discrimination that negatively impacts many segments of society. The *ACA Code of Ethics* (ACA, 2005) addresses this, which states that "counselors advocate at individual, group, institutional, and societal levels to examine potential barriers and obstacles that inhibit access and/or the growth and development of clients" (Section A.6.a). Such obstacles to development include racism, sexism, homophobia, discrimination against the mentally ill, religious oppression, and so forth.

The Case of Harriet

Harriet, a 35-year-old African American woman, comes to a community mental health center seeking counseling. During her intake with Robin, Harriet reports symptoms of depression including loss of appetite, feeling sad, and a general feeling of hopelessness. Harriet denies any recent personal losses, but states, "I've had lots of losses. My father's in prison, my brother was shot in gang warfare, and I'm struggling to feed and house my kids." Harriet also states she is working a minimum-wage job. Harriet says she wants to get her General Educational Development (GED) tests, but has not had the energy to study. Robin suggests a psychiatric screening for medication. Robin's belief is that the most effective method to help Harriet is to address her depressed mood by the use of an antidepressant.

What do you think of Robin's approach?

- What type of strategy would be most helpful for Harriet?
- What issues and barriers should Robin anticipate regarding helping Harriet?

Robin might have been more effective had she taken a wider-angle view of the multiple issues impacting Harriet. Instead of focusing solely on medication, she could have explored the resources and social supports available in Harriet's community. Robin's failure to engage Harriet on these possibilities is an example of a well-intentioned counselor missing the forest for the trees.

The following are skills and objectives suggested by Arredondo et al. (1996), Lee (2001), and Pedersen et al. (2002):

- Skill at accessing appropriate service agencies and resources in the client's community
- Repertoire of strategies for helping clients cope with culture shock and acculturative stress that may arise from immigration experiences
- Ability to anticipate consequences of events in other cultures
- Fluency in the languages of other cultures
- Comfort in functioning in other cultures
- Skill at finding common ground with members of other cultures while retaining your own racial or ethnic identity
- Skill in helping clients to effectively intervene with institutional barriers and in using community resources when appropriate
- Active involvement in activities aimed at reducing prejudice and enhancing cross-cultural counseling knowledge in the community

ETHICS AND MULTICULTURAL COUNSELING

The *ACA Code of Ethics* (ACA, 2005) offers guidelines to assist counselors in their efforts toward multicultural competent counseling. The critical issue in multicultural competence is for individual counselors to put these guidelines into practice (Sue, 1996). Standards regarding nondiscrimination and honoring diversity are found throughout the code in numerous sections addressing the counseling relationship, assessment, professional responsibility, counselor education and supervision, and research. Multicultural competence requires counselors to keep in mind that the ethical reasoning of counselors is embedded within the counselor's worldview, which is shaped by sociocultural conditioning of which we are often unaware (Helms & Cook, 1999; Remley & Herlihy, 2007).

The *ACA Code of Ethics* (ACA, 2005, Section C.5) states that counselors do not condone or engage in discrimination based on age, culture, disability, ethnicity, race, religion, gender, religion or spirituality, sexual orientation, marital status, partnership, language preference, socioeconomic status, or any basis protected by law. Many counseling professionals take the *ACA Code of Ethics* a step further, emphasizing that counseling professionals must take an advocate role to prevent and fight against societal discrimination and prejudice (Saltzman & D'Andrea, 2001). For example, a counselor may advocate for physically disabled clients to have access to school buildings; for a gay woman to have a say in the medical care of her long-term partner; for an older client battling age discrimination, and so on.

For student counselors working in practicum and internship placements, this could also mean confronting racist, sexist, and homophobic jokes and culturally offensive language. A simple method of supporting culturally sensitive counseling involves an intense self-examination regarding one's own language, attitudes, and behavior. Student counselors can also join the Association for Multicultural Counseling and Development, and read materials related to multicultural competence (e.g., *Journal of Multicultural Counseling*, and texts such as *Multicultural Issues in Counseling: New Approaches to Diversity*, *Multicultural Counseling Competencies*, etc.).

The Case of Paul

Paul is a gay African American minister of a Christian congregation that actively maintains that being gay is a sin. Although Paul does not agree with the stance his church takes, he is nevertheless very committed to his religious faith. For the past year, Paul has met and begun dating a man he met at a church conference. They have been very careful to keep their relationship a secret, but as the relationship grows,

Continued

they wish to make it permanent. However, both partners are struggling with the knowledge that continuing the relationship would mean having to leave their church. Confused about how to proceed, Paul comes to see James, a counselor at a Pastoral Counseling Center. James, a religious person, believes homosexuality is morally wrong. However, he is touched by Paul's story and feels torn between his religious convictions and his ethical obligation as a counselor. James seeks advice from his clinical supervisor.

- What are the issues James must address in providing counseling to Paul?
- What ethical issues are involved in this scenario?
- If you were James' supervisor and he came to you for advice, how would you counsel him to proceed?
- How does a counselor balance ethical practice and his or her own moral code?
- Would James be guilty of unethical practice if he refused to counsel Paul because of his religious beliefs? Why or why not?

Shades of Oppression

David is a Jewish counselor educator at a public university in the northeastern United States. During David's presentation on preventing discrimination at an ACA conference, Hussein, a young Palestinian professor, stands and begins calling David a hypocrite because of David's well-known support for the State of Israel. David tries to regain control of the presentation, but the crowd has been engaged and is divided over the issue. David's supporters maintain that Hussein's criticism is based in anti-Semitism; his opponents claim David is supporting a totalitarian society. Many in the audience are confused, because they see both David and Hussein as representatives of oppressed cultures.

- If you were a leader in ACA, how would you proceed in this case?
- What are the difficult issues involved in the conflict?
- How might the *ACA Code of Ethics* inform whatever action is taken?

In this case, we see professionals representing two cultures, both of which have faced severe discrimination. Advocacy, in such cases, may well lie in encouraging and facilitating dialogue among such disparate points of view. Counselor educators and professional counseling organizations are clearly in a position to facilitate difficult dialogues. A conversation between David and Hussein might facilitate lasting change; failure to dialogue on issues of conflict is simply abdicating professional responsibility.

FINAL THOUGHTS

The *ACA Code of Ethics* also prohibits counselors from discriminating against groups that currently do not fall under the current federal nondiscrimination code. Groups that do not fall under legal protection include gay and lesbians, the poor, and those practicing diverse forms of spirituality (e.g., Wiccans). Some states have recently passed legislation that allow for gay and lesbians to marry and many cities and municipalities have enacted nondiscrimination laws designed to protect underrepresented groups. The *ACA Code of Ethics* also opens the door to further in-depth discussions regarding what is and what is not unethical behavior when the topic revolves around diversity.

Another complication regarding multiculturalism and discrimination, involves the relatively recent expansion of the counseling profession into non-Western societies. In many societies, current cultural practice would be at odds with ACA's nondiscrimination clause, particularly regarding the role of women, sexual orientation, and religion to name a few "hot button" topics. There are some societies that provide no equal rights to women and no legal protection from domestic abuse, and where, most egregiously, being gay or lesbian and practicing a religion other than the official government sanctioned one are each punishable by death (Hodges, 2009).

There are no easy answers to multicultural and societal conflicts such as the ones just mentioned. The counseling profession, at least the *Western* counseling profession, has posited itself as a pluralistic one and advocates for the rights of disadvantaged groups (e.g., women, gays and lesbians, the poor). But, it is fair to state that many non-Western societies would not agree with ACA regarding much of ACA's nondiscrimination statement. A critical question is how ACA, and affiliate organizations, will remain consistent with their egalitarian policies without, ironically enough, seeming culturally insensitive? This will likely become a serious issue in the future as the counseling profession becomes more visible in foreign countries across the globe.

Counseling in a diverse world carries many challenges and rewards. A multicultural counseling perspective encourages counselors to become aware of their own biases, values, and assumptions by increasing their awareness of other cultural groups. A multicultural framework also involves developing culturally appropriate intervention strategies to address the particular needs of clients with regard to ethnicity, culture, spirituality, gender, disability, sexual orientation, and socioeconomic standing to name a few. Because of the wide variation in global cultures, no one can reasonably claim to be an expert. Therefore, it is highly recommended for counselors to continue their education well beyond the classroom through workshops, networking, and reading texts on multicultural counseling.

RECOMMENDED READING

Barret, B., & Logan, C. (2007). *Counseling gay men and lesbians: A practice primer*. Florence, KY: Wadsworth.

Cashwell, C. S., & Young, J. S. (2005). *Integrating spirituality and religion into counseling: A guide to competent practice*. Alexandria, VA: American Counseling Association.

Fukuyama, M. A., & Sevig, T. D. (1999). *Integrating spirituality into multicultural counseling*. Thousand Oaks, CA: Sage.

Harley, D. A., & Dillard, J. M. (Eds.). (2005). *Contemporary mental health issues among African Americans*. Alexandria, VA: American Counseling Association.

Henriksen, R. C., Jr., & Paladino, D. A. (2009). *Counseling multiple heritage individuals, couples, and families*. Alexandria, VA: American Counseling Association.

Lee, C. C. (2006). *Multicultural issues in counseling: New approaches to diversity* (3rd ed.). Alexandria, VA: American Counseling Association.

Pedersen, P.B., Draguns, J. G., Lonner, W. J., & Trimble, J. E. (2008). *Counseling across cultures* (6th ed.). Thousand Oaks, CA: Sage.

Perez, R., Debord, K. A., & Bieschke, K. J. (2009). *A handbook of counseling and psychotherapy with lesbian, gay, and bisexual clients*. Washington, D.C.: American Psychological Association.

Roysircar, G., Sandhu, D. S., & Bibbins, V. E. (Eds.). (2003). *Multicultural competencies: A guidebook of practices*. Alexandria, VA: American Counseling Association.

Sue, D. W., & Sue, D. (2002). *Counseling the culturally diverse: Theory and practice* (4th ed.). New York: John Wiley & Sons, Inc.

Vernon, A., & Clemente, R. (2005). *Assessment and intervention with children and adolescents: Developing multicultural approaches*. Alexandria, VA: American Counseling Association.

CHAPTER 8

Managing Stress During Your Practicum/Internship

Among most mental health professions, the counseling profession is unique in that it was conceived with a strength-oriented wellness approach (Gladding, 2009; Myers, Sweeney, & Witmer, 2000; Witmer & Granello, 2005). Such an approach promotes a healthy and balanced life, not only for clients but also for counselors themselves. This chapter will help you maintain a healthier and more balanced life as you proceed through practicum and internship. As a future counseling professional, it is essential that you maintain a healthy lifestyle. Healthier counselors will likely be better counselors, and have more productive years in the profession.

As graduate students in a counseling program, you will also meet counselors, psychologists, social workers, and other mental health professionals who do not practice what they teach. Unfortunately, there are far too many counselors and other mental health professionals who struggle with addictions, codependence, do not manage their anger well, have dangerously inflated egos, and whose behavior you will not want to emulate. All professions have members who are poor representatives of their respective professions. You are not expected to have perfect behavior, never get upset, or have a total lack of conflicts. You are expected to learn to manage the challenges of your practicum and internship (and, more significantly, the demands of your life!). As a young graduate student, I had much difficulty in managing the stress involved in working virtually full-time, taking classes, and working at my practicum and internship. I hope this chapter will provide some insights in recognizing stressors that accompany counseling people who are struggling. Furthermore, it is worth mentioning that for some students, their supervisors and fellow graduate students may provide more stress than the population they counsel! Workplace conflicts are after all the primary reason people leave their jobs (Bolles, 2009).

DEVELOPING AND MAINTAINING A HEALTHY AND MINDFUL LIFESTYLE

There are many different pathways, plans, theories, approaches, books, journal articles, and other sources devoted to living a healthy and fulfilling life. The fact that so many authors, counselors, theologians, personal trainers, coaches, and such attempt to provide counseling, coaching, and information to manage stress, mindfulness, healthy living, and so forth, is indicative of just how stressful daily life has become. As graduate students on a practicum or internship, you are no stranger to the challenges of external demands. The practicum or internship experience placed atop family responsibilities, a job, academic work, and financial demands can create great stress in your life (Remley & Herlihy, 2007). The irony of life as a graduate student in counseling is that while you are working to assist your clients to live healthier, more fulfilling lives, the demands of graduate school and practicum/internship can potentially derail your own sense of harmony and balance.

In this chapter devoted to managing stress on the practicum and internship, I have created several exercises for the purposes of self-reflection. Self-reflection is a critical task not only for counselors but also for anyone in any occupation or walk of life. Self-reflection is a process of looking at oneself during times of difficulty or success. The ability to step back from an experience, however successful or disappointing, can be a key skill for personal success as a counselor. I have referred to this first section of the chapter, "Developing and Maintaining a Healthy and Mindful Lifestyle." It is important for me to acknowledge that I have likely not created anything new in addressing the issues of healthy lifestyle, or "wellness" as it is often referred to in the counseling field (Myers, Sweeney, & Witmer, 2000). Regardless of how we decide to refer to managing stress, living a balanced life, and mindful living, we are usually addressing the same common themes of how to live a fulfilling, meaningful, and healthy life. I will also offer a list of additional resources at the conclusion of this section for counseling students to consider.

One of the first topics to address is that of stress. Stress is simply an everyday fact of life for everyone. Stress is an external change that we are required to adjust our lives to. Generally, we think of stress as being negative, such as death of a loved one, unemployment, divorce, and other such challenges. But positive changes in our lives can also bring about stress as well. For example, getting married or partnered, moving across the country for a new job, buying a home, and, of course, entering graduate school are all exciting experiences, but they can also bring about new stressors.

We can experience stress from three different sources: the environment, our thoughts, and in somatic ways (Davis, Eshelman, & McKay, 2008). Environmental stressors can be the workplace, harsh weather, pollution, overcrowding, and living in unsafe areas. Environmental stressors are the ones we commonly see played up in the media, such as the catastrophic oil well leak off the coast of Louisiana, slums in major cities, and the trauma brought about by natural disasters such as that of the Katrina hurricane, the recent earthquake in Haiti, or the tsunami in Sri Lanka a few years ago. Environmental issues clearly illustrate the connection between harmony with the environment and a less stressful life. Other common forms of environmental stress might be difficulties with your spouse/partner, roommates, colleagues at the office and so forth.

The second source of stress is somatic, or how your body interprets stress. High-paced work settings, poor diet, sleep disturbances, and addiction all stress the body. Our reactions to these external demands is influenced by a genetic "fight or flight" response inherited from primitive ancestors, who dealt daily with life and death issues. These genetic traits were passed on through the subsequent generations to assist people in their adaptation to environmental demands. Consequently, we all have as part of our physiological system the innate tendency to prepare the body to face the stressor or to flee from it. An adaptive example of "fighting" might be the coworker who requests to speak with the party he or she is having conflicts with. Unhealthy fighting is when the same coworker screams obscenities at the other party. Adaptive "fleeing" is when someone takes a temporary break from the stressful event (say an argument with their spouse), then returns and asks to speak with the party they are having the conflict with. Unhealthy fleeing is when the hurt person says, "They don't bother me," when in fact the other person's comments or actions do in fact bother him or her. Denial is a type of "unhealthy" fleeing. The critical factor here is "healthy" fighting and fleeing.

The third source of stress derives from our thoughts. How you interpret or label stressful events will in great measure determine how well you resolve stress (Ellis, 2001). One of the ways our thoughts can add to stress is when we overinterpret messages. For example, interpreting your supervisor's grimace to mean she is mad at you will likely create stress for you. Remember, your supervisor's facial expressions may or may not have anything to do with you. This is where checking out the received message is important.

Effects of Stress

Stress is difficult to define in a precise manner because it is a highly subjective phenomenon that differs for each of us. Experiences that are stressful for some are pleasurable for others. We respond to stress in different ways: some people eat less when stressed, other overeat, some turn pale whereas others blush, some use healthy coping skills such as exercise and talking with friends, and others self-medicate with alcohol and other drugs. Here are some common signs of stress:

1. Frequent headaches
2. Disturbed sleep
3. Trembling of limbs
4. Neck ache, back pain, muscle spasms
5. Dizziness
6. Sweating
7. Frequent colds
8. Stomach pain
9. Constipation or diarrhea
10. Hyperventilation
11. Frequent urination
12. Decreased sexual desire
13. Excessive worry or anxiety
14. Increased anger or frustration
15. Decreased or increased appetite
16. Depression or mood swings
17. Difficulty concentrating
18. Feeling overwhelmed
19. Feelings of worthlessness
20. Suicidal thoughts
21. Social withdrawal
22. Excessive defensiveness
23. Reduced work efficiency
24. Constant fatigue
25. Feeling less hopeful

Adapted from the American Institute of Stress (2010).

Tips for Managing Stress

Because stress is a reality in daily life, you cannot eliminate it. You can, however, manage the stress that comes into your life. The following are several tips for managing stress.

Tip # 1: Recognize stress and deal with it accordingly.

- Learn to say "no." This may take some practice. Know your limits to projects and stay within them.
- Limit time with people who cause you stress. If someone consistently causes stress in your life, minimize your time with him or her.
- Take a break from stressors. If traffic causes you unmanageable stress, take a different route or use alternative forms of transportation (e.g., car pooling, mass transit, cycling, etc.). If the evening news stresses you, take occasional breaks from reading the paper, online news, or watching TV.
- Refrain from discussing upsetting topics. If discussing politics, religion, sex, or even sports causes you too much conflict, do not discuss them. If people try

and engage you in arguments over these topics, simply inform them, "I don't discuss these topics."

■ Prioritize your schedule. Make "to do" lists in order of what is most important. If there are unnecessary tasks, move them to the bottom of the list or eliminate them.

Tip # 2: Be proactive.

■ Find constructive ways to express your feelings instead of suppressing them. Practice expressing your feelings with a friend. This way you will be more prepared to do so on your practicum/internship.

■ Learn to be assertive. There will be more on assertiveness later in the chapter.

■ Manage time effectively. Poor time management skills will lead to additional stress. Prioritize your workload and this will help reduce your stress level.

■ Be willing to compromise in conflicts. Do not make all the compromises, but make the ones you can.

Tip # 3: Reframing problems.

Reframing is a basic counseling technique. Here are some examples of how you might use reframing:

■ Reframe personal conflicts as "growth opportunities" and seek to resolve them.

■ Be realistic and let go of perfectionism. You are going to make mistakes on your practicum/internship. Make them and learn from them. Ask your supervisor for advice.

■ Step back from stress and ask: "How big an issue will this be in 6 months or a year?"

■ On a regular basis, take time to reflect on the successes and blessings in your life.

Tip # 4: Accept what you cannot change and change what you can.

■ You cannot control other people. So, focus on how you react to their behavior and strategize more effective ways to deal with challenging people.

■ Get support. Talking concerns over with close friends can be very helpful. For one, you realize you are not alone and also sharing a concern may provide an outside perspective you might find useful.

■ Forgiveness. No one is perfect and, most of the time, other people are not out to make our lives miserable. Learning to forgive perceived slights can free you from negative energy. If you have trouble with forgiving others, counseling may be a viable option for you.

■ Self-reflection. What do I need to change about myself? You might ask a few trusted friends to help you with this. Do they see areas you could improve on? How could you improve on these areas?

A Healthy Assets Ledger

To build on your wellness practice, consider the following responsive questions. These questions are for you to use for purposes of self-exploration regarding personal, professional, and spiritual growth.

Reflective Questions to Consider

■ How well-developed and balanced are the personal, occupational, social, and spiritual dimensions of your life?

■ Who do you say you are? Also, how does who you say you are compare to how others appear to view you? Or, how great is the distance between who you really are and who you want to be? Be realistic, but be honest about this "divide."

- How does this self-view correlate with how significant people in your life view you (you may wish to discuss this with relevant people in your life)?
- What is your most fulfilling time of the week? Why?
- How would you describe this stage of your life?
- What issues and/or challenges are creating difficulty for you?
- How could you begin to lessen or better manage these challenges?
- What are your key strengths?
- What skills, hobbies, interests, and talents do you possess?
- What areas of your life would you like to explore? (Note: This could apply to personal relationships, travel, continuing education, career, or anything you deem important.)
- In what ways are you dependent on others?
- In what ways are you self-reliant?
- What conflicts are inhibiting your personal growth and professional effectiveness?
- How could you take steps to resolve these conflicts?

Regarding Major Successes and Failures in Your Life

- When you consider your successes, what has worked well and why?
- Regarding your failures, what seemed to go wrong and why?
- What could you do differently next time either to build on success or to ensure you did not fail in the next opportunity?

Figure 8.1 represents a self-monitoring system using scaling questions. This assessment technique provides a sense of where you are in the respective domains. The self-rating questions are intended to help provide a constructive method of self-care. This approach is not intended as a substitute to replace good personal, professional, and spiritual growth, but to serve and support wellness in these areas.

Additional Considerations for Managing Stress

Setting Limits with Others

- Do you have difficulty saying "no" to other people? If you do, how could you begin to say "no" when you know doing so is necessary? What makes setting limits difficult for you? Guilt? Fear? Something else? How could you begin to practice setting limits with others? For example, saying "no" when you mean no?
- What healthy risks can you undertake to enhance your personal and professional growth?
- When you think about the type of people who cause you stress, what is they do that is stressful for you? Okay, now that you have identified what is stressful about their behavior, how could you manage your stress level around them?

Developing Connections

- Would you want to make friends with someone like yourself? Why or why not?
- If you feel isolated, how could you begin to develop meaningful relationships?
- If you are in a marriage or partnership and you are not feeling fulfilled, how could you begin to create a greater sense of fulfillment in that relationship?
- If you are not in a relationship and would like to be, how could you begin to create such a relationship? (Or, what qualities would you like in a partner?)
- Recall a difficult period in your life. How did you navigate you way through this time?
- How do you go about creating meaning in your life?
- Make a list of at least five skills you already possess that you can use to keep yourself well and fit.

FIGURE 8.1   Dimensions of a Healthy Lifestyle

Spirituality/Religious Life

My spiritual/religious life provides a sense of purpose and helps me address major life challenges.

(Note: An alternate phrasing for nonspiritual/nonreligious people might be: "My sense of life meaning/purpose provides fulfillment and helps me address the challenges in my life.")

1	2	3	4	5	6	7	8	9	10

(1 = *no help at all*; 10 = *strongly helps*)

If your score was less than five, how could you improve your situation?

Personal Vision

"I have a clear vision in my personal, spiritual, and professional life."

1	2	3	4	5	6	7	8	9	10

(1 = *No vision*; 10 = *I have a clear vision*)

If you do not have a clear personal, spiritual, or professional vision, how could you develop one? Visioning is a key component to success in all these areas.

Self Worth

"I feel worthwhile as a human being and have a strong sense of self-acceptance. Although I am not perfect, I feel good about myself."

1	2	3	4	5	6	7	8	9	10

(1 = *I am worthless*; 10 = *My self worth is very strong*)

If you are experiencing low self-esteem, how could you begin to feel better about yourself? What actions could you take to begin to feel more self-confident?

Goal Setting

"I feel self-confident about setting and meeting goals and demands in my life."

1	2	3	4	5	6	7	8	9	10

(1 = *I lack confidence in my ability to meet demands and the goals I set*; 10 = *I feel very confident in setting, planning, and meeting goals and demands*)

If you lack clear goals in your life, how could you begin to create some clear goals?

Rational Thinking

"I believe I perceive my life and life situations in a rational manner. I seldom engage in overly negative thinking."

1	2	3	4	5	6	7	8	9	10

(1 = *I frequently engage in irrational thinking*; 10 = *I am very rational in my beliefs*)

If you have rated yourself as frequently engaging in irrational beliefs (e.g., "I am a loser," "I am worthless," "No one could ever love me," etc.), how could you begin to think in a more rational manner? (Or, if you are unsure as to whether your beliefs are rational, you might consider asking someone you trust for feedback.)

Emotional Understanding and Regulation

"I am in touch with my emotions and am able to express the full range of emotions appropriate to the situation. I also am not governed by my emotions."

1	2	3	4	5	6	7	8	9	10

Continued

FIGURE 8.1   Dimensions of a Healthy Lifestyle *Continued*

(1 = *I am not able to regulate my emotions and often express emotions inappropriate to the situation*; 10 = *I am able to regulate my emotions and experience emotions appropriate to the situation*)

If you find you are not experiencing an appropriate range of emotions, or you find you are too often ruled by your emotions, how could you begin to change this? Remember, you will have "negative" emotions, so the task is to regulate them appropriately.

Resilience

"I am a resilient person, and able to analyze, synthesize, and make a plan to deal with challenges and projects that come my way."

1   2   3   4   5   6   7   8   9   10

(1 = *I do not feel resilient*; 10 = *I am very confident in my resiliency*)

If you do not feel resilient (or you are not as resilient as you would like) or do not have the ability to resolve difficulties in your life, what could you do to begin to develop more resilience? (Note: If you feel stuck on strategizing with this component, perhaps begin by making a list of ways you feel resilient. Or, ask someone who knows you well to list ways they see you as being resilient.)

Sense of Humor

"I possess a healthy, appropriate sense of humor that helps me deal with the stresses of life."

1   2   3   4   5   6   7   8   9   10

(1 = *I have no sense of humor*; 10 = *I have a healthy sense of humor*)

If you do not feel your sense of humor is either strongly developed, appropriate, or provides an effective release of stress, what could you change to improve the situation?

Fitness or Recreation

"I have a regular weekly fitness/recreational routine that helps me stay physically and emotionally fit."

1   2   3   4   5   6   7   8   9   10

(1 = *I have no activity routine*; 10 = *I have an active physical/recreational routine*)

If you do not have a regular weekly fitness routine, what could you do to change this? (Remember, you do not need to become a marathoner, competitive cyclist, swimmer, or dancer. It is simply about developing a regular routine of 20 minutes a day, at least 3 days a week.)

Healthy Diet

"I regularly eat a balanced diet, including healthy vegetables and fruits."
(Note: Healthy is not meant to imply you *never* eat unhealthy foods because that is not realistic. In fact, sometimes it is good for the psyche to eat ice cream, cookies, and so forth. Just do not do it too often. Rather, it is about eating unhealthy food in moderation.)

1   2   3   4   5   6   7   8   9   10

(1 = *My diet is unbalanced and unhealthy*; 10 = *My diet is balanced and healthy*)

If your diet is unhealthy (eating high-fat food, "junk" food, fast food too often), how could you begin to eat a healthier diet? (For in-depth help, you may wish to consult a dietician.)

Continued

FIGURE 8.1   Dimensions of a Healthy Lifestyle *Continued*

Mindful Living

"I maintain a mindful lifestyle by not abusing alcohol or other drugs, by wearing a seat belt, having regular medical exams, and by refraining from high-risk activities (e.g., casual sex, binge drinking, binge eating, restricting food, etc.)."

1   2   3   4   5   6   7   8   9   10

(1 = *I do not live a healthy, mindful life*; 10 = *I maintain a healthy, mindful lifestyle*)

If you find you are not living a healthy, mindful life, what steps could you take to change this?

Managing Stress and Anxiety

"Through my diet, workout routine, friendships, and so forth, I have the ability to manage stress and anxiety. When I find I am unable to manage the stress and anxiety in my life, I check in with close friends and family or if the need arises, I see a counselor."

1   2   3   4   5   6   7   8   9   10

(1 = *I am regularly unable to manage the stress and anxiety in my life*; 10 = *I am able to manage the stress and anxiety in my life*)

If you find you regularly have difficulty managing the stress and anxiety in your life, how could you begin to manage that stress and anxiety better?

Sense of Self

"I feel that my self identity is strong and well developed."

1   2   3   4   5   6   7   8   9   10

(1 = *My sense of self is incongruent with who I am because I try too hard to be who others want me to be*; 10 = *My sense of self is very congruent with who I am*)

Some people struggle with their own identity for various reasons, such as enmeshment with family, codependence with a loved one, low self-esteem, and so forth. If you find you are struggling with an inability to develop your own identity, what are some options for exploration? (Options that would reduce your struggle or help you resolve your personal identity struggles.)

Connection to Family or Culture

"I feel a strong connection to my family or culture."

1   2   3   4   5   6   7   8   9   10

(1 = *I feel no connection to my family or culture*; 10 = *I feel a strong and healthy connection to my family and culture*)

In the event you feel no connection to your family or culture, what would you say accounts for this? Also, how could you begin to make stronger connections to your family and culture?

Career/Vocational Development

"I feel a sense of satisfaction in my career (or the career I am pursuing)."

1   2   3   4   5   6   7   8   9   10

(1 = *No satisfaction*; 10 = *Maximum satisfaction*)

If your career does not provide personal challenge and satisfaction for you, what steps could you take to create more fulfillment and satisfaction in your career? (Or, if you are unemployed, how could your job search become more fulfilling? Or, how could this period of unemployment be more productive?)

Continued

FIGURE 8.1   Dimensions of a Healthy Lifestyle *Continued*

Hobbies

"My hobbies help me relax and provide a sense of enjoyment."

1   2   3   4   5   6   7   8   9   10

(1 = *I have no hobbies or they provide no sense of enjoyment or relaxation*; 10 = *My hobbies are a pure joy*)

If you lack hobbies or outside interests from work, how could you create some fulfilling pursuits?

Social Life

"I have healthy relationships that provide me a sense of emotional connection and help make life more rewarding."

1   2   3   4   5   6   7   8   9   10

(1 = *I have no significant relationships, they are shallow, or provide little in the way of emotional connection*; 10 = *I have healthy and fulfilling relationships and they are an important part of my life*)

If you lack significant personal connections or your relationships do not provide you a sense of emotional connection, how could you begin to address this? (Or, how could you begin to create fulfilling relationships?)

Intimacy

"Intimacy, or love, is a central part of my life and my relationship with my spouse/partner provides the grounding, intimacy, and close connection I need. (Note: Intimacy could involve sexual intimacy or even a close, nonsexual relationship)."

1   2   3   4   5   6   7   8   9   10

(1 = *Intimacy is largely absent from my life*; 10 = *Intimacy is a large part of my life and provides me with great satisfaction*)

If intimacy seems absent from your life, or seems unhealthy or unfulfilling, what do you need to do to change this situation?

Work and Career

- Are you pursuing the career you truly belong in? Why or why not?
- Why did you choose to pursue counseling as a career?
- What is your dream job or dream career? (Describe in some detail: title, location, etc.)
- How can you begin to create your dream job? What steps are necessary?
- Setting goals is important for success. What are your major goals for the next 5 years?
- In what ways have you changed since entering your graduate counseling program?

Mentoring

- Who are some people who have inspired you? Note: They need not necessarily be people you have met. For example, many have been inspired by the likes of Martin Luther King, Gandhi, Mother Teresa, Dalai Lama, Stephen Hawking, and so forth, even though they have never met these people.

- Name five people and state how they have inspired you.
- Who are some people who share your hobbies and interests?
- Cite some organizations you are actively involved in.
- List some people who share your spiritual beliefs (or, who share your personal convictions).

CONFLICT MANAGEMENT SKILLS

A big part of health and wellness involves managing conflict (Weinhold & Weinhold, 2009). As a future counselor, you will have many opportunities to help clients and fellow students identify, address, and manage conflict. Conflict between people is actually a very natural occurrence; yet many people find conflict to be traumatic and stressful. Conflict need not necessarily be traumatic, however, and if well managed and addressed, it may provide the foundation for personal growth. The critical factor regarding conflict is that we acknowledge it, and then strategize on how to resolve it.

The first step in managing conflict is to admit that it exists. Because counseling can be demanding and stressful work, it is likely you will have ample opportunities to work on developing competence in dealing with conflict. I have listed common assumptions about conflict, and then, a reframed response to these assumptions.

Assumption 1: "All conflict is bad and should be avoided."
Reframed response: Conflict is not necessarily "bad." Acknowledging and addressing conflict can be liberating and improve self-confidence.

Assumption 2: "Conflict is awful and terrible."
Reframed response: Conflict is neither "awful" nor "terrible," although refusing to admit or address it can result in poor health.

Assumption 3: "I simply can't deal with conflict."
Reframed response: Dealing with conflict is sometimes unpleasant for me. However, the more experienced I become at addressing conflicts, the more confident and effective I become at resolving them.

Assumption 4: "When I have conflicts they always 'blow up' into something unmanageable so it's just better to ignore them."
Reframed response: Sometimes my attempts at conflict resolution go awry and tempers can escalate. However, in many, if not most cases, I am able to navigate conflict without causing further injury.

Now, a critical factor beyond admitting the existence of conflicts is how we go about resolving them. Fortunately, people can improve their conflict resolution skills with practice. As a counselor operating from a cognitive framework, I believe conflict resolution is grounded in childhood experiences of observing and participating in family conflicts. Our parents or guardians consciously or unconsciously modeled styles of conflict resolution, which we internalized and then repeated in our conflicts with siblings and peers. Some families are more functional at addressing conflict; children raised in more functional homes will have an early advantage at conflict resolution. Children raised in less-functional, dysfunctional, abusive, or neglectful homes will have more struggles in resolving conflict.

Conflict Resolution Styles

- The Denier: "Conflict? What conflict?" "Everything's just perfect."
- The Minimizer: "It's not anything to worry about." "No big deal."
- The Overly Responsible Type: "It's all my fault."
- The Avoider: "It's better to avoid conflict regardless of the cost."
- The Aggressor: "You have to get in people's face! That's how you resolve conflicts."
- The Mindful Type: "Ok, there's a conflict. What steps can I take to resolve it?"

Examine the types and think about which type best fits how you generally behave when faced with conflict. No one will always choose only one type; but decide which of the conflict resolution styles most frequently describes you. Now, think about which of these styles you would prefer.

The following questions are aimed to focus your awareness on your current conflict resolution style and how you would like to modify it.

- Which of the mentioned types would usually describe the manner in which I deal with conflict?
- What do I fear about conflict?
- What types of conflict situations do I find most challenging?
- Who were my role models in learning how to address conflict?
- What are my strengths in resolving conflict?
- How effective is my style of conflict resolution?
- In what situations does my approach to resolving conflict work?
- In what situations does my approach to resolving conflict seem ineffective?
- What would I want to change about my style of conflict resolution?
- How could I begin to change my approach to conflict resolution?
- What is one small change I can make that will help me address conflict more effectively?
- My biggest challenge in improving my conflict resolution skills is . . .
- Think of someone who seems effective in resolving conflict. What conflict resolution skills do they possess?
- What, in my professional training and background, assists me in resolving conflict?
- What types of conflict resolution work do I see myself performing in the future?
- What types of conflict resolution roles would be inconsistent with my future practice as a counselor?
- How would a skill in conflict resolution assist me in becoming an effective counselor?

Conflict Scenario One

You have just commenced your practicum. You get along very well with most of the staff and fellow graduate students. However, after a few weeks, you discover another practicum student seems to be constantly belittling you ("You haven't learned much about counseling, have you?" "Your approach to counseling is all wrong."). You decide not to address the issue, hoping it will just resolve itself. Then, one of the graduate students informs you the student in question is bad mouthing you to the others.

Continued

How would you resolve this apparent conflict? (If possible, role-play the scenario out with a classmate or friend. The more you practice resolving conflicts, the more skilled you will become at resolving them.)

Conflict Scenario Two

You have completed practicum and are beginning internship at your placement. Your new supervisor seems very harsh with his criticism and is somewhat sarcastic during supervision sessions, making comments such as "This is terrible work!" and "I can't believe your last supervisor saw your work as worthy of passing practicum." Your supervisor also discloses he really did not want to supervise you, but was forced to do so by the director of clinical services. Intimidated and discouraged, you soon discover yourself avoiding him whenever you can; as weekly supervision arrives, your stomach is upset and you feel very anxious. You realize this is an unhealthy situation and you would like to switch supervisors, but worry the answer will be no and that your supervisor may hold your actions against you. What steps might you make to deal with this conflict?

THE COUNSELING STUDENT AS CLIENT

Counseling work can certainly be very stressful, as clients bring in difficulties of their own, and there may be job conflicts with coworkers. As a graduate student in a counseling program, you have the added complication of course work, along with seeing clients, balancing a home life and numerous additional demands. Many counseling programs now mandate a few counseling sessions for their students. Counselors who have had the experience of being clients themselves have a more complete understanding of the therapeutic process (Norcross, Strausser, & Faltus, 1988). Putting yourself in the vulnerable position as a client also provides you the opportunity of experiencing the "other side" of the therapeutic experience and likely can help you develop more empathy for clients and their struggles.

I can state from experience that many counselors and other mental health professionals are reluctant to seek counseling services for themselves, out of their fear or arrogance, or simply being unaware of the extent of their personal issues. As a future professional counselor, graduate school is the optimal time to begin addressing your own mental health to ensure whatever personal concerns you have do not impact your counseling work. (This is not to say you must be perfect to be a counselor; every counselor, no matter how successful and well-adjusted, has some personal "baggage.")

If you decide that entering personal counseling would be a good idea, you should be aware that many counselors, psychologists, social workers, and other mental health professionals have already reached similar conclusions. Mahoney (1997) reported that 87% of mental health professionals surveyed admitted they had entered personal counseling at some point in their careers. Personal counseling was rated by mental health professionals as second to practical experience as the most important influence in their professional lives. A study of 500 counselors and psychologists revealed that 93% rated the experience from mildly positive to very positive (Baird, Carey, & Giakovmis, 1992). Other notable counseling professionals such as Sam Gladding (2009) have posited personal counseling as a critical growth experience for counselors.

Pope and Tabachnick (1994) conducted a study of more than 800 psychologists, in which 84% admitted to having been in personal therapy. The most often cited reasons for mental health professionals to seek counseling were (in descending order): depression, divorce or relationship difficulty, struggles with self-esteem, anxiety, career, work or study concerns, family of origin issues, loss, and stress (Pope & Tabachnick). Among those surveyed, 85% described the therapeutic experience as very or exceptionally helpful. What these and other studies suggest is that personal counseling can be very important for our own emotional health and personal growth.

In addition to counseling, support groups can serve an important role for counselors and certainly for graduate students. I am not aware of counseling programs that require student participation in support groups, but I think it is a worthwhile concept, given the stressful nature of graduate study, practicum and internship demands, and because the Council for Accreditation of Counseling and Related Educational Programs (CACREP) Standards (2009) essentially mandate training reflective counseling professionals. In my own graduate counseling program, we were required to participate in an intensive growth experience for 3 days. I was both a participant as a master's degree student and later, a group facilitator as a doctoral student. My experience in both groups was educational and very informative regarding the power of the group experience on individuals. However, my belief is that an ongoing support group would be more impactful.

FINAL SUGGESTIONS FOR SELF-CARE

Kenneth Blanchard, famous for the best-selling book, *The One Minute Manager*, cowrote a follow-up book titled, *The One Minute Manager Gets Fit* (1986). He was motivated to write this book after realizing that he was so consumed with chasing success that he forgot the most important thing: to keep his life in balance (Blanchard, Edington, & Blanchard, 1986). He ate junk food, failed to workout, his weight ballooned, and his blood pressure rose to dangerously high levels (Blanchard et al.). In the book, he listed the following as a means of assessing fitness level:

- I love my job. (Most of the time)
- I use safety precautions like wearing a seat belt in moving vehicles.
- I am within five pounds of my ideal weight.
- I know three methods to reduce stress that do not include the use of drugs or alcohol.
- I do not smoke.
- I sleep six to eight hours each night and wake up refreshed.
- I engage in regular physical activity at least three times per week. (Including sustained physical exertion for twenty to thirty minutes—for example, walking briskly, running, swimming, biking—plus strength and flexibility activities)
- I have seven or fewer alcoholic drinks a week.
- I know my blood pressure.
- I follow sensible eating habits. (Eat breakfast every day; limit salt, sugar, and fats like butter, eggs, whole milk, breakfast meats, cheese, and red meat; and eat adequate fiber and few snacks.)
- I have a good social support system.
- I maintain a positive mental attitude. (p. 36)

The list contains many common sense items, yet it is clear that many people, including some counselors, struggle with many of them. Regular medical check-ups on an annual basis are also highly recommended. Graduate students who lack health insurance should check with their student health service as medical care is usually subsidized by student fees and significantly less expensive than off-campus providers.

CONCLUSION

The practicum and internship experience can be a very demanding and, occasionally, stressful time for a graduate student. The good news is that survival rates are very high and it is likely you will manage stressful times quite well. You should expect occasional times, however, when you feel overwhelmed or "stressed out." These times, though unpleasant, also provide some of the greatest opportunities. You will get to practice the same stress management techniques and skills you have been teaching your clients. This is where self-reflection, reframing, meditation, exercise, friendships, and so forth, are so valuable and rewarding. Be aware of your stress and anxiety levels and monitor them closely so that you remain physically and emotionally healthy. A burned out counselor—one who tries to be everything to everyone—fails to set limits, lacks assertiveness, eats a poor diet, and has no significant friendships, is likely to be of limited value to his or her clients. So, understand yourself and your emotional and physical limitations and work to stay within them.

RECOMMENDED READING FOR MANAGING STRESS

Brinkman, R., & Kirschner, R. (2002). *Dealing with people you can't stand: How to bring out the best in people at their worst.* New York: McGraw-Hill.
Davis, M., Eshelman, E. R., & McKay, M. (2008). *The Relaxation and stress reduction workbook* (6th ed.). Oakland, CA: New Harbinger.
Greenberger, D., & Padesky, C. A. (1995). *Mind over mood: A cognitive therapy treatment manual for clients.* New York: Guilford.
Myers, J. E., & Sweeney, T. J. (Eds.) (2005). *Counseling for wellness: Theory, research, and practice.* Alexandria, VA: American Counseling Association.
Williams, M. B., & Poijula, S. (2000). *The PTSD workbook: Simple effective techniques for overcoming traumatic stress symptoms.* Oakland, CA: New Harbinger.

RECOMMENDED READING FOR CONFLICT RESOLUTION

The following books are good resources for ideas, self-reflection, and skill building regarding conflict resolution:

Barsky, A. E. (2007). *Conflict resolution for the helping professions* (2nd ed.). Belmont, CA: Thomson/Brooks-Cole.
Fisher, R., & Ury, W. (1981). *Getting to yes: Negotiating agreement without giving in.* New York: Penguin Books.
Weinhold, B. K., & Weinhold, J. B. (2009). *Conflict resolution: The Partnership way* (2nd ed.). Denver: Love Publishing.

CHAPTER 9

Crisis Intervention in Practicum/Internship

No area of professional counseling practice creates as much stress and anxiety as crisis situations. For purposes of this chapter, crisis will be defined as situations in which a client poses a danger to self or others. This includes clients who may be potentially suicidal, those who threaten to harm a third party (e.g., homicidal ideation), and cases of child abuse and neglect.

Most practicum and internship settings, whether in schools, agencies, residential treatment centers, hospitals, and so forth, will try to screen potential crisis clients away from practicum and internship students. Because no screening system is perfect, however, counseling programs must prepare students for the possibility that they will encounter crisis clients on practicum. In fact, many supposed "safe" clients assigned to the practicum or internship student may, because of stressful circumstances, suddenly escalate into a crisis. This chapter will discuss what to do in the cases of such clients.

THE DUTY TO WARN

Before we discuss crisis situations, it is necessary to review confidentiality and its exceptions, which are discussed in detail in chapter 3. Confidentiality is not absolute, and federal and state laws mandate several exceptions where confidentiality must be broken (state laws vary, so you must know the laws of your jurisdiction). These situations include:

- Potential suicide
- Credible threats made against third parties
- Abuse (children, the elderly, or vulnerable persons)
- Court-mandated disclosure

As discussed in chapter 3, the landmark court case involving confidentiality is the *Tarasoff* case (*Tarasoff v. Regents of the University of California*, 1976). In the wake of the *Tarasoff* ruling, when clients disclose a viable threat to themselves or another party, the counselor must breach confidentiality and notify appropriate parties (e.g., the police and potential victims). Failure to adequately address a crisis or to warn appropriate parties could result in legal and ethical sanctions (Remley & Herlihy, 2007; Wheeler & Bertram, 2008).

SUICIDAL CLIENTS

There are several commonly held myths regarding suicide. Sadly, you may even hear mental health professionals repeating them. Common suicide myths include:

- Discussing suicide will cause the client to attempt it.
- Clients who talk of suicide will not attempt suicide.
- Suicides increase around Christmas and New Year's Eve.
- Only insane people attempt suicide.
- When a suicidal patient improves, it is a sign the danger is over.
- Suicide is more prevalent among poorer classes of people.
- Suicide generally happens without warning.
  (Sommers-Flanagan and Sommers-Flanagan, 1999)

Many counselors fear they might say the wrong thing and precipitate a suicidal attempt. Fortunately, there is virtually nothing you could say to induce suicide (Granello & Granello, 2007; Sommers-Flanagan & Sommers-Flanagan, 1999). In my experience with crisis clients, all of them seemed visibly relieved when I inquired about the possibility of suicide. Captain (2006) agrees that counselors need not fear asking clients about suicide. Most clients who are contemplating suicide are actually relieved to discuss the topic and generally are appreciative that someone has asked (assuming of course that the topic is discussed in a caring, nonjudgmental way). It is also important to ask the client whether he or she has a plan (ask for details) and the likelihood to carry out that plan. The client's responses will give you a sense of his or her intent (Capuzzi & Gross, 2008).

Some students have also told me that they worry the client will get mad if they ask about suicide. In my opinion and clinical experience, if the client does become angry, it is likely a positive sign, as it may indicate that the client has not given up hope. I am far more nervous with suicidal clients who appear calm. Such rationality and composure may indicate that the client has made a decision to commit suicide and is at peace with the idea (Capuzzi & Gross, 2008; Granello & Granello, 2007).

Ethical and Legal Mandates Regarding Suicide

The *ACA Code of Ethics* (American Counseling Association [ACA], 2005) clearly addresses the issues of suicide and client welfare:

> The general requirement that counselors keep information confidential does not apply when disclosure is required to protect clients or identified clients from serious and foreseeable harm or when legal mandates demand that confidential information be revealed. Counselors consult with other professionals when in doubt as to the validity of an exception. (Section B.2.)

State laws also mandate that counselors and other professionals (e.g., psychologists, nurses, physicians, etc.) also breach confidentiality when the issue of self-harm arises (Remley & Herlihy, 2007). As a counselor, you must also be prepared to take appropriate measures to prevent suicide. Appropriate measures would generally include a thorough risk assessment, consulting with your supervisor, notifying the appropriate parties, and documenting the actions you took.

Talking With a Suicidal Client

Here are some suggestions for discussing the issue of suicide with a client:

- Do not panic or show any signs of discomfort. You want the client to believe you are under control.
- If you are concerned that a client might be suicidal, specifically ask, "I'm wondering if you might be considering suicide."
- Do not try to argue with the client about his or her plan or give him or her minimizing advice. ("It'll get better," "It's really not that big a deal," "What will your family think?" etc.)
- It is critical that the suicidal client feel "heard" and not judged. Listen empathically and let the client know you accept him or her even though he or she is in crisis. It is also worth remembering that suicidal clients feel very isolated. You are very possibly the first person the client has disclosed his or her intent for self-harm.
- Most crisis clients have thought of suicide but have not made a plan. If this is the case with your client, get him or her rescheduled at the soonest possible time (the next day if possible). Provide the client with a 24-hour crisis number so he or she knows help is available.
- Remember, when the client discloses thoughts or even a suicide plan, he or she is saying "Help me" to the counselor. The fact they have admitted life is presently beyond their management is a sign they are asking for help.

How to Assess Suicidal Risk

Because suicide assessment is not an exact science, counselors would be wise to apply a broad approach to treating suicidal clients. McGlothen, Rainey, and Kindsvatter (2005) suggest that professionals consider five aspects for all potentially suicidal clients:

- Plan. The verbalization of a plan of how the client would attempt suicide suggests lethality. The more detailed and specific the plan, the greater potential lethality.
- Intent. The stated intent to follow through on a suicide plan also suggests higher lethality.
- Means. The means by which the client plans to use in a suicide attempt. The more deadly the means (e.g., gun), the greater the lethality.
- Prior attempts. Previous suicide attempts also suggest the client has previously seen suicide as a viable option. This suggests higher lethality.
- Substance abuse. A history of substance abuse increases lethality, because substance abusers often display less management of crisis situations. (McGlothen et al., 2005)

McGlothen et al. (2005) also suggest the following general guidelines in gauging lethality:

- Low lethality. Suicidal ideation (thoughts of suicide) is present but intent is denied, and the client does not have a concrete plan and has never attempted suicide in the past.
- Moderate lethality. More than one general risk factor for suicide is present, suicide ideation and intent are present but a clear plan is denied, and the client is motivated to improve her or his psychological state.
- High lethality. Several general risk factors for suicide are present, the client has verbalized suicidal ideation and intent, and he or she has communicated a well thought-out plan with immediate access to resources needed to complete the plan.
- Very high lethality. The client verbalizes suicidal ideation and intent, and he or she has communicated a well thought-out plan with immediate access to resources needed to complete the plan, demonstrates cognitive rigidity and hopelessness for the future, denies any available suicide support and has attempted suicide in the past.

Essential Factors of Suicide Risk Assessment

- Assessment of each person is unique.
- Assessment is complex and challenging.
- Assessment is an ongoing process.
- Assessment uses multiple perspectives.
- Assessment tries to uncover foreseeable risk.
- Assessment relies on clinical judgment.
- Assessment is treatment.
- Assessment errs on the side of caution.
- Assessment takes all threats, warning signs, and risk factors seriously.
- Assessment asks the tough questions.
- Assessment tries to uncover the underlying message.
- Assessment is done in a cultural context.
- Assessment is collaborative.
- Assessment is documented.
   (Granello & Granello, 2007, p. 184)

Assessing suicide in adolescents may be particularly difficult because of the fact that this population is still developing coping mechanisms, understanding crisis is a temporary situation, and they tend to be more impulsive. In 1996, Juhnke adapted the SAD PERSONS checklist for use with adolescents and called it the Adapted SAD PERSONS checklist. The adapted scale can be used to assess suicidal risk factors and provide general intervention recommendations for school counselors and counselors working youth.

The adapted version does not assign specific points for most of the items; rather, the counselor assigns from 0–10 points for each item based on the severity of risk.

Adapted SAD PERSONS Scale (A-SAD)

S—Sex (males = 10 points; females = 0 points)
A—Age (older adolescents are at higher risk and receive more points)
D—Depression or affective disorder (the more serious the disorder, the more points)
P—Previous attempts (score recent attempts and more lethal attempts higher)
E—Ethanol/Drug abuse (score drug or alcohol use or abuse higher)
R—Rational thinking loss (score evidence of rational thinking loss higher)
S—Social supports lacking (score lack of close friendships or social supports higher)
O—Organized plan (score specificity and lethality higher)
N—Negligent parenting (score neglect, abuse, family stress, and suicidal modeling higher)
S—School performance (score aggressive behaviors, vandalism, or deterioration of academic performance higher)

Scoring Guideline

Assign points (0–10) to match severity for each risk factor. Total scores can range from 0–100.

Scores of 0–29: Students should be encouraged to participate in counseling services and be given information about crisis services.

Scores of 30–49: Students should be strongly encouraged to receive counseling and close follow-up services. School counselors should contact parents or guardians and make a thorough suicide assessment.

Scores of 50–69: Students in this range should be strongly considered for an evaluation for hospitalization.

Scores of 70+: Scores in this range suggest both environmental turmoil and severe emotional distress. Scores at this extreme end of the continuum warrant immediate hospitalization. Child protective services should be contacted in cases where family turmoil does not allow adequate assurance of care.

Caution: Suicide risk assessment is a complex process and cannot identify all persons who will suicide. The Adapted-SAD PERSONS Scale should not be used as the sole or primary assessment to determine, measure, consider, or estimate suicide risk or suggest interventions. The Scale and its generally suggested actions should be used as merely one component of a structured, multi-component, and thorough suicide assessment process facilitated by a suicide assessment, threat, or safety committee minimally comprised of multiple clinicians, clinical supervisors, legal counselor, and a client or student ombudsman or advocate.

Reprinted by permission from Juhnke, 1996.

There are other assessments for suicidality and depression (which is a significant risk factor for suicide). Perhaps the most widely used instrument for assessing depression is the Beck Depression Inventory (BDI), second edition (Beck, Steer, & Brown, 1996). The BDI-II is often considered as the preferred instrument because of the large amount of research validating its effectiveness (Beck et al., 1996). It is a 21-item self-report that assesses levels of depression and predicts the likelihood of suicide in adolescents and adults. It is completed by the client and usually takes less than 10 minutes. According to Beck et al. (1996), BDI-II scores ranging from 0–13 represent *minimal depression*; total scores from 14–19 suggest *mild depression*; total scores from 20–28 represent *moderate depression*; and total scores from 29–63 suggest *severe depression*. For more information about this instrument, go to http://psychcorp.pearsonassessments.com and search on Beck Depression Inventory.

According to Beck et al. (1996), finding a way to instill hopefulness in clients is of critical importance to suicide prevention. This may involve encouraging the client to cultivate friendships, seek ongoing counseling, consider medication (at least temporarily), incorporate a fitness routine and healthy diet, seek appropriate opportunities through work or schooling, reduce use of alcohol and drugs, and many other things.

Additional Risk Factors

Most people who attempt suicide have a diagnosable mental disorder (Granello & Granello, 2007) such as major depression or bipolar disorder. Here are some additional risk factors that may increase the risk for suicidality:

- Substance abuse
- Posttraumatic stress disorder (PTSD)
- An eating disorder
- An Axis II diagnosis (Borderline Personality Disorder, Histrionic Personality Disorder, etc.)
- Mental illness such as schizophrenia
- A history of previous suicide attempts
- Gender: Males are three to five times more likely to commit suicide than females (Granello & Granello, 2007)
- Age: Elderly Caucasian males have the highest suicide rate. In addition, suicide is the second leading cause of death among college students and is rising among adolescent high school–age adolescents. (Sommers-Flanagan & Sommers-Flanagan, 2000)
- A recent and major precipitating event (death of a loved one, divorce or breakup, loss of job, major disappointment, academic difficulty, loss of home, etc.)
- For children and adolescents, peer taunting and shunning has been associated with several high-profile suicide cases in recent years (Moore, 2010).
- Access to firearms or other lethal means.

Steps to Take When a Client Is Contemplating Suicide

The most effective means of preventing suicide is to recognize the warning signs and respond to them. As mental health professionals, counselors are expected to read and interpret the signs of suicide and to intervene appropriately. Counselors should heed the following suggestions:

1. Take all suicide threats seriously. This is the first and most significant guideline of suicide prevention.
2. Of all suicidal individuals, 75% give some type of warning sign. Examples of warning signs might be vague threats ("I might not be around much longer"), giving away treasured possessions, risky behavior (driving very fast, illicit drug or alcohol abuse, risky sexual behavior, etc.), nonlethal self-injurious behaviors (cutting, burning, numerous injuries, etc.), withdrawal from social activities, pessimism, sleep problems, increased alcohol use, a plan for suicide, and so on.
3. When you do encounter a potentially suicidal client, do not simply advise him or her not to commit suicide, because that is unlikely to work. Instead, ask them to postpone an attempt of suicide. When you get an agreement to delay suicide, this provides an opening for additional possibilities other than self-harm.
4. Remember: When a client discloses an intention of suicide, what they are saying to you is, "Help me!"
5. Fortunately, most clients who bring up suicidal thoughts or intent never make a plan for suicide. Of those who make a plan, few follow through on the plan. (But again, treat each gesture seriously.)
6. Get the suicidal client to commit to ongoing counseling. In addition, get the client a referral for a medication screening as they may need antidepressant medication at least temporarily. If the client refuses, be sure to document your suggestions for legal and ethical reasons.
7. Never leave the suicidal client alone. If you need to consult with a colleague or supervisor regarding a suicide-prevention plan, get a colleague or secretary to stay with the client while you consult.
8. Always consult with your immediate supervisor about the situation. Moreover, document the situation, how you assessed the client, and consultation, and the plan you made. Does the client need to be hospitalized? If the client needs hospitalization, the police or other authorized personnel should provide transportation. Suicidal clients will probably need to be screened for medication by a psychiatrist or other healthcare professional. Does the client live alone? Does the client have the means to attempt suicide? If so, get the means away from him or her.
9. Have the client sign a safety contract. (Some research suggests that safety contracts may not be a good idea. Experts seem to be divided on this issue. I include safety contracts because I have yet to find any research indicating contracts are unwise. I also believe signing one's name is a concrete act of commitment.)

10. Remember, it is not your role to prevent suicide, but rather to provide the best treatment plan to interrupt any suicide plan (Remley & Herlihy, 2007). Basically, your job as a counselor is to provide the client with the best chance for recovery.
11. After the crisis has passed, review the case with your colleagues and supervisor to learn from the experience.

Assessing Suicidal Risk in Schools

Although it could be argued that assessing suicide risk is the same regardless of the setting, middle and high schools pose unique challenges because of the educational and social nature of children and adolescents. Capuzzi (2009) has proposed 15 steps in assessing suicide risk in schools.

1. Remember the meaning of the term crisis management. This initial step refers to the need to assess a crisis and manage the situation until the risk has passed. Rapid decisions must be made by counselors and other school officials to prevent suicide.
2. Be calm and supportive. Remember that a suicidal adolescent likely feels hopeless. The demeanor and attitude of the counselor or intervener is crucial.
3. Be nonjudgmental. Statements such as "This is no big deal, it'll pass," are minimizing statements that ignore the seriousness of the student's issue and may precipitate the adolescent to slip further into depression.
4. Encourage self-disclosure. The act of talking about painful issues is the first step in getting needed help. If the adolescent feels she or he can be honest, the assessment will be more accurate.
5. Acknowledge the reality of suicide as a choice, but do not "normalize" suicide as a choice. For example, you might say, "It is not unusual for adolescents to feel upset with relationships or other disappointments. Suicidal thoughts may sometimes come up in such situations, but there are other choices, such as what you are doing now — talking about the issues."
6. Actively listen and positively reinforce. Make appropriate eye contact, encourage the student to continue talking, be soft in your voice tone, etc. Allowing the adolescent to be heard conveys respect.
7. Do not attempt in-depth counseling. You want to establish the relationship and get the student assessed as quickly as possible. When the crisis has passed and the student is more stable, in-depth exploration and goal setting can begin.
8. Contact another professional. A second school counselor, psychologist or social worker may be able to catch issues you might miss. No matter what plan you establish, document all that was done.
9. Ask questions to explore lethality. The following questions may help determine the risk:
   - What has happened to make life so difficult?
   - Are you thinking of suicide?

- How long have you been thinking of suicide?
- Do you have a suicide plan?
- Do you know someone who has committed suicide?
- How much do you want to live?
- How much do you want to die?
- What do you think death is like?
- Have you attempted suicide in the past?
- How long ago was the previous attempt? (or most recent attempt)
- Have you been feeling depressed?
- Is there anyone to stop you? (significant relationships can make a difference)
- On a scale of 1 to 10, with 10 being high and 1 being low, what is the number that best predicts the possibility you will attempt suicide?
- Do you use alcohol or drugs?
- Have you experienced significant losses during the past year or earlier losses you have never discussed?
- Have you been concerned, in any way, with your sexuality?
- When you think about yourself and the future, what do you visualize?

10. Make crisis-management decisions. Develop a crisis intervention plan for the suicidal adolescent to be followed until the crisis is over and long-term counseling is initiated.
11. Notify parents or legal guardians. Parents or legal guardians must be notified in crisis situations. Naturally, students may be very nervous about bringing their parents into the situation, but this must be done both for legal and clinical reasons. When the crisis has passed, the parents or guardians should be part of treatment planning. Family counseling may be in order.
12. Consider hospitalization. All suicidal adolescents should be screened for hospitalization, though many will not be hospitalized. In some cases, short-term hospitalization may be required.
13. Write contracts. Though suicide contracts are not foolproof, professionals may use contracts as a concrete method of getting the adolescent to committing to long-term safety. Contracts should include:
    - Agreement for safety
    - The adolescent's agreement to obtain enough food and sleep
    - The adolescent's agreement to discard items that could be used in a suicide attempt (e.g., guns, weapons, or medications)
    - A specified time span for which the contract is in force
    - The number of an after-hours crisis line so the adolescent has 24 hours access to help
    - Phone numbers of people to contact if the feeling of crisis escalates
    - Healthy ways the adolescent will structure his or her time (e.g., walks, talks, or movies)
14. Organize suicide watches. If hospitalization is not readily available due to insurance issues or remote location, family and friends may take shifts staying with the adolescent until the crisis passes.

15. Refuse to allow the youth to return to school without an assessment by a mental health counselor, psychologist, psychiatrist, social worker, or other qualified mental health professional. Some fear that the assessment may alienate an adolescent, but it establishes that treatment is ongoing and that the school took the crisis seriously. (pp. 40–47)

All middle and high schools (and colleges also) should have a written crisis management plan to deal with crisis situations such as suicide. The plan should identify key personnel (counselors, psychologists, social workers, the principal, etc.). The treatment team at the school should regularly review the plan so that everyone knows their role. The plan should identify who is responsible for ensuring that crisis management is carried out. Just as schools have conducted drills for natural disasters such as tornados and hurricanes, they should practice their crisis management plan in simulated crisis situations. This provides school personnel the opportunity to refine and improve their potential response in the face of an actual crisis. With high-profile school suicides and school shooter tragedies (e.g., Columbine High School, Jonesboro High School, Paducah High School, and also higher education, with tragedies at Northern Illinois University and Virginia Tech) in the past 15 years, school personnel must have a disaster management plan. Counselors and other trained school personnel must be facile in recognizing and checking out the warning signs for suicide and homicide and intervening before such plans are actualized. Because counselors will not be able to cover all possible eventualities, some suicides, and tragically some homicides as well, will occur, schools must have a plan for debriefing after such tragedies.

After-Crisis Counseling

Fortunately, few clients will attempt suicide (Granello & Granello, 2007; Sommers-Flanagan & Sommers-Flanagan, 2000). Because clients who have previously contemplated or attempted suicide are vulnerable to further attempts (Sommers-Flanagan & Sommers-Flanagan), you will to lay therapeutic groundwork to help them work through difficult times without becoming suicidal. A significant part of after-crisis counseling involved assisting clients in developing resilience (Beck et al., 1996).

Now, developing and cultivating hope is not an easy or simple matter, particularly for a client who feels beaten down by life experiences. Marketing hope to a client is scarcely as simple as getting a physician to prescribe medication (Glasser, 2004). Nevertheless, I have outlined some questions to help you challenge clients' negative beliefs. The self-reflection exercises are structured to assist the client to see beyond their present difficulty and to entertain the belief that the difficult period is temporary and will pass.

- What have you learned` during this difficult period that will help you deal with stress, disappointment, or future trauma?
- In your opinion, what do you believe you most need to work through a difficult time?
- If a good friend of yours were to have attempted suicide or have contemplated suicide, what would you want to see this friend change?

- What are your strengths? Cite three core strengths you possess. If you cannot come up with three, then ask close friends, trusted family members, coaches, ministers, teachers, or coworkers you respect.
- On a scale of 1–10, with 1 meaning *you have no hope in your life* and 10 meaning *you have a great sense of hope and meaning,* what score would you give yourself? If your score is, say, 1, what do you need to do to raise it to a 2?
- Examine the various people in your life: family, friends, fellow students, coworkers, and members of a club or organization you are involved in. Now, find three people you admire in your various contacts. When you are ready, ask how they developed self-confidence and hope.
- How could you begin to develop self-confidence and hope in your own life? What steps could you begin to take? (Note: If you cannot think of specific steps, then ask close family and friends what steps they would like to see you take.)
- Having recently been through a crisis period in your life, what advice do you have for counselors, psychologists, the clergy, teachers, parents, and anyone else regarding how to be helpful to people in crisis? What could or should have been done that would have helped you?
- Consider the following questions for self-exploration: Who am I? Who do I want to be? How can I begin to become the person I desire to be? What strengths can you use to help you get there?
- On a scale of 1–10, how committed are you to making the changes that will promote your personal resilience and become the person you desire?

These exercises are not enough alone, as you will need to set limits with clients, hold them accountable for their behavior, encourage them, and challenge them. Some clients will need medication, a healthier diet, friendships, meaningful work, and so forth. In short, it takes many things to prevent and develop resilience against suicide. Moreover, work with your supervisor or another senior clinician to add to this list of interventions.

ASSESSING DANGER TO OTHERS

Like assessing suicide, predicting potential risk to third parties is not an exact science (Sommers-Flanagan & Sommers-Flanagan, 2000). There are numerous methods of prediction, which involve a multimodal approach. Appelbaum (1985) developed a three-stage model of assessing the threat of violence to others, which involves assessing the threat for violence, taking appropriate intervention, and monitoring the case.

Assessing the Threat for Violence

Assessing a client's potential for violence should come in the intake portion of the interview. The intake interview should consist of assessment, client history, review of case records (medical records, psychiatric records, previous counseling records, incarceration, etc.), and the client interview. A few structured assessments are available for counselors to use in determining the risk level for violence. One of the more popular threat assessment instruments is the Structured Assessment of Violence Risk in Youth (SAVRY) that has 24 at-risk factors (e.g., history, social or contextual, and individual) as well as an additional six protective factor items (Borum, Bartel, & Forth, 2002).

The following are a sample of questions counselors can use to determine the potential for violence:

- First and most importantly, does the client have a history of violence (bullying, cruelty to animals, domestic violence, assault, workplace violence, etc.)?
- Does the client make references to violence and see violence as a means to meet his or her needs?
- Does the client tend to get physically or verbally aggressive when abusing substances such as alcohol or other drugs?
- Does the client have a history of mental illness? Although mental illness alone is not a predictor of violence, mental illness plus substance abuse can be a significant factor (Sudders, 2010).
- Does the client have a history of being the victim of violence? Clients who have been the victims are more likely to be perpetrators of violence.
- Does the client have a history of using physical and verbal violence to control people?
- Does the client have a documented history of cruelty to animals or bullying?
- Has the client made threats of violence to third parties?
- Does the client have access to weapons?
- Does the client belong to a social group that advocates and encourages violence?

Additionally, if possible, consider asking family members and significant others questions about the client's propensity for violence.

Appropriate Interventions

The following guidelines can assist you in developing a plan of intervention:

- If the danger does not seem imminent (e.g., no specific plan for violence, no access to weapons, etc.), then continue with counseling.
- Ask the client to participate in disclosing the information to third parties (provided the client agrees to do so). Be very honest with the client that you may need to notify the police. You want to ensure the client is not surprised by disclosure to the authorities.
- Get client screened for medication or medication change, if necessary, and arrange to get lethal weapons taken away from client.
- Keep up-to-date and accurate records. Record the name of the threatened party, date of threat, and nature of the threat (be specific, e.g., client threatened he would "get his ex by slashing her car"). In addition, explain why you took the course of action you took. Naturally, you will have included your

supervisor in the plan of action and note that you made the plan in conjunction with your supervisor.

■ Disclose only the minimal amount of information needed to the intended victim.
■ Keep your supervisor informed of any and all issues related to the case. You do not want your supervisor to be surprised by any action you have taken. (Appelbaum, 1985)

Monitoring the Case

You need to carefully monitor the case until the danger has passed. Monitoring activities should include follow-up with the police, the intended victim, the client, and other pertinent agencies such as parole, probation, child protection, and so forth.

Managing Risky Clients and Situations

The following are the top ten risk management strategies:

1. Risk Management Tool Kit: Create a file or binder in which you keep all copies of relevant risk management materials, which includes the following:
   a. Ethical codes
      ■ Relevant code(s) of ethics: ACA, American School Counselor Association (ASCA), American Mental Health Counselors Association (AMHCA), and so forth
      ■ Ethical decision-making model (Corey, Corey, & Callanan, 2007)
   b. Laws or statutes
      ■ Counselor licensure statute and rules
      ■ Abuse reporting laws
      ■ Civil commitment (mental health and/or substance abuse)
      ■ Health Insurance Portability and Accountability Act (HIPAA)
   c. Subpoena checklist
      ■ Consult an experienced attorney
      ■ If needed, a written release from the client to release requested case notes (note: consult with your attorney first)
      ■ Have your attorney file a motion to "quash" the subpoena
      ■ Under instructions from your attorney, send a letter to the attorney who initiated the subpoena with language such as the following:
         "In order to testify or release records or other protected health information, I must receive one of the following: (a). written, informed authorization from the client to release the information requested; (b). a court order to release the information or testify, as commanded by the subpoena. Remember, you are a HIPPA-covered entity, and must follow HIPPA guidelines."
         (adapted from Wheeler & Bertram, 2008, pp. 71–72)

    d. Attorney. List of local attorneys who have expertise in mental health and health law. Also, annually review these documents to ensure current familiarity and update when/as appropriate.

2. Colleague consultation: Two heads are better than one. Obtain colleague consultation when confronted with difficult counseling situations. To that end, identify colleagues from whom you have professional regard and establish in advance of the need a reciprocal consultation relationship.

3. Informed consent: Develop an informed consent process (written document, verbal explanation, and commitment to reviewing consent as circumstances change); be sure the process clearly defines confidentiality, privilege, and privacy guidelines as well as limits and exceptions to confidentiality, privilege, and privacy.

4. Institution policies: Know the internal policies that regulate the practice of counseling in your school or agency. Adhere to these policies. If there are policies that are at odds with legal or ethical requirements, bring these to the attention of appropriate officers within the institution.

5. Termination and abandonment: Avoid terminating a client who is in crisis. Otherwise, termination should be accomplished, when appropriate, after giving adequate notice and referrals. As "adequate" is not specifically defined, make sure you have documented the client's progress (or lack thereof), timeline for preparing the client for termination, and a clear rationale for why the client is being terminated or referred. The rationale should include consulting with your supervisor or a senior colleague.

6. Document clinical decision making: Properly and fully document the circumstances surrounding difficult or dangerous client situations (abuse, threats of harm to self or others, etc.), decisions made, action taken, and follow-up.

7. Manage co-occurring relationships: Co-occurring relationships (dual roles) must be effectively managed to prevent harm to clients. This is true regardless of whether the co-occurring relationship is a regular part of your job responsibilities (school counselors who counsel students and also have other relationships) or evolve from unforeseeable circumstances, or are an intentional or conscious choice. Be mindful of your state licensure board's position on boundary issues, as well as updated guidance in the 2005 *ACA Code of Ethics* on roles and relationships with clients, supervisees, and others.

8. Practice within your scope of competence: Recognize and respect the limitations of your competence; expand competence by securing the appropriate education, training, or supervision.

9. Supervision: Supervisors and supervisees are at risk if supervision is not properly administered. Supervisors and supervisees should be mindful in the selection process to ensure a good fit (theoretical approach, supervision style, availability of supervisor, etc.), clearly define the mutual expectations

of both supervisor and supervisee, and monitor to ensure fulfillment of the expectations. If required, engage in regular supervision as defined by statute or policy.

10. **Professional liability insurance:** Obtain and maintain professional liability insurance, preferably coverage that will provide attorney representation if a complaint is brought against you by the state licensure board as well as attorney fees and settlement/damages resulting from a civil lawsuit. (adapted from Wheeler & Bertram, 2008, pp. 209–210)

A Few Additions to the Preceding List

As a longtime counselor and former director of counseling programs, I would also make a few additions to the preceding list:

1. Maintain professional memberships for the duration of your professional life. Professional memberships illustrate you are active in your field. All counselors should join ACA and their respective division (ASCA, ARCA, AMHCA, etc.)
2. Read at least one professional article in a counseling journal each time you receive a copy (e.g., *Journal of Counseling and Development*, *Professional School Counselor*, *Journal of Mental Health Counseling*, etc.).
3. Attend regular relevant professional trainings (on managing clients in crisis), either at a national, state or local conference or through health providers.

CHILD ABUSE AND NEGLECT

As discussed in chapter 3, counselors are mandated reporters of suspected child abuse and neglect. The ASCA (2003) defines abuse and neglect as follows:

> *Abuse:* The infliction of physical harm upon the body of a child by other than accidental means, continual psychological damage or denial of emotional needs (e.g., extensive bruises/patterns; burns/patterns; lacerations, welts or abrasions; injuries inconsistent with information offered; sexual abuse involving molestation or exploitation, including but not limited to rape, carnal knowledge, sodomy or unnatural sexual practices; emotional disturbance caused by continuous friction in the home, marital discord or mentally ill parents; cruel treatment).

> *Neglect:* The failure to provide necessary food, care, clothing, shelter, supervision or medical attention for a child (e.g., malnourished, poorly groomed, dirty, without proper shelter or sleeping arrangements, lacking appropriate health care; unattended, lacking adequate supervision; ill and lacking essential medical attention; irregular/illegal absences from school; exploited, overworked; lacking essential psychological/emotional nurturing; abandonment). (p. 1)

Signs of potential physical abuse include:

- Sudden changes in behavior or school performance
- Appears very wary, as if anticipating danger or disruption
- Overly compliant or overly responsible
- Has unexplained bruises, burns, black eyes, and so forth
- Seems frightened of his or her parents and uncomfortable when time to go home
- Appears initially frightened at the approach of an adult
- Reports injury by a parent or another caregiver

Signs of potential sexual abuse include:

- Reports sexual abuse by parent or caregiver
- Suddenly begins sexually acting out
- Runs away or discloses he or she is considering running away
- Displays unusual sexual knowledge or behavior
- Complains of pains in the vaginal or anal area
- Becomes pregnant or contracts a venereal disease

Signs of potential emotional abuse include:

- Seems overly fearful at speaking up in class or in peer groups
- Appears to isolate himself or herself when on the playground or during recess
- Appears depressed and seems unattached to parents or family
- May display either overly compliant or acting out behavior regarding disagreements with peers or authority figures

Signs of potential neglect include:

- Frequent absence from school
- Often has no money for lunch or no lunch packed from home
- Frequently has medical concerns such as ear infections, dental problems that go untreated, or is underweight
- The child or the adolescent often looks poorly groomed, disheveled, or dirty
- Abuses alcohol or drugs
- Discloses he or she is responsible for own care, despite being a minor

Reporting Child Abuse or Neglect

Counselors, like physicians, nurses, teachers, and other health and mental health professionals, are mandated reporters and must report cases where they believe child abuse or neglect is occurring (Remley & Herlihy, 2007). Counselors and other professionals must be trained in recognizing child abuse and neglect before being licensed to practice or prior to accepting educational and treatment jobs (Remley & Herlihy). Confidentiality must be breached in cases where the counselor believes there is reasonable cause to suspect abuse or neglect. All states and U.S. territories have "hold harmless" provisions that prevent mandated reporters from litigation when they report in good faith.

Cases of abuse and neglect must be reported even when the minor does not want it reported (Remley & Herlihy, 2007). There may be numerous reasons why a child or adolescent would not want abuse or neglect reported, including the potential breakup of the family, fear of retribution by an abusive adult, fear of being removed from the home to the unknown (i.e., foster care), stigmatization by peers, and judgment that they snitched on family members. Counselors need to inform and prepare the child for all eventualities when they prepare to report suspected abuse or neglect. Extended counseling services are clearly in order, especially regarding victimization and displacement.

Beginning counselors should be aware of the "double-edged sword" regarding reporting child abuse and neglect. In some communities, child protection agencies may be perceived more as the villain than the alleged perpetrator because of a history of removing children from the home for perceived unfair reasons. Counselors may even find themselves under pressure from some authorities not to report some instances of abuse.

RECOMMENDED RESOURCES FOR SUICIDE PREVENTION

Capuzzi, D. (2006). *Suicide across the lifespan: Implications for counselors.* Alexandria, VA: American Counseling Association.

Granello, D. H., & Granello, P. F. (2007). *Suicide: An essential guide for helping professionals and educators.* Boston: Pearson.

McGlothin, J. M. (2009). *Developing Clinical skills in suicide assessment.* Alexandria, VA: American Counseling Association.

Westefeld, J. S. (2009). *Suicide assessment and prevention.* Hanover, MA: Microtraining Associates. (DVD)

ORGANIZATIONS FOR THE PREVENTION OF SUICIDE

Because suicide prevention tends to be the most common type of crisis situations counselors encounter, here is a short list of organizations that provide education for counselors and others.

American Association of Suicidology (AAS; www.suicidology.org). AAS provides information to counselors, schools, colleges, and so forth.

Youth Suicide School-Based Prevention Guide (www.theguide.fmhi.usf.edu/). Provides accurate and user-friendly information

American Foundation for Suicide Prevention (www.afsp.org). Provides research and information to professionals and nonprofessionals.

Suicide and Mental Health Association International (SMHAI;
www.suicideandmentalhealthassociationinternational.org/). SMHAI is
dedicated to preventing suicide and related mental health issues.

National Organization for People of Color Against Suicide (NOPCAS;
www.nopcas.com/).

International Association for Suicide Prevention (IASP; www.med.uio.
no/iasp/). IASP provides information for a broad forum of academics,
practitioners, and suicide survivors.

Youth Suicide Prevention (www.yspp.org/). An educational program providing education and training for parents and teenagers.

SUICIDE HOTLINES

Note: Always know the local suicide prevention hotline and make that available
to clients. In addition:

National Hotline Network: 1-800-SUICIDE
National Suicide Prevention Lifeline: 1-800-273-TALK
Specialized hotline for teenagers: 1-800-252-TEEN
Specialized hotline for gay, lesbian, bisexual, and transgender (GLBT)
teens: 1-800-4UTREVOR
Specialized hotline for elderly persons: 1-800-971-0016

CONCLUSION

Assessing and managing crisis situations are likely to be the most challenging
part of your practicum and internship experience. Probably the most important
thing to remember is that you do not have to go through the experience of crisis intervention alone. It is crucial that you involve your supervisor as soon as
possible. Regardless of whether these issues are suicide prevention, counseling
victims of trauma, or dealing with a child endangerment case, chances are very
good that you will be helpful in providing resolution that will bring a reduction
in stress level for the client.

CHAPTER 10

Protecting Yourself During Practicum/Internship

The risks of encountering violence during your practicum/internship vary considerably depending on the nature of your setting and population. An elementary school will be considerably less risky than a maximum security prison or certain psychiatric facilities. But all practicum and internship settings carry with them the inherent risk of violence. Therefore, all students should be prepared to deal with violence and the aftermath of potential physical and psychological symptoms of violence.

My first job after graduating was in a large residential psychiatric center that provided treatment for children and adolescents. I was assaulted twice (although not seriously) and was threatened by one adolescent with a broken bottle. Nothing in my graduate counseling program had prepared me to deal with violence directed against me. After all, I was a counselor and counselors are "nice" people and naturally no one would want to hurt us, right? Being threatened and physically attacked was a "slap" of reality for me. Fortunately, most counselors complete their practicum and internship experience without any danger. Still, the potential for violence must be accounted for in counselor education programs as well as when out on the job as a professional counselor.

Studies of violence against mental health professionals have yielded varying estimates on the potential that a counselor or other therapist will be assaulted (Baird, 2005). Work conducted by Tully, Kropf, and Price (1993) and Reeser and Wertkin (2001) are among the few in the field. Thackery and Bobbit (1990) reported that among the participants in a regional conference, 59% of clinical staff and 28% of nonclinical staff indicated they had been attacked at least once. Similar percentages were reported by Perkins (1990, as cited in Baird, 2005) in a British study where 116 psychologists were surveyed. Of this group, 52% said they had been assaulted at least once by a client, and 18% reported being assaulted in the year prior to the study. Other potentially dangerous and intimidating behaviors have also been reported in the mental health profession. Romans, Hays and White (1996) reported that out of a sample of 178 counseling staff, roughly 6% reported being stalked, and 10% had a supervisee who had been stalked. Others suggest that violence may be underreported in the field and that therapists are likely to face assault at some point in their careers (Whitman, Armao, & Dent, 1976).

These studies should not be taken to mean that most clients are dangerous. In fact, most clients do not pose a significant risk to assault, stalk, harass, or threaten counselors. The studies do suggest there is some inherent risk over a long career. It would also be worth mentioning that driving an automobile over the course of a lifetime is also somewhat risky, yet few people cease driving because of the risks involved. Still, the potential of assault is real and counseling programs must prepare students to deal with it. In this chapter, we will explore various ways you can identify, defuse, or deal with violence during your practicum/internship.

PREDICTORS OF CLIENT VIOLENCE

Kinney (1995) cites several risk factors as rough predictors to use in assessing the potential for a person to commit workplace violence. These, I think, are useful to keep in mind when dealing with clients in your practicum/internship setting.

- Emotionally disturbed status.
- Extreme stress in personal life circumstances and/or job.
- Substance use or abuse.
- Frequent disputes with supervisors or authority figures.
- Routine violation of company/agency/school policy or rules.
- Sexual and other harassment/bullying of coworkers or peers.
- Threats of violence, either verbal or written (including electronic communication).
- Preoccupation with weapons and violence.
- An isolated person with a minimal support system. (p. 25)

There are other factors that you should keep in mind that may help you identify a potentially violent client:

A history of violent behavior. A fundamental tenant in the therapeutic world is that the best predictor of future behavior is previous behavior. If a client has a history of violence, it is wise to understand the circumstances that facilitated the client's violence (e.g., a history of violence toward women, bullying others, etc.). Other factors to recognize are the triggers of violence, such as stress, alcohol, drugs, confrontation, and so forth.

A history of victimization. Many perpetrators of violence are themselves victims of violence. Most victims of violence will not become violent themselves (Granello & Granello, 2007). However, some victims learn that violence is a viable method of controlling others and resolving conflicts. Does the client have a history of sexual, verbal, or physical abuse? Some traumatized clients may be more prone to perceiving potential threats and striking out against those they consider a viable threat (Granello & Granello).

Substance use and abuse. The use of alcohol and drugs plays a major role in precipitating violence (Beck, Wright, Newman, & Liese, 1992). Granted, in most therapeutic settings, clients will not be under the influence of alcohol or drugs. However, counselors will frequently work with clients who become aggressive when under the influence of a chemical substance.

Going off of psychopharmacologic medications against medical advice. The use of medications in mental health therapy has a long and controversial history. There is a little doubt, however, that medication, properly used, can aid in counseling. One of the issues to be aware of are clients who suddenly cease taking their medications. This is particularly problematic for clients taking antipsychotic drugs to help manage their violent behavior. If you are counseling clients who have been prescribed antipsychotics, you need to monitor their behavior carefully. Have aggressive incidents suddenly increased? If so, a critical question to ask such a client is, "Have you gone off your medications?"

Although psychoactive medications usually reduce the risk of violence, there is some evidence that certain medications may actually increase the propensity for violence (Baird, 2005). Haller and Deluty (1990) reported a significant relationship between antipsychotic medication and violent attacks on psychiatric staff. An important footnote here is that it seems the patients reacting with violence appear to be a minority.

Access to weapons. A big factor in assessing violence potential involves the client's access to weapons. In inpatient settings, the risk of handguns is minimized, although makeshift weapons (scissors, broken glass, and other sharp instruments) are a concern. Even when staff has carefully screened a patient or client for weapons, fists, legs, and the like can become a risk.

One colleague of mine was counseling an estranged husband, who was upset with his wife's decision to file for divorce. The client admitted to the counselor he had a plan to shoot his ex. After being informed by the counselor that the police would need to be notified to detain him and take charge of the weapon, the client seemed calm. He replied, "That's why I brought this in," reached into his coat, took out a handgun, and handed it to the astonished counselor! Although this situation ended peacefully, it illustrates the potential risk inherent in counseling work. The potential for violence, though usually small, is always present.

Stress. Stress is frequently the catalyst for behavioral regression (Beck et al., 1992) and clients under a good deal of pressure should be viewed with caution, particularly if they do have a history of violence.

Ability to manage behavior. Clearly, some clients are able to manage their behavior and make healthier choices than others. Several factors impact a client's ability to regulate behavior. Mental disorders or neurological conditions, for example, may impair a client's judgment, especially under stress. Substance use or abuse will also impair a client's ability to manage his or her behavior.

Clients who have gone off medication, or who have been inconsistently medicated, may not be able to respond to reason from staff. Some mental illnesses (such as some types of schizophrenia) can manifest in intense paranoia, and any attempt to dialogue with clients in this state is likely to be counterproductive. Sadly, clients who cannot manage their behavior may need to be restrained by the staff. Needless to say, graduate students should not be involved with physically restraining clients unless the health and safety of themselves, staff, or other patients dictate such a response.

Identifying Children or Adolescents at Risk for Violent Behavior

The following checklist of early warning signs can serve as a practical technique for counselors in schools and other settings to use when assessing the potential for violence among children or adolescents. Although this is not a comprehensive list, it provides basic information for violence prevention.

1. Expresses self-destructive or homicidal ideation
2. Expresses feelings of hopelessness
3. Has a history of self-destructive behavior
4. Begins giving away formerly valued possessions
5. Appears withdrawn
6. Engages in bullying peers
7. Has significant changes in mood
8. Has difficulty with impulse control or regulating emotions
9. Experiences difficulty sleeping and has significant changes in appetite
10. Evidence of significant behavioral change
11. Has a history of trauma and tragedy
12. Engages in substance abuse
13. Has been a victim of child abuse
14. Has become involved in a gang
15. Has experienced a significant loss
16. Has been tormented or teased by others
17. Preoccupied with fighting or violence
18. Preoccupied with violent TV shows, movies, DVD games, and so forth
19. Has a history of antisocial behavior
20. Has a history of being violent
    (American Academy of Experts in Traumatic Stress, 2010)

DEALING WITH AGGRESSIVE BEHAVIORS

Dealing with the possibility of client assault involves recognizing risks and learning how to de-escalate potentially dangerous situations before they become violent. Prevention is the best measure: When you accept a practicum or internship placement, it is wise to inquire about the safety plan. (If the school or agency does not have one, you should be concerned.)

If you have reason to believe a client is likely to harm you, a coworker, or anyone else, you must discuss the potential threat with your supervisor immediately. Do not try to deal with a potentially dangerous situation alone. Keep in mind a few basic factors:

1. Unusual behavior (speaking to oneself, hallucinations, etc.) may be unsettling, but usually does not necessarily indicate violent or dangerous behavior. (Keep in mind non-mental health professionals will likely feel more threatened by "unusual" behavior and may want counselors and other mental health professionals to have such people committed. Remember: Unusual behavior is not necessarily a predictor of violent behavior.)
2. Developing good relationships with clients may be a good way to lessen the risk of violence. In fact, the stronger your relationship with a client/student/inmate, the more likely it is you will be able to de-escalate a potentially violent situation.
3. Be aware of a client's issues so that you may notice signs of aggression and intervene before violence occurs.
4. In residential placements, be aware of bullying and how it may precipitate violence among peers. When you witness bullying, immediate intervention is necessary.
5. Be aware that developmental issues may determine the seriousness of potential violence. A 6-year-old who makes a vague threat to "get you!" obviously does not carry the same level of seriousness as a 35-year-old male prison inmate making a specific threat. Regardless, take all threats seriously and follow-up on the threat through the established channels (e.g., agency, legal, etc.).
6. However, notwithstanding the previous point, take all verbal threats seriously. Report them immediately to a supervisor or a colleague.
7. Know the violence prevention plan and the response to violence plan at your practicum/internship.
8. Get training if it is offered. Many residential treatment centers (for example) will have active and ongoing trainings on dealing with violent patients.
9. Do not attempt to intervene alone. Although numerous strategies go into preventing and dealing appropriately with violence, a common first response is for staff to make a show of numbers; in some places that I have worked, the first response to any potentially violent situation was for all available staff to converge on the scene. Even very agitated patients may become compliant in the face of a large number of staff. Certainly, never approach a potentially violent client or patient on your own.

DEFUSING VIOLENCE

People use violence for various reasons. For most, violence occurs when an individual perceives a threat and responds out of fear. Fortunately, most people are not violent when they are afraid. *The Gift of Fear: Survival Signals That Protect Us from Violence* (DeBecker, 1997) says people who use violence can be understood by considering their justifications, alternatives, consequences, and abilities. Someone using violence feels justified doing so, sees few alternatives, is willing to accept the consequences, and has the ability (physical, mental, etc.) to do so (DeBecker).

However, most people who get angry do not become violent (thankfully!). People who successfully manage their anger will see other options instead of violence. For example, options other than violence might be:

- Attempting to use reason to defuse a tense encounter
- Calling for a mediator
- Walking away from the encounter

When someone is angry and potentially violent, it is helpful to try to determine why he or she is angry. Using a calm tone, you might ask, "I can see you're upset. What's led to your being so upset?" You want to send the message that you acknowledge their anger and wish to understand it. Approaching the client from the standpoint of understanding is likely the best chance of defusing a potentially violent situation. If the client's hostility level decreases, you may be able to reason with him or her and create the beginning of his or her self-understanding.

Unfortunately, it should be acknowledged that remaining calm and centered is very difficult in the face of an overt threat when adrenaline is coursing through the autonomic nervous system. Remaining calm in the face of hostility and imminent violence takes a lot of practice. Law enforcement officials and first responders who regularly face threats undergo training to practice remaining calm under duress (Tunnecliffe, 2007).

If the client continues to be agitated, you might calmly state, "I see you are very upset. I want to understand why and be helpful." This is far more likely to be effective than raising your voice tone, invading the client's physical space, or loudly demanding that the client calm down. In fact, telling an upset person to calm down will likely sound insulting and could well have the opposite effect. Your body language and voice tone may do far more to defuse the situation than anything else.

Another factor in calming angry people is to establish a dialogue. Some people may be angry because they feel misunderstood and marginalized. My counseling experience working with the unemployed, underemployed, incarcerated, and people on probation has shown me how many people feel unimportant and disempowered. When people feel such marginalization, it is no surprise they respond by lashing out in anger.

Your most effective response with angry people is to acknowledge them and then to establish a dialogue. By engaging the frustrated, angry, and potentially violent client in a conversation, you build a stronger relationship and increase the chances of being able to defuse a potentially violent situation. The following is an example of a dialogue with an upset client.

Client: I've had it with these fucking rules! This is bullshit! (Client is becoming more and more agitated, red in the face, and looking physically aggressive.)

Counselor: Steve, I can see you are upset. What's going on? (The counselor speaks softly, but firmly, and asks a reflective question to get Steve to think. The counselor's question also demonstrates respect, as opposed to simply being concerned about the rules.)

Client: I'm tired of the counselors always picking on me . . . always assuming I'm using again! I'm not fucking using! (Steve is still very upset. Remember, success may not come quickly, but keep the upset person talking and see if his or her anger deescalates.)

Counselor: Ok, well, I'm happy to hear that you feel so strongly about working your program and staying sober.

Client: I do! But just like prison, no one believes me!

Counselor: Well, I know Sonya had given you some real positive feedback in our last group. You seemed pretty happy about that, right?

Client: Yeah . . . (Calms down when he recalls the praise.) Yeah, she did . . . I guess I forgot.

Counselor: Steve, I'd like you to feel I was trying to be helpful to you as well. What needs to happen so that you feel we're working together?

Client: (He pauses, considering what the counselor has just said.) I don't exactly know for sure . . . maybe just what you're doing now . . . taking time with me.

Counselor: Alright, maybe this is a start.

Now, in this example, Steve begins feeling very angry and implying everyone is against him. The counselor, mainly by listening and soliciting information, is able to deescalate the situation before it erupts into violence. The counselor's question, "What needs to happen so that you feel we're working together?" is an example of turning the tables on an angry client in a therapeutic manner. Now, Steve, who has complained that no one understands him, is confronted with someone who wants to understand him. Steve then puts serious thought into the question and at this point, therapy can begin to take place. A potentially dangerous situation has just been transformed into a therapeutic encounter. This is what therapy is all about.

SELF-DEFENSE TRAINING

To my knowledge, few, if any, graduate counseling programs provide students any training or information on how to protect themselves if assaulted. No agency, hospital, prison or addictions treatment center can *guarantee* to protect you. Therefore, it is important that you receive training in ways to protect yourself.

There are many different types of self-defense training that may be worth looking into. The reality, of course, is that a diminutive female or male counselor may have limited ability to protect herself against a large male client. Still, some degree of training is better than none at all. My recommendation would be to find a reputable self-defense class that offers training, with an emphasis on defensive techniques. This should also include physical training, which has many health and stress-relieving benefits beyond the safety aspect. Better physical conditioning and some knowledge of self-defense will likely increase your confidence and that may be an asset if you are confronted by a hostile client.

Regardless of your physical size or level of training, your best asset is good common sense. Your first option is always to try to calm a potential assailant. In fact, a counselor's ability to reason with a hostile client or patient is likely far more important than physical conditioning. Many angry clients are actually frightened; if you can help dispel their fear, you may avoid an assault. Basically, you want to reason with the client and point out how avoiding a fight is to his or her benefit. Another possibility, at least in some situations, is to flee from the situation. If you cannot calm the client and you are backed into a corner and forced to defend yourself, then use whatever defense you can muster. Certainly, protect vital areas and call for help as loud as you can. Use your legs for kicking as they generate more force than arms and leave you less exposed. If you can just momentarily slow down your attacker, you may be able to reach help.

It goes without mentioning, of course, that preventing an assault is the best protection of all. Prevention also involves agency policies and procedures regarding staffing, training, a viable safety plan, and making sure clients understand that the repercussions for violent behavior will be serious.

WORKPLACE VIOLENCE PREVENTION PLAN

All schools, agencies, and so forth, need plans to assess for violence, prevent violence, and to deal with the aftermath of violence. A few basic steps for violence prevention are the following:

1. Identify vulnerabilities in the school agency or treatment facility. Does the facility have a means of assessing violence? Is there an emergency plan to deal with violence after it occurs?
2. Naturally, violence prevention is the most important goal. Develop early intervention systems to identify and intervene before violence occurs (e.g., mediation programs, peer helping programs, bullying prevention programs, etc.).
3. Develop a threat protocol to assess for violence and a plan to deal with the aftermath of violence. Then, practice the plan routinely through emergency drills to ensure everyone knows their role in trauma management. In addition, when threats occur (verbal, written, text messages, etc.) always take them seriously and follow up with an investigation.

4. Establish who in the school, college, or agency will be responsible for communication to the staff, families, media, and so forth. This reduces rumors and assists with timely information and sends the message that the facility has a plan.
5. Develop feedback measures to assess how the violence prevention program is working. Use focus groups for detailed insight and survey the staff.
6. Review past incidents of violence to see how successfully they were managed. (Kinney, 1995, pp. 46–47)

WHAT TO DO AFTER AN ASSAULT

If the worst has come to pass and you have been assaulted, you need immediate assistance. Notify staff, medical personnel, your supervisors, and law enforcement officials (if necessary). Get a medical checkup to ensure you are not injured. If you have been injured, be aware of who is responsible to pay the cost of treatment (the practicum/internship placement? you? your insurance? your counseling program?). This is often a gray area. It goes without saying you should have your own personal insurance. In my own experience as a former clinical director and current professor of counselor education, this is an overlooked area of practicum and internship.

Afterward, you need to document what happened and why you responded the way you did. You also need to speak with your immediate supervisor as soon as possible, because he or she will likely need to file an incident report for the agency or for insurance purposes.

After you have received medical care, made the report, and spoken with your supervisor, it is important to debrief the traumatic experience with a supportive colleague (Tunnecliffe, 2007). Debriefing, followed by longer-term counseling, can assist you in making the transition back to feeling healthy. It should be stated, however, that in the aftermath of an assault, you are likely to experience a transition period before regaining your emotional equilibrium (Van der Kolk, 1994). Feeling tense, frightened, having higher blood pressure, and experiencing flashbacks are all normal symptoms of recovery and are nothing to hide or be ashamed about. These are all symptoms of a normal and healthy response to trauma. Most victims of trauma have symptoms that will significantly remit in 30 days. So, give yourself time to let your body and your psyche heal. As a counselor who has been the victim of an assault, I can tell you that healing does take time and will involve at least some of the symptoms mentioned earlier. Fortunately, most survivors do not develop posttraumatic stress disorder (PTSD; Tunnecliffe, 2007; Van der Kolk, 1994).

Another factor regarding healing involves the perpetrator who assaulted you. Residential treatment programs will have sanctions for assault and, depending on the severity of the assault, there may be legal charges. My recommendation is that students as well as professional counselors, psychologists, and other staff press charges when assaulted. Pursuing legal action sends a clear message that assault is taken seriously and that sanctions will follow. Most treatment facilities will likely back you up if you decide to pursue legal action, although it is realistic to note that some may not (often because of concerns about negative publicity). Victims of violence who feel unsupported by their employers are likely to feel revictimized and may experience more significant trauma (Kinney, 1995).

Some type of restitution should be made between the perpetrator and the victim. Many schools and agencies have a written policy on this regard. Some communities have programs such as Victim–Offender Reconciliation Programs (VORP) that bring the victim and offender together (with the victim's approval) so that the offender can apologize and the victim can discuss how the violence has impacted him or her on a personal, medical, familial, and occupational level.

CONCLUSIONS

Predicting violent behavior is at best difficult to discern. Perhaps the best type of defense for counselors to employ is to understand the population they counsel and take appropriate precautions. Appropriate precautions would mean building appropriate relationships with clients/students/inmates/etc. so that they view you as helpful and not an authority figure. Be informed regarding the specific mental health and behavioral issues of the clients assigned to your care. Do your best to develop a caring relationship that incorporates techniques to calm angry clients. As previously mentioned, speaking calmly, and somewhat quietly, is a prudent behavior in the face of hostility. Also, it is important to ask the aggrieved person, "How can I be helpful?" This may force the angry client to self-reflect, which might calm him/her somewhat. Never adopt a challenging attitude in the face of anger as that is likely to be received as a challenge at best and disrespect at worst. An angry client who feels disrespected is more likely to lash out physically.

As previously mentioned in this chapter, self-defense training is a very good idea for everyone, especially for counselors working in correctional facilities. It must be re-emphasized, naturally, that physical defense should be the refuge of last resort. No matter the size or self-defense expertise of the counselor, physical self-defense is dangerous. So, use force only as a last resort. If you can, flee from the situation or call for assistance. Also, know your agency's/school's/prison's/etc. safety plan. Once again, you will likely be safe throughout your practicum and internship. But, be prepared!

CHAPTER 11

Termination in Counseling

Up until recently, the process of termination in counseling has largely been avoided in the literature (Gladding, 2009; Maholick & Turner, 1979). Research by Ward (1984) concluded that the reason for this deficit is twofold. First, termination is associated with loss, which is often an avoided topic in our society. Second, termination, unlike establishing the counseling relationship, is not directly related to the skills that promote counseling. This chapter will focus on methods of termination and also will illustrate some issues that impede termination both for the counselor and the client. It is worth mentioning that for some clients, the counseling relationship may represent the best relationship they have had. For clients whose primary positive human connection is during counseling, it is natural they would seek to remain in counseling indefinitely.

Gladding (2009) postulates that more emphasis has recently been placed on termination because of a greater societal acceptance of loss. Although much of Western society has traditionally been one of death-denying societies (Kubler-Ross, 1969), loss and grief are now popular topics in the counseling field, as numerous book, journal articles, and workshops target grief counseling. Termination and endings are now associated with new beginnings and new adventures regarding the counseling relationship and it is this latter point that is critical for successful client termination. It should also be acknowledged that a lack of termination training in counselor education programs results in incomplete education and could be a potential liability for counselors unskilled in ending counseling relationships. After all, endings are a significant part of the life process (Maholick & Turner, 1979) and to begin a new phase in life, a former experience must be completed (Perls, 1969). Termination can also serve as a springboard for clients to move on to healthier, more growth-oriented behavior (Yalom & Leszcz, 2005). Basically, termination is an important part of the counseling process for both client and counselor.

Endings in counseling also serve as important reminders of the life process. Relationships with family begin at birth, grow and develop throughout the life span, and terminate in death. Along the way, friendships end with relocation, marriages end in divorce, and collegial relations change as people accept new jobs and leave previous ones. Healthy adjustment to change depends on acknowledgement and mourning the end of relationships and transitioning to new ones (Perls, 1969). Termination, although it may be painful, also presents the opportunity to create new and, often, more fulfilling relationships. Counseling is also a relationship that by its very nature should grow toward separation.

Termination has become a more common topic in recent years, especially with the emergence of time-limited approaches, such as narrative and solution-focused counseling (Gladding, 2009). These approaches begin with the assumption that each session may be the last and that consequently, the counselor should be preparing the client for termination (O'Hanlon, 1994). Acknowledging that time in counseling is limited could also help the client in becoming more proactive and doing less procrastinating. Understanding the limits of counseling may also spur the client to make more use of his or her time and change jobs, go back to finish college, end unhealthy relationships, and set new goals.

Successful counseling will result in attitudinal and behavioral changes in clients' lives. Such growth should naturally be a clear focus of counseling. Counselors also should encourage their clients to practice their new skills each week in their personal lives. Part of the therapeutic process also involves the counselor preparing the client for the ending of the counseling relationship. This also can involve a role play. By role playing termination, clients and counselors acknowledge and honor the relationship. As Gladding (1990) says, termination puts "insights into action" (p. 130).

Finally, termination serves to reinforce that the client is ready to graduate from counseling as a healthier, more mature person (Rogers, 1961). (Personally, as both a counselor and a former client, I much prefer the term *graduation* over termination because it implies goals have been met.) Through the crucible of the counseling relationship, the client has matured and mastered many of the obstacles that originally brought him or her into counseling. The client's increased ability to manage the demands of life results in increased self-confidence and a healthier and more meaningful life (Yalom & Leszcz, 2005). The lack of appropriate termination would actually rob the client of a lot of potential growth!

In this chapter, I will discuss some issues around when and how to terminate counseling.

WHEN TO TERMINATE A COUNSELING RELATIONSHIP

Knowing when to terminate a counseling relationship is an inexact proposition. In the managed care system, typically insurance companies determine the session parameters of counseling. Other factors that will influence termination are legally set limits (by a judge, probation officer, etc.) and whether the client is in a residential treatment setting. In my experience, clients often make the decision to end the relationship before the counselor. Still, it is important to dialogue with the client to ensure that he or she has thought through the process. If counseling ends too soon, clients may not be able to maintain the healthy behaviors they learned in therapy. Conversely, if termination is not addressed in a timely manner, counseling may drag on with no real focus, wasting time that could be used for needy clients (to say nothing of the cost). There are several issues to address when considering termination (Gladding, 2009):

- Have clients achieved behavioral, cognitive, or affective goals? When both clients and counselors have a clear idea about whether particular goals have been reached, the timing of termination is easier to figure out. The key is to establish a mutually agreed-on contract before counseling begins.
- Can clients concretely show they have made progress in what they wanted to accomplish? Specific progress may be the basis for making a decision about termination.
- Is the counseling relationship helpful? If either the client or the counselor senses that what is occurring in the counseling sessions is not helpful, termination may be appropriate.
- Has the context of the original counseling arrangement changed? In cases where there is a move or a prolonged illness, termination (as well as a referral) should be considered. Examining whether the client's initial problem or symptoms have been eliminated or significantly reduced.
- Does the client appear capable of coping with demands in his or her life?
- Is the client better able to relate to others and to give and receive love?
- Has the client progressed in her or his ability to be productive in career and life tasks?
- Can the client "play" and enjoy life? (pp. 177–180)

I have also found it helpful to consider another factor: Is the counselor confident the client is ready for termination? This is nothing scientific, but experienced counselors often develop a sixth sense regarding a client's likelihood for success. Wise counselors will attend to this "sense" and explore the client's own readiness for termination.

It is up to the counselor to explain termination clearly to the client at the earliest possible time. The initial intake is the ideal time to cover the topic, especially as essentials such as confidentially, fees, and related topics are covered during that session. This way, the client understands that at some point in the future, the counseling relationship will end. Termination should also be framed in terms of success. For example:

Counselor: Now, at some point in the future, when you have met your goals for counseling, you will graduate from counseling.

As mentioned earlier, if the client has been mandated by a judge, probation officer, or another party, then termination will likely have more fixed parameters.

Counselor: Steve, the terms of your probation specify 12 sessions of anger management. Provided you have attended all sessions and have made progress, termination will occur at that point. Do you have any questions?

As another example:

> **Counselor:** Jade, your health plan provides eight individual counseling sessions. Now, in the event we both feel you could use more, I can ask the HMO to authorize two additional sessions. Another option after eight sessions is to get you into a local support group.

These are all examples of the counselor explaining at the onset that the counseling relationship will end. This reduces the likelihood that the client will be surprised by termination.

DISCUSSING TERMINATION WITH THE CLIENT

In many cases, termination may be a shared decision between the counselor and the client. For example, a client may say, "I believe I have made a lot of progress the past 3 months. I'm thinking one more session would be enough. What do you think?" Or, the counselor may initiate the conversation by saying, "You appear to be in a very solid place. I'm thinking we could wrap up our relationship in two more sessions. What do you think about that?" In these examples, both the client's and the counselor's termination statements imply client growth and resolution of whatever issues brought the client into counseling. Both statements also involve checking the message out with the other party. I encourage counselors to include the client in any discussion of termination; including the client in significant discussions demonstrates your respect and trust in the client (Miller & Rollnick, 2002). The following is an example of a discussion of termination to a client:

> **Counselor:** Shoshanna, I have seen you make a lot of progress over the past 9 weeks. Your depression, as evidenced by the Beck Depression Inventory Scale, seems to have dropped significantly. You have also mentioned that you are managing your grief much better and that recently, you have been able to reach out and initiate social events with friends. These were the issues that brought you into counseling. So, I'm wondering how you feel about terminating from counseling in the next 2 weeks?
>
> **Client:** You know I'm kind of thinking the same thing. I do feel a lot better . . . still sad about my mother's death, but she did have a full life and she was old. I would like to have at least one more session to wrap up. Okay?
>
> **Counselor:** Absolutely. We can also revisit the option of the grief support group.

In the example, the counselor raises the topic of termination and frames it in such a fashion that client progress is noted in a concrete manner. The counselor also solicits the input of the client and thereby demonstrates trust and respect for the client's judgment. They agree on at least one more session and the counselor mentions a support group in the event the client would like more emotional support.

Cormier and Hackney (2008) believe that when counseling relationships last more than 3 months, the final 3–4 weeks should be spent discussing the impact of termination. They suggest counselors inquire how their clients will cope without the counselor's support. Counselors may also address topics, such as what has changed since the client has entered therapy, what the client has learned, and how the client's life will be different in the postcounseling phase. In my experience, it has been helpful to acknowledge the growth and hard work of the client, as most clients will appreciate having their personal work acknowledged by the counselor.

De Shazer and Berg (1988), proponents of Solution-Focused Counseling, advocates using scaling questions to assess client growth. The following dialogue is an example of using scaling questions to discuss termination:

Counselor: Well, we are now at the end of counseling. On a scale of 1–10, with 10 being *high* and 1 being *low*, how helpful has counseling been?

Scaling questions provide some concrete idea of progress and allow the client to provide explicit feedback regarding what has and has not been helpful. Scaling questions focused on therapeutic effectiveness provide a forum for client and counselor discussion. Now, suppose the client answers in the following manner:

Client: On a scale of 1–10, today's session has been a 2.

Counselor: Okay, what can we do next time to move it to a 3?

In this case, the counselor does not become defensive and argue with the client, but rather accepts the client's verdict and reframes it to elicit what could be more helpful in the next session. Scaling questions could also be used at termination to help the counselor understand how he or she can be more helpful in the future.

Counselor: Okay, I ask this question to all clients about to graduate from counseling. On a scale of 1–10, with 1 being counseling was *not helpful* to 10 being counseling was *very helpful*, how would you rate your experience in counseling?

Client: I would rate it a 6.

Counselor: Well, it sounds like our time together was worthwhile. Now, what could we have done to make our rating a 7?

When using scaling questions, it is best to keep improvements small so as to make them appear more attainable (De Shazer & Berg, 1988). As much as possible, the counselor should make the termination session as positive as possible and discussing outcomes and soliciting feedback from the client is the most direct way to achieve this.

THE TERMINATION PLAN

If you think a client may be ready for termination, there are several logistical issues to consider:

1. Does the client have adequate resources outside the counseling relationship to sustain whatever gains were made in counseling? Resources might include supportive family, friends, colleagues, support groups, and so forth.
2. Have you spent adequate time preparing the client for termination? Ideally, the counselor begins to prepare the client for eventual termination at the onset of therapy. Some professionals recommend an approach called *fading* (Dixon & Glover, 1984) involving a gradual decrease in counseling. For example, going to 30-minute sessions, or spacing sessions 2 weeks or more apart instead of meeting weekly. Another technique involves reminding the client about the remaining number of sessions: "Now, remember, we have three more sessions remaining." You do not want an abrupt termination or else you can undo successful therapeutic gains and potentially be liable for abandonment.
3. Have you and the client agreed on an aftercare plan (if needed)? Has the client agreed to join a support group, if necessary?
4. Have you documented in the case notes why you terminated the client?
5. In cases of mandated counseling, has the client met the conditions set down by the court, probation officer, place of employment, disciplinary board, or other concerned institutions? Does the client need a letter stating he or she has met the conditions? If subpoenaed for a court hearing, could you defend termination?

These issues will not apply equally to all clients, but they should be considered and discussed with the client before making a decision regarding termination. Counselors should also discuss termination issues with their supervisor.

CLIENT'S RESISTANCE TO TERMINATION

Counselors should be aware that some clients will resist termination. There are several reasons why a client might desire to remain in counseling even after the reasons that brought them to counseling have been resolved. A client's resistance to termination is most common when the counseling relationship has been long term or involves a strong connection between the counselor and the client, or involves factors such as grief, fear of rejection, and previous abandonment (Cormier & Cormier, 1998; Welfel & Patterson, 2005).

Some clients have few close relationships and find counseling hard to give up. It is worth mentioning that healthy friendships involve both parties engaging in a two-way relationship. Counseling relationships, although friendly, are not true friendships, because counseling is all about the client. Counseling is also a professional relationship, involving an ethical code, fees, time limits, and boundaries regarding time and social distance. It may be helpful for counselors to discuss the various differences between counseling relationships and friendships, should the client be reluctant to terminate.

Witness the following exchange of dialogue between the counselor and a client reluctant to terminate:

Counselor: Ellen, we have spent the last 6 months together. I have seen you make a lot of progress on your stated goal of managing your depression, establishing personal contacts, and recently you were able to go back to work part time. I think it's time to talk about termination.

Client: I'm just not ready. Yeah, I am back at work, but I just went back a month ago and it's hard to get back in the swing of things. Also, I have made some progress making contacts, but have yet to make a real friend. It's true that I do feel better—maybe a combination of new medication and such, but coming to see you weekly is something I can't let go of.

Counselor: I appreciate that you have found our time together valuable. But, as I mentioned two sessions ago, we are running up to the end of your insurance benefits in 2 weeks. I can work with you two more sessions then we refer you to a support group run by a colleague.

Client: I think a support group is okay . . . and I'm willing to begin, but I want to continue counseling with you.

Counselor: Well, we are up against a couple of issues. One, as your benefits expire, our agency requires we have a minimum charge of $60 per session. The more pressing issue is that you appear ready to graduate from counseling. You have met all your goals and seem to be well on your way.

Client: I might be able to get the money through out-of-pocket pay. So, I can continue, right?

There is no simple way to terminate with a client who is not ready to hear about termination. The counselor in this dialogue might have inquired of the client for some idea of how she would know when she would be ready for termination. Another possibility is, if the counselor believes she has taken the client as far as she can, perhaps a referral to another counselor. In such cases, the counselor should discuss the situation with his or her supervisor, get support, and make a plan to address client resistance to termination.

A client's fear of termination is an issue to address directly. For example:

Counselor: Erica, I want to follow up on the topic of termination. As I mentioned previously, we have two more sessions left. I know you have some concerns regarding termination.

Client: Yes. I am not ready to let go of the support I'm getting here. I agree that I've made a lot of progress the past 4 months, but I want to keep our relationship. I don't think I can make it without you.

Counselor: I appreciate the hard work you have put into counseling and both of us have noted the gains you have made, especially the past 2 months. Given how you felt when counseling began, I believe you are selling yourself short regarding your own resilience.

Client: But I'm not ready to end our relationship.

Counselor: The reality is that our time is coming to a close. My belief is that you are ready for the next step. I think it would be wise to explore your feelings and beliefs regarding termination today and the next couple of weeks. There are also some options.

The client in this scenario is very reluctant to end counseling. This hesitancy is best addressed delicately, but firmly. Clients reluctant to end counseling may be overly reliant on counseling. The counselor in this scenario could use some creativity. For example, the sessions could be staggered to bimonthly instead of every week, thus providing a little more transition time. However, extending the counseling relationship in such a manner might reinforce the client's neediness and be countertherapeutic. The counselor would be wise to have the client explore her feelings regarding termination, including a list of her fears about termination as well as what she may gain by ending the counseling relationship. As previously mentioned, support groups are always an option, provided they exist.

It must be admitted, however, that some clients will be highly resistant to ending counseling. Several years ago, I encountered a woman who had been a client at an agency for more than 20 years. The agency, wisely, had recently decided that long-term clients (2 or more years, those whose insurance coverage had run out, and those who seemed more appropriate for case management) would be moved to the case management area, where they would participate in support groups, peer groups, social activities, and meet weekly with a caseworker, not a counselor. In most cases, this policy was working well. This particular client, however, demanded to speak to the clinical director (me). When I went to retrieve her file from the office, it was as thick as the *DSM-IV* (*Diagnostic and Statistical Manual of Mental Disorders*, fourth edition)! For this client, counseling was more about avoidance than growth. Over her strenuous objections, she was referred to the case management program.

As a new counselor, you will notice that clients have many ways to resist termination, whether at the end of the session or the end of the counseling relationship. They may request additional counseling after their goals have clearly been met, or sabotage what appears to be successful therapeutic progress because they want the counseling relationship to continue. Some clients may insist that their current counselor is the "only one" who has ever been helpful, thus using manipulation in an attempt to entice counselor guilt. With apologies to De Shazer who once held a mock funeral for client resistance (in Corey, 2009), client resistance is alive and kicking!

COUNSELOR RESISTANCE TO TERMINATION

Although the ultimate goal in counseling is to help the client move toward independence from the counseling relationship, some counselors occasionally resist termination (Corey, Cory, & Callanan, 2007). Sometimes counselors will encounter clients they feel a special bond with, or, unfortunately, clients they become infatuated with. Counselors, especially beginning counselors, must take special care to ensure they are working in the best interest of the client whenever the issue of termination arises. Counselors who find themselves reluctant to terminate a client are encouraged to consult with a supervisor or trusted colleague to critique their motivations. Good-year (1981) has cited reasons why counselors may have difficulty with termination:

1. When termination signals the end of a significant relationship.
2. When termination arouses the counselor's anxieties about the client's ability to function independently.
3. When termination arouses guilt in the counselor about having not been more effective with the client.
4. When the counselor's professional self-concept is threatened by the client abruptly and angrily leaving.
5. When termination signals the end of a learning experience for the counselor (e.g., the counselor may have been relying on the client to learn more about the dynamics of a disorder of a particular culture).
6. When termination signals the end of a particularly exciting experience of living vicariously through the adventures of the client.
7. When termination becomes a symbolic recapitulation of other (especially unresolved) farewells in the counselor's life.
8. When termination arouses in the counselor conflicts about his or her own individuation.

In my observation, some counselors also form an unhealthy attachment based on an attraction to the client and are reluctant to see the relationship end. The ethical issues involved in dual relationships are covered in chapter 3. Beyond ethical parameters, it must be mentioned that counseling is entirely about the client. Clients, particularly those with a history of unhealthy relationships, may mistake the counselor's professional concern with that of actual friendship. Counselors then must take special care to set and respect the boundary separating the professional from the personal. Termination for clients who believe they have a special relationship with the counselor may be particularly difficult. Such clients are likely to resist ending the relationship.

Self-Reflections for Counselors Reluctant to Terminate With a Client

- List the reasons why you are reluctant to terminate with the client.
- Now, in examining these reasons, whose needs are being served by keeping the counseling relationship going?
- What would be in the best interests of the client? Also, what would be in your own best interest (ethically, legally, professionally, personally, etc.)?
- If a friend or colleague were in the position you are in, how would you advise that friend?
- What do you need to do to be ready to "let go" of this client and facilitate termination?
- What have you learned from this situation? How will that knowledge help you in future situations?

When counselors find they are having difficulty in ending a counseling relationship, it would be prudent for them to carefully assess the reasons for their reluctance. It is well worth mentioning that counselors certainly will have their own personal issues, inadequacies, and struggles. The problem develops when counselors have not adequately addressed these issues or struggles. Counselors with a history of abandonment may be particularly vulnerable to fears of termination (Guy, 1987).

In cases where termination has been difficult for whatever reason, Welfel and Patterson (2005, p. 124–125) offer four suggestions for counselors:

1. "Be aware of the client's needs and desires and allow the client to express them." The client may wish to express gratitude. Counselors should accept such expressions with gratitude with a simple "Thank you." Do not minimize the value of the client's expression.
2. "Review the major events of the counseling experience and bring the review into the present." This suggestion provides the client the opportunity to the progress she/he has made during counseling.
3. "Supportively acknowledge the changes the client has made." The counselor should let the client know she or he recognizes the progress the client has achieved.
4. "Request follow-up contact." Counseling relationships eventually end, but the client needs to know the counselor is invested in their continued well-being. But, use discretion here as more "needy" clients may see this as an opening to extending the relationship. Put parameters on future contact such as, "Give me a brief call . . ." (In Gladding, 2009, p. 187)

Case Example: Jordan and Yvonne

Jordan has been counseling Yvonne for six sessions. Yvonne originally presented for counseling after a particularly painful ending to a romantic relationship. From the beginning, Jordan noticed he and Yvonne seemed to have a stronger than typical counselor–client attachment. Although he feels Yvonne is ready for termination, he is reluctant for their relationship to end because he enjoys spending time with her. Yvonne has also mentioned that she would like to be in a relationship with someone who "listens to me like you do." Jordan knows that ethically he should refer her or terminate with her, given both their feelings. Yet, he really enjoys seeing her. If Jordan came to consult with you, how would you advise him? What ethical issues and concerns would you want Jordan to consider?

REFERRALS AND FOLLOW-UP

Unfortunately, it goes without saying that most counselors will not be able to help 100% of the clients who pass through their door. My experience is that beginning counselors frequently struggle when they encounter clients who make marginal progress. Counselors need to be realistic regarding making referrals when productivity ends. A referral involves arranging continued therapeutic assistance for clients when the current counseling relationship is not making a satisfactory progress (Pietrofesa, Hoffman, & Splete, 1984). There are numerous reasons referrals are made:

- The client has an issue the counselor does not know how to handle.
- The counselor is inexperienced in a particular area (e.g., substance abuse, couples therapy, etc.).
- The counselor knows of a nearby expert who would be more helpful to the client.
- The counselor and client have incompatible personalities.
- The relationship between the counselor and the client is stuck in an initial phase of counseling. (Goldstein, 1971)

The client may resist a referral, perhaps feeling that such action implies a sense of failure on his or her part. Likewise, a client may feel rejected by the counselor. Thus, the counselor needs to make it clear that the reason for the referral to another professional is neither failure nor fault of either client or counselor. Counselors should also mention the professional to whom they are referring the client, and then volunteer to make the referral for the client, or at the very least, encourage the client to make the call before the sessions end. Ideally, the counselor would bring up the possibility of a referral during the informed-consent phase of the intake, so that the client understands from the outset that a referral is a possibility.

When the counselor begins to believe that another counselor (or other professional) would be more beneficial for the client, he or she should raise the issue for discussion with the client. Discussing the possibility of a referral provides the client a voice in the matter and also establishes a forum for the counselor and client to discuss the issue. Dialoguing on the pros and cons of referral may also take some pressure off both parties because addressing the topic of referral establishes that, perhaps, another counselor is more appropriate for the client's issue. Welfel and Patterson (2005) recommend a counselor spend at least one session with the client in preparation for the referral. Some clients may need several sessions before a referral can be made.

Following up with a client after counseling has ended has become more common in recent years (Okun & Kantrowitz, 2008). Following up with former clients also provides the counselor valuable client feedback regarding the effectiveness of counseling. It can also serve to reinforce that the counselor is still concerned about the client's progress even after counseling has ended.

Follow-up can be conducted on either a short-term (3–6 months after counseling has ended) or long-term (more than 6 months after counseling has ended) basis. One of the difficulties, especially for more mobile clients, is that counselors may no longer have an accurate address. Many clients also are less invested in participating in follow-up activities when they are no longer seeking counseling services. In fact, the percentage of clients who respond to counselors' follow-up efforts is, in my experience, quite small.

Follow-up with former clients can take many forms. In the counseling centers where I have worked, follow-up consisted of a simple evaluation form accompanied by a self-addressed stamped envelope. This provides the client the opportunity to evaluate the services provided. Having had some time and distance from counseling may also be beneficial for the evaluation process as the client may have a clearer idea of how counseling has benefited him or her. In the immediate aftermath, gains that seem so promising may look less so a few months later when the supportive structure of counseling has been removed. Conversely, clients may have a clearer understanding of the gains they have made through the counseling process. This method of sending the client an evaluation is a safe method of follow-up, although some may see it as impersonal.

A second method of follow-up is to invite the former client in for a session to discuss the progress he or she has made after counseling has concluded (Cormier & Cormier, 1998). This method is more personal and provides the counselor the most direct feedback. For counselors working in schools, bringing in former clients may present no problem. However, the time and expense of scheduling former clients for a check-in session in many clinical settings can be prohibitive. Does the client need to pay? Is the follow-up session free? If the counselor works in an agency, college center or another high-volume center with a waiting list, bringing in former clients for follow-up sessions is not feasible. It is also likely that the only clients who would show for a follow-up session are ones who felt counseling was a real success.

Another common way for counselors to check on clients is to call them on the phone, or to request the former client to call in after 3–6 months after counseling has concluded. This method provides easy access and is both time and cost efficient. This approach does involve some preparatory work, as the counselor should ask the client for permission to call before doing so. E-mail could also be used, although there are concerns about the privacy and security of such a method.

Although follow-up can be time-consuming, it can be very important to the counseling process. Follow-up provides the counselor a concrete method of evaluating the success of counseling. In my experience, most clients appreciate the opportunity to have a voice in the evaluative process. Counselors can also receive some helpful feedback regarding their own sense of effectiveness and what techniques worked best for the particular client. Counselors may also discover the client had a different idea of what was and was not helpful. Counselors must also be ready to receive critical feedback regarding themselves, their approach, and their effectiveness. The important thing for counselors (particularly beginning counselors) to remember is that the feedback and evaluation process provides valuable feedback into the effectiveness of their work. This piece of the counseling process may well be the most important of all.

CONCLUSIONS

Terminating with clients can be difficult for both the counselor and the client. It is natural for clients to want to "hang-onto" a relationship that has been positive and growth-oriented for them. After all, for some clients, the counseling relationship may have been their closest relationship. Nevertheless, termination is necessary for continued growth and development of the client. Counselors would do well to frame termination up as "continued growth" and portray it as a type of "commencement."

For counselors, especially graduate student counselors-in-training, learning to "let go" of clients they have worked with for extended periods can be very difficult, especially if the client has made significant progress. It is important for counselors to remember that the welfare of the client is of utmost importance. An important aspect of client welfare is acknowledging the completion of major treatment goals and the subsequent "graduation" from counseling. Counselors having difficulty with termination should seek out their supervisor for advice on the matter. It is also recommended that counselors engage in self-reflection and ask themselves, "What make termination with this client so difficult for me?" The difficulty may arise from issues within the counselor that need addressing.

Then again, as covered in this chapter, some client will resist and perhaps even sabotage termination. Work with your field site supervisor and university supervisor to manage such challenging situations. The good news is that the more experience you gain with termination, the more competent you will become with such endings.

CHAPTER 12

Completing the Practicum/ Internship and Preparing for the Future

This chapter is devoted to completing the practicum/internship sequence and preparing for your job search. The first part of the chapter addresses termination of the field supervisor–intern relationship. The latter section will be devoted to preparing for the job search, including preparing a résumé or curriculum vitae (CV), letters of reference, cover letters, interviewing, and issues of licensure and credentialing.

As you complete your final semester of field placement, it is important to keep in mind that you carry the reputation of the counseling program with you during internship. Counseling students who perform well on internships show their counseling program in a favorable light. Conversely, counseling students whose performance is subpar, or who have ethical issues, potentially harm their program's reputation. Because future practicum and internship placements depend on the willingness of the field placement site, it is important that you always be mindful about how you complete your final internship placement.

TERMINATING THE FIELD SUPERVISOR–INTERN RELATIONSHIP

In the previous chapter, we reviewed termination with clients. A key question during that process is, "Has this client made adequate progress in counseling?" A similar question could be asked of graduate counseling interns prior to termination: "Has this intern made the type of progress we would expect a beginning counselor to have made?" Because interns are usually in the final stage of their graduate program, field supervisors are preparing them to be future counseling professionals (Remley & Herlihy, 2007). As completion of the final internship is a critical step in the education of future counselors, field supervisors and interns should ensure ample time is set aside for evaluation and discussion of the intern's development before termination occurs.

Most interns will experience some formal type of evaluation process (Remley & Herlihy, 2007; Williams, 1995). A sample evaluation form is shown in Figure 12.1. Such evaluation forms should be filled out then forwarded to the graduate counseling program. Before the form is sent on to the appropriate faculty member, the field supervisor and intern should meet to discuss the evaluation.

| FIGURE 12.1 | Internship Evaluation |

**Site Supervisor's Evaluation of Student Counselor's Performance
(Return to: Counseling Program, Niagara University, College of Education)**

Note: This form should be completed at the conclusion of each practicum and internship. Clinical supervisors are encouraged to go over the results with their student.

Name of Student Counselor: _____

Name of Clinical Supervisor: _____

Directions: The supervisor will circle the number most closely approximating the student counselor's skill rating in each area below.

GENERAL SUPERVISION RATING:	POOR		SATISFACTORY		EXCELLENT	
1. Demonstrates a personal commitment to developing professional competencies.	1	2	3	4	5	6
2. The student possesses a good working attitude.	1	2	3	4	5	6
3. Accepts and uses constructive criticism.	1	2	3	4	5	6
4. Communicates well with peers and supervisors.	1	2	3	4	5	6
5. Recognizes both strengths and limitations and works to improve clinical skills.	1	2	3	4	5	6
6. Punctual with case notes and other documentation.	1	2	3	4	5	6
7. Keeps appointments on time.	1	2	3	4	5	6
8. Researches client information prior to session.	1	2	3	4	5	6
9. Appears relaxed and confident in dealing with counseling and clinical issues.	1	2	3	4	5	6
10. Presents a nonjudgmental attitude regarding clients and their issues.	1	2	3	4	5	6
11. Able to gain client trust.	1	2	3	4	5	6

Continued

FIGURE 12.1	Internship Evaluation *Continued*

12. Facilitates client's exploration of personal issues.	1	2	3	4	5	6
13. Student is professional and ethical.	1	2	3	4	5	6
14. Student is able to deal with mandated or hostile clients.	1	2	3	4	5	6
15. Recognizes and deals with client manipulation.	1	2	3	4	5	6
16. Uses silence effectively in counseling.	1	2	3	4	5	6
17. Uses self-disclosure appropriately.	1	2	3	4	5	6
18. Student is aware of own biases and how they impact the therapeutic relationship.	1	2	3	4	5	6
19. Student is skilled in using confrontation in session.	1	2	3	4	5	6
20. Facilitates realistic goal setting with the client.	1	2	3	4	5	6
21. Writes clear, appropriate treatment plans.	1	2	3	4	5	6
22. Explains, administers, and interprets tests correctly.	1	2	3	4	5	6
23. Terminates/refers clients at appropriate times.	1	2	3	4	5	6
24. Able to use appropriate techniques and interventions properly.	1	2	3	4	5	6
25. Makes sound clinical decisions in counseling.	1	2	3	4	5	6

Additional Comments (Use back if necessary): _____

_____

_____

_____

Clinical Supervisor _____ Date: _____

Student Counselor _____ Date: _____

The most difficult part of the evaluation process lies in the giving and receiving of critical feedback (Herlihy & Corey, 1997, 2006). As a longtime supervisor, I have witnessed interns who receive 95% positive feedback and perhaps 5% critical feedback. It is always the 5% that the intern focuses on! Although it may be human nature to focus on the deficit, interns must learn to address both, keeping strengths and deficits in the proper perspective. Praise can help the intern develop confidence, and constructive criticism assists the intern in shoring up the areas of concern.

One method of soliciting constructive criticism is for the field supervisor to require the intern to write a self-evaluation, identifying his or her strengths as well as areas of concern (Baird, 2005; Capacchione, 2000; Hodges & Connelly, 2010). This exercise requires the intern to engage in intense self-reflection, which is required for future success as a counselor (Covey, 1996). Then, when the supervisor and intern meet, they can compare and contrast the two evaluations. My recommendation is for the field supervisor to go over the intern's self-evaluation first; this not only provides a window into the intern's thinking, but also sets the stage to compare and contrast the intern's evaluation to the supervisor's.

Many field supervisors may simply ask the intern to write up a narrative of their strengths and areas of concern. Others may simply ask the intern to do this verbally. For posterity's sake, my recommendation is for the intern to write the self-evaluation because this provides more structure and organization to the reflection process. A sample written self-evaluation is shown in Figure 12.2.

Interns who have had a good working relationship with their supervisor will likely experience only mild anxiety heading into the formal evaluation meeting. In such cases where the intern has already completed a self-evaluation and has had the benefit of several months (or in some cases years) of feedback from the supervisor, the fear factor regarding the final evaluation is likely quite low. Regardless of the field supervisor–intern relationship, I would encourage the student to prepare for the formal evaluation by considering the following suggestions:

- Do not become defensive. Even if you disagree with the supervisor's evaluation, do not react with anger. It is sometimes very difficult to receive critical feedback, but doing so with respect and a cool head is good preparation for the future. After all, the final internship evaluation will not be the last time you receive critical evaluation. Remember, you do not have to agree with the feedback; you do need to remain present and respectful during the evaluation meeting.
- If you find yourself feeling overly anxious about the formal evaluation, find ways to combat the stress—a workout routine, talking with friends, family, a support group, through counseling, and so forth.
- Make a "worst case/best case" list of what you may hear in the evaluation meeting. After each item on the list, write out a respectful response (which may include saying nothing and listening). On the other hand, if a compliment, a simple "thank you" may be appropriate.

FIGURE 12.2　Intern's Self-Evaluation of the Practicum/Internship Performance

On the following issues, rate yourself based on the scale as follows:
1 = *Needs Improvement;*　**2** = *Below Average;*　**3** = *Average;*　**4** = *Above Average;*
5 = *Excellent;*　**N/A** = *Not Applicable*

1. Counseling skills:

　　　1　　2　　3　　4　　5

2. Writing clear, concise case notes:

　　　　1　　2　　3　　4　　5

3. Competence and confidence in leading a group session:

　　　　1　　2　　3　　4　　5　　N/A

4. Competence and confidence in leading a psychoeducational presentation:

　　　　1　　2　　3　　4　　5　　N/A

5. Understanding and applying the ethical code (ACA, AMHCA, ASCA, etc.):

　　　　1　　2　　3　　4　　5

6. My professional dispositions on the placement (e.g., being on time, completing case notes in timely manner, showing respect to the staff, dressing appropriately, managing critical feedback, etc.):

　　　　1　　2　　3　　4　　5

7. Taking initiative by reading relevant books, journal articles, viewing DVDs and attending offered trainings and workshops (if offered):

　　　　1　　2　　3　　4　　5　　N/A

8. My own work ethic while on the practicum/internship:

　　　　1　　2　　3　　4　　5

9. Readiness for the job market through my growth on the practicum/internship and having an updated résumé/CV, cover letter, and practiced interviewing skills:

　　　　1　　2　　3　　4　　5

10. Because of my experience on the practicum/internship, I have clear and measurable professional goals:

　　　　1　　2　　3　　4　　5

11. Overall, I would rate my progress during this placement as:
(Note longer scale: **1** = *Poor,* **5** = *Average;* **10** = *Excellent*)

　　　　1　　2　　3　　4　　5　　6　　7　　8　　9　　10

Continued

FIGURE 12.2   Intern's Self-Evaluation of the Practicum/Internship
Performance *Continued*

Narrative Section

In the space provided below, please comment on additional areas of interest related to your development while on the practicum/internship. Use an additional sheet of paper if you need more space.

12. As a counselor, my greatest strength appears to be _____

_____

13. The area I most need to improve in is _____

_____

14. Additional comments regarding my experience in practicum/internship:

_____

_____

_____

_____

_____

_____

_____

_____

_____

_____

_____

_____   ____/____/____

Practicum/Internship Student's Signature   Date

- If you feel the need, practice a mock evaluation session with a friend, family member, or counselor. During this "mock evaluation," write down both strengths and weaknesses you believe the supervisor will point out. Then, have the mock supervisor mention these. Practice provides a greater likelihood you will manage the evaluation session.
- Let the supervisor control the meeting. This conveys respect and illustrates maturity.
- The supervisor may ask if you have questions or comments regarding the evaluation. This is your opportunity to clarify anything that seems unclear to you. Again, work to manage your emotions even if the evaluation is disappointing in some areas. If you have made it to the end of the placement with this particular school, agency, or university counseling center, the strengths likely outweigh the weaknesses.
- At the conclusion, regardless of how the meeting has gone, thank the supervisor for the opportunity to work at the setting. Remember, your counseling program needs practicum and internship placements and a respectful departure will help maintain good relations between your program and the field organization.

In addition to the field supervisor's evaluation of the intern, some counseling programs have the interns complete a field supervisor evaluation form, even though such evaluations are not always shared with the field supervisor. A sample student evaluation of field supervisor form is available in Figure 12.3.

If you are asked to evaluate your field supervisor, you need to be prepared to offer honest and constructive insights, yet use discretion when delivering critical feedback. First, you would be prudent to ask for a form, such as the one shown in Figure 12.3. A form provides you with a format to convey your opinions in a reasonable way. Reflect on the following considerations prior to evaluating your field supervisor:

- How strong is your relationship with the supervisor? If the relationship is strong, you will likely feel more confident in evaluating him or her.
- What is your level of trust in your supervisor?
- What do you know about this supervisor's ability to receive criticism? Have you seen the supervisor take constructive criticism? Does the supervisor occasionally solicit critique from coworkers?
- How important is this supervisor's recommendation for you? If this supervisor has been the only one you have had, the reference is critical. If this supervisor is one of two or three, then perhaps his or her reference is less weighty for you.
- You may wish to practice providing feedback. Have a friend, classmate, family member, counselor, and so on, do a role play with you.
- If you are still concerned, consider speaking with your faculty advisor, another professor, or someone you trust for advice.
- An alternative to providing face-to-face feedback would be to write the supervisor a letter after you have completed all work at the site and grades have been turned in. (It may be wise to consider whether such a letter might jeopardize a future reference from the supervisor.)

FIGURE 12.3   Student Counselor's Evaluation of On-Site Supervisor

Directions: Circle the number that best represents how you, the Practicum/Internship Student, feel about the supervision received from your on-site (agency) supervisor. This information will not be shared with your on-site supervisor without your consent.

My Supervisor:	Poor		Fair		Good	
1. Gives appropriate time for individual and/or group supervision.	I	2	3	4	5	6
2. Provides constructive feedback in supervision sessions	I	2	3	4	5	6
3. Recognizes and encourages further development of my clinical strengths and capabilities.	I	2	3	4	5	6
4. Encourages and listens to my ideas and suggestions.	I	2	3	4	5	6
5. Helps to define specific, concrete goals for me during the practicum or internship experience.	I	2	3	4	5	6
6. Is available when I need consultation.	I	2	3	4	5	6
7. Through her/his professional behavior, my supervisor models ethical practice.	I	2	3	4	5	6
8. My supervisor makes the effort to remain current in the counseling field.	I	2	3	4	5	6
9 Maintains confidentiality within the clinical setting.	I	2	3	4	5	6
10. Helps me formulate my own theoretical approach to counseling.	I	2	3	4	5	6
11. Explains her/his criteria for evaluating student interns in clear terms.	I	2	3	4	5	6
12. Applies her/his criteria fairly in evaluating my counseling performance.	I	2	3	4	5	6
13. Demonstrates respect to clients, staff, and student interns.	I	2	3	4	5	6
14. Encourages me to discuss concerns encountered in the practicum or internship setting.	I	2	3	4	5	6
15. Through my work with this supervisor, I have learned new counseling techniques, interventions, or assessments.	I	2	3	4	5	6
16. The supervisor has helped to make this practicum/internship a valuable experience.	I	2	3	4	5	6
17. Because of my experience with the supervisor and this agency, I would recommend this site to other students.	I	2	3	4	5	6

Additional Comments and/or suggestions:

_____

_____

_____

Date: ____/____/____   Student: _____

Good supervisors will desire feedback on ways to enhance their supervision skills. Regardless of the outcome, a two-way evaluation where both the supervisor and the intern provide feedback is the healthiest process when termination arrives.

Self-Reflection Exercise for the Conclusion of the Internship

Through your practicum and internship experience, you have gained a broader understanding of how to identify and address the educational, career, emotional, and mental health needs of the students and clients you have counseled. Another aspect of your field placement is how what you have learned fits into the needs of your chosen career. Examine and respond to the following questions.

1. What specific skills and interests have you gained through your practicum and internship experience?
2. The practicum and internship experience is a challenging one. During this process of counseling others, what have you learned about yourself?
3. What lessons have you learned from working with different types of people (clients, supervisors, colleagues, fellow students)?
4. In what ways have you benefitted from your practicum and internship experience?
5. What specific skills, talents, and interests are you likely to use in your new counseling position?
6. What type (or types) of counseling setting are you considering for your first job after graduate school?
7. Regarding item number 6, what specifically interests you about working with the settings you have listed?
8. What advice would you give to a fellow graduate counseling student regarding choosing a practicum or internship?
9. Considering your experiences on practicum/internship and in your graduate counseling program in general, what changes would you like to see (e.g., course or curricular changes, changes to the practicum/internship, changes in the counseling profession, or anything that seems relevant)?

PREPARING FOR THE JOB SEARCH

I feel that because the practicum/internship is all about preparing to become a professional counselor, this book would not be complete without some basic orientation to prepare for a job search. Although this section of the text is a brief overview (there are many more comprehensive job search books and Web sites available), it will provide some basic information and point the way for further information.

A job search involves many facets: planning, résumé writing, mock interviewing, applying, interviewing, following up, dealing with rejection, entertaining an offer, and negotiating salary to name a few. The remainder of the chapter will focus on the basics of this process.

THE VISIONING PROCESS: CREATING YOUR DREAM

Career professionals will tell you the first step to success is the ability to visualize a desired goal. The second, and more important task, is to strategize on how to achieve the goal. One of the most popular methods for strategizing is creative visualization, or *visioning* for short (Capacchione, 2000). Successful people in every occupation tend to use some type of visioning process. Some notable visionaries are Nelson Mandela, Mohandas Gandhi, Martin Luther King, and Mother Teresa. Vision includes optimistic thinking, which is strongly correlated with success (Seligman, 1998). Visioning is a simple process requiring just a few basic pieces of information:

- Personal history. How did you arrive at where you are? What experiences led you to becoming a professional counselor or counselor educator?
- Values. What values are important to you? Psychologist Milton Rokeach (1979) conducted extensive research in the study of values. His findings suggest that the most successful people find work congruent with their personal values. For example, if your spirituality is important to you, then perhaps you should find a spiritually affiliated school or agency. If working with inner-city youth is where your passion lies, a job in a wealthy suburban school may not be a good fit for you.
- Professional identity. Sure, you know you want to be a professional school/ rehabilitation/career/mental health counselor. However, labels such as "counselor" do not tell the entire story. For example, some mental health counselors may decide to become school counselors or vice versa. In addition, many experienced counselors may move into administrative roles, such as clinical director, and do more administrative work and little counseling. Would your long-term goals include moving into administration? Would those changes be healthy for you?
- Goals. What are your immediate, short-term, and long-term career goals? Are you interested in running a school counseling center? Being director of a college counseling center? Becoming dean of students at a large university? Moving overseas? Becoming president of the American Counseling Association (ACA), American School Counselor Association (ASCA), American Rehabilitation Counseling Association (ARCA), American College Counseling Association (ACCA), and the like? Goals are fluid and subject to personal changes over time, but it is still a good idea to set goals and to revise them periodically.
- Action Plan. Everyone with a vision needs an action plan to achieve it. An action plan is a rough roadmap to success and should consist of concrete steps leading up to the vision. The visioning process should also involve estimated time frames to get a sense of how you are proceeding toward your goal.

Sample Action Plan

If your ultimate goal is to become president of the ACA, your action plan might look something like this:

I. Become active in the state affiliate of ACA (1–3 years).
2. Transition into a state leadership role through the following steps (1–2 years):
   a. Serving on the planning board for the state conference
   b. Serving on the editorial of the state journal
   c. Running for president, vice president, or another office of the state organization
   d. Submitting manuscripts to the state journal and national ACA-affiliated journals
3. Attend the annual ACA conference for networking opportunities.
4. Volunteer, make presentations, and host receptions at ACA conferences to boost your profile with the organization (3–6 years).
5. Get published in academic journals, national newsletters, and in venues such as *Counseling Today.* Sit on ACA subcommittees to further boost your profile and understand the organization (3–4 years).
6. Run for secretary or vice president of ACA (2 years).
7. Finally, you run for president, using everything you have learned previously regarding visibility, a coherent platform, networking, and so forth. You win!

Even if you are not presently interested in becoming ACA president, this example illustrates that setting a clear goal helps you strategize how to work to reach that goal. You should also be flexible with timelines and remember that you will have some failures along the way. Do not let failures get you too down as they offer the opportunity for self-reflection and reassessment. In fact, failures can provide the incentive and the wisdom for future success.

Thus, when creating a visioning plan:

1. Be conscious of the present. Think long term as in the previous example. However, do not let long-term planning trip you up in the present. Doing well in your present is the first step to achieving your long-term goals.
2. Set a time frame. Remember, long-term goals will take time and you will need to revise them when setbacks and life circumstances change (e.g., marriage, divorce, children, moves, promotions, job loss, etc.).
3. Be flexible. You goals will change and that may be good. For example, you may start out with the long-term goal of running a university counseling center but decide over time you are more interested in being a training director at a college counseling center. This would be an example of clarification, or simply learning that the original goal was not as congruent with your values and interests as previously thought. Remember, life is dynamic and all about change.

4. Review your action plan periodically. You need to check on your progress regularly. If you are not being successful, why not? In addition, what does success actually mean to you? Have your interests and values changed?
5. Be mindful. Be grounded in the center of your own being while connected to others. Make sure the goals you have set actually fit with your values. This may be the most difficult process you encounter in your career journey. You may need years of struggle, professional counseling, and some type of meaningful self-reflecting practice to a mindful career.

Some techniques for career visioning are as follows:

■ Open-ended questions. "What do I want in my career?" and "Now that I know what I want career-wise, how can I create it?"
■ Meditation. Many people have a meditation practice that calms and centers them. Some people use meditation as part of the creative process.
■ Visualization. When you picture yourself 5, 7, or 10 years down the line, what does that picture look like? What does your job involve? Where are you living? Who else is in the picture?
■ Focusing. This assists in clarifying how to plan and prioritize the preceding visualization process. For example, what needs to happen before you can open your own private practice?
■ Career journaling. For many people, journaling allows them the opportunity to document how their career is proceeding, what challenges, satisfactions, struggles, changes, failures, successes, and so on, they face. Not everyone finds journaling helpful, but for those who enjoy it, journaling can be a type of self-discovery regarding career and personal insights.
■ Collage making. Do not denigrate this potentially creative exercise. Collage making can be fun as well as helping you create a picture of your career dreams.
■ Interviewing. Choose two or three people whom you respect and who know you well. Ask them to address the following questions about you:
 1. What qualities do you possess that will help make you successful in your career?
 2. What steps do you need to take to realize your career goal(s)?
 3. What is your strongest quality?
 4. What is your chief weakness?
  (Hodges & Connelly, 2010, p. 14)

THE CAREER CENTER

The career center on your campus can offer numerous services for the soon-to-be-graduated intern.

One of the most valuable services is the letters of reference bank. With this, your field supervisor(s) can write a letter of reference for you and it can be stored at the center. Reference letters can be open or closed. Open references mean that the student has the right to inspect the letter. Closed letters cannot be read by students.

Students frequently ask me "Should I have an open or closed file?" I always feel somewhat torn, because I believe when we agree to serve as a reference it should be an open process. However, I also know that some hiring committees view closed files as more authentic. So, make the best decision you can. You may feel more confident in closed files if you are confident about the people who are writing the letters. I have written reference letters both for open and for closed files and my letter would be the same for both.

The career center staff can also critique your résumé and cover letter (you might show them to your supervisor as well). It never hurts to have fresh eyes examine your materials for errors, accuracy, and to make sure they present you in the strongest possible light.

REQUESTING REFERENCES

As you complete your final internship and prepare for the job search, you should be soliciting letters of recommendation from professors and field supervisors. Your letters of reference ideally should be written by counseling professionals—professors in your counselor education program, faculty advisor, major professor, field supervisors, and possibly supervisors or professionals in related fields who may be able to address pertinent areas related to counseling work. These references may be required to either write a formal letter on your behalf, or merely be accessible for a verbal discussion about you with a potential employer. Although most counseling applications typically require three references, some may ask for five. So, be prepared for the possibility of needing additional references.

Prior to sending off your résumé or cover letter, you must *ask* each person on your list if he or she would be willing to serve as a reference. This may seem elementary, but you might be surprised how many times I have received a phone call from an employer asking about an applicant who never asked if I would serve as a reference. Such unexpected calls are always embarrassing and usually sink the counselor's candidacy.

Consider the strength of the referral before asking anyone to serve as a reference. As one who has written scores of reference letters for the past 2 decades, my guideline is I must be able to write a strong letter of reference or I will refuse to write. Be aware that weak or nebulous references are worse than none at all. So, as soon as possible during your final semester, line up your references. As you do so, consider the following:

1. Provide your referral sources with a résumé or CV. This helps them fill in the gaps they may not know about your vocational life. No mater how well I know a student, I always learn something from his or her résumé or CV.
2. Make sure you do not ask your references to write a letter at the last moment. This shows poor planning on your part. Ideally, give your references at least 2 weeks to write letters of reference.

3. Make sure you keep your references informed as to how your job search is proceeding. I personally appreciate hearing how my students are progressing on the job search. When you land a job, let your references know—they will be happy to know their supervision and hard work has paid off.
4. Although many of your applications may not require a mailed letter of reference, it is a good idea to provide your references with self-addressed stamped envelopes.

DEVELOPING A RÉSUMÉ OR CURRICULUM VITAE

A résumé or CV provides a summary description of your educational and occupational life. The résumé or CV provides a sketch of you for a potential employer's perusal. This is no time to be overly modest; your résumé is your calling card and summary of your professional life. Be your best self. But, be honest! Overly embellishing on a résumé can cost you a job and maybe even a career.

The recommended reading list at the end of the chapter offers many comprehensive references to help you craft a résumé and conduct other aspects of your job search. I highly recommend you consult one or more of them. Here are some basic tips to get you started (Hodges & Connelly, 2010, p. 34):

- Your education and transferrable skills are of critical importance. Your experience, training, education, and skills serve as a bridge to desired employment. Make sure you design your résumé or CV in a manner that clearly highlights your training and skills areas. List all degrees, degrees in progress, certifications, work history, awards, and so forth.
- Make sure your résumé makes chronological sense. Begin with the most recent position and work your way back. In addition, I recommend that you list your graduate assistantship just as you would list a job—because in essence, it is.
- Claim the highest skills ethically possible. For example, if you have cofacilitated counseling groups for 2 years, certainly list that. Do not, however, list that you developed and oversaw the group treatment model at your school or agency if this is untrue.
- Be able to elaborate on anything you list. For example, if you list that you are advanced in Dialectical Behavioral Therapy (DBT), you must be prepared to demonstrate you have mastered the basic concepts of the subject.
- Include membership in relevant professional organizations. Membership demonstrates a stronger commitment to the profession. It also suggests you are more likely to keep informed of research and emerging trends in the counseling field.
- Make your résumé or CV reader friendly. When a search committee member first looks at your résumé or CV, he or she will give it a 30- to 45-second speed

read (Bolles, 2009). Make sure it is clearly organized. Use a common 12-point font (such as Times New Roman).

- Do a spelling and grammar check. Have a career counselor or someone else you trust read it for content and mechanics.
- There is no one "right" résumé or CV format. Make sure your résumé makes sense, flows logically, is factually accurate, and fits with the counseling position for which you have applied.
- Cover your most recent years of work experience in the greatest detail, depending on your age and years in the field. Do not be discouraged if you are a recent graduate of a counseling program. At your age and experience level, you are not expected to have many years of professional experience. After all, everyone starts somewhere.
- Holding multiple jobs is no longer the problem as it was in previous generations. In this era, people are expected to hold three, four, or even more jobs (Bolles, 2009). In higher education, the general understanding is that you must "move out to move up," and that is likely to be reflected in your résumé or CV.
- Be factually correct. You are responsible for anything you list in your résumé or CV. If you are caught lying or embellishing, the least you will lose is a job. In some cases, you may forfeit your career. Be warned!
- Provide all contact information. List landline and cell phone numbers, e-mail, and so forth.

In developing your résumé and cover letter, I encourage you to use language that describes your experience, skills, and interest in a concise, descriptive, and eloquent voice. The best way to illustrate your work in the cover letter and résumé is with action words that present your case in a lively manner. Here is a sampling of action words:

Accomplished	Directed	Negotiated
Achieved	Drafted	Organized
Advised	Edited	Planned
Assisted	Established	Presented
Chaired	Facilitated	Presided
Collaborated	Implemented	Reorganized
Consulted	Integrated	Researched
Counseled*	Lectured	Revised
Developed	Monitored	Supervised

*Use of this word should be a given after completing practicum and internship!

Figure 12.4 displays a sample résumé. Remember, there is no one right résumé format. The books listed at the end of this chapter will give you plenty of additional styles to choose from.

| FIGURE 12.4 | Sample Résumé |

Reggie Martinez, Master's Candidate, BA, AA
327 Springdale Ave.
Palouse Hills, WA 96332
(817) 555-0234 (c)
rmartinez@hotmail.com

Profile

Master's degree candidate seeking a challenging counseling position at a community mental health clinic.

Summary of Qualifications:

■ Five-year experience supervising college students in collegiate living groups, providing peer advising, crisis intervention, and educational programming.
■ Nearing completion of 700-hour practicum/internship in community counseling agency.
■ Trained in grief counseling during practicum/internship.
■ Developed an outreach program for Latino youth.
■ Selected as the Graduate Student of the Year at Washington State University.

Education

Master's Degree Candidate (will graduate in June 2010) in Clinical Mental Health Counseling, Washington State University, Pullman, WA (CACREP-accredited program)

Bachelor's of Arts (2008) in Cultural Anthropology at Western Washington University, Bellingham, WA (Minor: Psychology)

Associates of Arts (2006) in Psychology at Seattle Area Community College

Related Work Experience

Mental Health Counseling Practicum and Internship (2008–2009), The Rainbow Center, Moscow, ID.

■ Provided individual and group counseling to clients in Spanish and English.
■ Cofacilitated support groups for parents of gay and lesbian children.
■ Developed a grief support group for parents who have had children die.
■ Presented psychoeducational workshops to schools, service organizations, and law enforcement officers.
■ Served as crisis counselor for evening crisis call center.
■ Assisted in rewriting the *Rainbow Staff Employee's Manual*.

Continued

FIGURE 12.4   Sample Résumé *Continued*

Resident Director, Department of Housing and Residence Life, Washington State University, Pullman, WA (2008–2010)

■ Director of International Student residence hall, with students from 33 countries.
■ Oversight of 150 undergraduate and graduate students and scholars-in-residence.
■ Supervisor for five residence advisors.
■ Responsible for coordinating educational programming in residence hall.
■ Mediated conflicts between residents in the residence hall.
■ Provided crisis intervention and referred students to the university counseling center.
■ Participated in Safe Haven training for gay, lesbian, and transgender students.

Resident Advisor, Department of Residential Life, Western Washington University, Bellingham, WA (2007–2008)

■ Floor supervisor in coeducational collegiate residence hall (30 students).
■ Responsible for educational programming.
■ Served as peer counselor for students.
■ Referred students to the counseling center, health services, and the career center.
■ Mediated disputes between students on the floor.

President, Student Government Association, Seattle Area Community College, Seattle, WA (2005–2006)

■ President of student organization representing 25,000 community college students.
■ Responsible for oversight of student fee budgeting, programming approval, and selecting committee chairs.
■ Voting member of Seattle Community College's Board of Trustees.
■ Charged with lobbying for student needs, such as a new student union, recreation center, and campus residence halls.

Awards:

2009–2010, Graduate Student of the Year. Presented by the Association for Gay, Lesbian, and Transgender Student Association, Washington State University, Pullman, WA

2005–2006, Seattle Area Community College's Presidential scholarship

Continued

FIGURE 12.4　Sample Résumé *Continued*

Publications:

Martinez, R. (2009). Barriers to providing counseling services to Latino clients: Some reflections from the trenches. *Journal of the Washington Counseling Association, 12*, 22–34.

Martinez, R. (2008). Experiences as a first generation Latino graduate student. *The Advocate, 10*, 3–5.

Martinez, R. (2008, October 15). Racism and homophobia: One Latino's struggle for acceptance. *Seattle Post, V.57*, p. A.1, 22.

Additional Training:

Trained in Dialectical Behavioral Therapy (Rainbow Center, 2009–2010)

Washington State Certified Mediator

Solution-Focused Counseling, Pullman, WA, June 22–25, 2009

Professional Memberships:

Chi Sigma Iota (Counseling Honorary)

American Counseling Association (ACA)

American Mental Health Counselors Association (AMHCA)

Washington State Mental Health Counselor's Association (WSMHCA)

Hobbies:

Running, cycling, traveling, and writing poetry

References:

Sam Cogan, PhD, Associate Professor of Counseling, Counselor Education program, College of Education, Washington State University, Pullman, WA (509) 633-0134,
e-mail: scogan@wsu.edu.

Angela Hermes, MS, LMHC, The Rainbow Center, Moscow, ID, (509) 714-1027, e-mail: hermesa@yahoo.com.

Harriet Wilson, EdD, Assistant Dean of Students/Coordinator of International Students, Washington State University, Pullman, WA, (509) 618-9090, e-mail: hwilson@wsu.edu.

WRITING A COVER LETTER

In writing the cover letter, you want to keep several elements in mind:

1. Open the letter with a respectful businesslike address such as "Dear Director," "Dear Search Committee," or another title that conveys respect. Do not use informal titles even if you know the persons to whom you are writing. Remember, the cover letter indicates you understand professional protocol.
2. As with your résumé, type using a standard 12-point font (such as Times New Roman or another conservative style). If you are delivering hard copies, have your résumé and cover letter printed on quality, heavy stock paper.
3. In the opening paragraph, explain why you are interested in the job and show that you understand the population the organization serves. For example, if you are applying for a position as a school counselor in an inner-city school or alternative school, briefly illustrate your knowledge of the student population.
4. Keep it brief: one to one and a half pages.
5. Hit the highlights of your qualifications for the position: cite your counseling experience (practicum/internship) and theoretical approach. (If the school or agency uses a particular approach, indicate your knowledge and experience with it if appropriate.) Additionally, if you have special training in a particular approach, indicate that as well.
6. If you have experience related to the counseling field, you certainly want to mention that. Related experience (such as working as a case manager, teaching assistant, resident advisor, bachelor's level addiction counselor, etc.) should also be mentioned.
7. In the final paragraph, wrap up by stating that you look forward to meeting to discuss your interest and fit for the job. Provide a phone number and e-mail.

Figure 12.5 shows a sample cover letter.

THE INTERVIEW

Some questions you will face in an interview will be generic, whereas others are specific to a school, agency, or college counseling center. The sample questions in this section are not comprehensive, but will hopefully give you a sense of the types of questions you should be prepared to answer. It may also be helpful to have a career counselor, classmate, spouse, or friend play the role of interviewer. As previously stated, practice is *highly* recommended.

Now, there are a couple of important points to consider before interviewing. If you do not know the answer to a question, say, "I don't know." This displays both honesty and a lack of pretension. After all, you have just completed a master's program and are not expected to know everything.

Secondly, you do not want to be too lengthy with your answers, as those interviewing you will lose interest. Bolles (2009) suggests the 50/50, 2-minute

FIGURE 12.5   Sample Cover Letter

March 13, 2010
1339 Easy Street
Vista View, AR 72301

Personnel Department
Hickory Ridge School District
5555 Cardinal Lane
Hickory Ridge, AR 72709

Dear Personnel Officer:

Please consider me an applicant for the school counseling position at Hickory Ridge High School. I noticed the advertisement in a recent online edition of the *Northwest Arkansas Times*. Currently, I am a graduate student completing my studies and will graduate with my master's degree in school counseling this May at the University of Arkansas. In addition to coursework, I have completed 700 hours of practicum and internship at a local high school. I have also served as a teacher's aide in a public school for 5 years and have a good understanding of both academic and personal issues that impact a student's learning environment.

My practicum and internship was spent at Fayetteville Technical High School, where I assisted the school counseling staff with academic, career, and personal counseling. This past semester, I cofacilitated two counseling groups for students at risk for dropping out of school. I also led an after-school group targeted at gang prevention.

During my counselor education studies at the University of Arkansas, I was selected for the counseling honorary Chi Sigma Iota, and have even served as president. During this past year, I also worked part time at the Beacon Light Center, where I provided personal, career, and academic counseling to at-risk adolescents.

My résumé and three letters of reference requested in the advertisement are being forwarded from the Career Center at the University of Arkansas. I would welcome the opportunity to discuss my interest in the school counseling position with you in the near future. If you have additional questions, please feel free to contact me at (123) 456-7890 or through e-mail at noone@hotmail.com.

Respectfully yours,

Althea Jefferson
Althea Jefferson

rule. The 2-minute maximum suggests that you keep your answers thorough, but brief. The longer you talk, the less interest the interviewer (or search committee) will have in your answers. After all, if you are too wordy at the interview, you may be too talkative as a counselor. In addition, the longer you speak during an interview, the greater the likelihood you will disclose something you would rather not disclose (Hodges & Connelly, 2010). Be brief, thorough, and discrete.

Here are some sample interview questions:

1. **Why do you want this job?** This is a critical question. You want the search committee to believe this school, agency, college counseling center, and so forth, is your primary interest and focus. Be able to tie your answer to the mission of the organization.

2. **Tell me about yourself.** This is your opportunity to take initiative in the interview. Now, what interviewers want to hear is how you can tie your brief biography into why you are a good fit for the job. I would suggest that you weave your personal experience and strengths into a 60-second answer that sums up your "fit" for the position.

3. **What special training or skills do you offer?** This is where additional training or related skills and experience come in handy. For example, if you are a trained or certified mediator, mention that. Or, say you have several years supervising collegiate residential living communities, or training in art therapy, or adventure-based therapy, mention that and tie the experience into how much it has enhanced your counseling ability.

4. **What is your experience with this particular clinical population?** This is where your practicum/internship comes in handy, as does any related experience. Again, use your professional and related experiences to answer the question.

5. **Could you describe your strengths and weaknesses?** Everyone has weaknesses, and you are no exception. An overused line I have heard too many times in job interviews goes something like, "I'm a perfectionist." To me, this sounds contrived. So, try to relate a weakness that can be turned around into a strength. For example: "Well, I am young and have just completed my graduate degree. But, I'm a quick learner and in a couple of years I will be older and more experienced." The strength aspect of this question is much easier. Cite your experience on practicum and internship, related work, and so forth.

6. **If offered this position, how long could you see yourself working here?** In most cases, it is best not to give a specific time. Instead, you might answer something like, "I would like to work here as long as I have fresh challenges and opportunities. And, I hope to be challenged and have opportunities here for several years to come."

7. **What theoretical counseling approach do you work from?** This is often a tough question for recent graduates of master's degree counseling programs, as the program may not have provided one single approach. So, cite the approaches you have used and under what situations you used them. Also, let the committee know you are open to learning new techniques and approaches.

8. **What are your professional goals?** Wise interviewees will tie their answer to the job at hand. For example, if you are interviewing for a school counseling position, you might express that you would like to direct a high school counseling office. You might also mention a few marking points along the way (such as attaining licensure, national certification, additional training, etc.).

9. **How do you handle conflict?** Be judicious with your answer, but be authentic. A possible answer to this question might be something like this: "I work to calm myself, then review the main points of the disagreement. Then, I try to seek out the other party from the standpoint of trying to understand their point of view. If we then cannot come to agreement, perhaps asking a colleague or supervisor to mediate might be a good idea."

10. **What if a parent, teacher, coach, and so forth, demands to know what you and a student or client is working on in counseling?** This is a question to see how well you remember your professional ethics (and legal issues as well!). You might want to briefly allude to the relevant legal issues in your answer.

11. **Regarding research, what is your specialty area?** If you are applying for an academic position, or a research position, you need to be able to articulate your research interests, experience, and publications. Additionally, check out the department's Web site to see how your research interests match those of the faculty.

12. **Have you ever been fired from a job?** If you were terminated for a cause, explain what that was. Emphasize how you have learned and grown from this experience. Remember, the world is full of successful people who were fired from previous jobs.

13. **What did you like about our organization that interested you enough to apply for the job?** This is a critical question. The interviewer wants to hear your in-depth knowledge of the organization and its programs, missions, goals, client population, talented staff or faculty, and so forth. Be brief but thorough. Illustrate that you are knowledgeable about what they do.

14. **What do you see as the pressing issues in the field for the next decade?** This question is designed to see how well you understand the profession and potential changes. Good answers also illustrate that you have kept up on professional reading in journals. The "pressing issues" are subjective, so be prepared to support any answers you give. For example, a potential answer might be, "I believe multiculturalism is the more important issue because of the large influx of immigrant and multicultural populations."

15. **How have you or how would you support multiculturalism?** Be prepared to address how you support multiculturalism and include specific examples. Concrete examples might include having served on the school district's diversity task force, having counseled a multicultural population, having worked abroad, and so forth.

16. **What professional counseling organizations do you hold membership in?** If you are preparing for a job search, get a membership in a professional counseling organization such as the ACA, ASCA, ARCA, and the like.

17. **What salary would you expect to receive?** Never quote a specific figure. Answer with something like, "Somewhere in the advertised range," or "Something reflecting my training or experience." Never state a dollar amount until you receive a job offer!

18. **What do you know about the mission of this university, school, or agency?** This is a question that is becoming more commonly asked in interviews. Make sure you have read and understood the mission, which should be posted on the organization's Web site. In addition, be prepared to explain why your experience and background fits the mission of the organization.

19. **Why should we hire you?** All interviews are an attempt to address this overriding question. This question usually comes at the end of the interview and is the candidate's opportunity to state his or her special qualifications and fit for the job. You need to be brief and sound confident, but not cocky. Here is one possible answer, "I believe myself to be the best candidate for the school counseling position because I have spent the past 2 years working in a school setting. I also have experience in vocational and academic counseling and art therapy and I am passionate about students' well-being and academic achievement. I have already articulated my ideas about educational programming earlier in the interview and would be excited about implementing them here at Salem High School. Hire me as a school counselor and I'll make you very happy you did."

20. **Do you have any questions for us?** Of course you do! This is your opportunity to take control of the interview and it comes at the tipping point. I cringe when I hear job candidate's state, "No, I have no questions." Such an answer implies the candidate did not do her or his homework. You must always have questions to ask, even if you already know the answers to them. Chapter 2 offered suggested questions when choosing a practicum/internship placement; many of those questions would also be appropriate for a formal job interview. (Hodges & Connelly, 2010, pp. 68–70)

Inappropriate Questions

Unfortunately, some interviewers will ask inappropriate questions during interviews. This may be unintentional (although ignorance is no excuse) or deliberate. Most public and private institutions sign an Equal Opportunity Employment Commission (EEOC) statement that pledges they will not discriminate based on race, creed, national origin, disability status, veteran status, gender, and so on. Many schools, agencies, and colleges also include sexual orientation as a status they will not discriminate on that basis. Thus, questions concerning any of these issues should generally not be raised in an interview.

Examples of inappropriate questions might include:

- "Are you married?" or "Do you have children?"
- "What church do you attend?"
- "Mind if I ask you some personal questions?"

- "What political party do you belong to?"
- "Do you have a *normal* sexual orientation?"
- "How many times a day do you pray?"
- "I don't see a ring on your finger. Are you dating anyone?"
- "Are you related to anyone who could help us politically?"

The professional way to respond to illegal or inappropriate questions is to be tactful and ask clarification-type questions.

Example of illegal/inappropriate question: "Are you married?"

Potential Answer: "How does that question relate to the job?" or "Why is this important information to know?" You might use humor to defuse the situation: "Hmmm . . . I don't think the interview police allow that question." A more low-key and humorous approach does not suggest that illegal or inappropriate questions are any laughing matter, but rather they provide the interviewee an opportunity to set a message in a manner that does inflame the situation.

Inappropriate or illegal questions should rightfully lead you to wonder about the day-to-day ethics of the workplace. Should you be asked illegal or inappropriate questions on an interview, you may wish to consider whether this is a place you will want to work. Once the interview is over, you may consider contacting the appropriate person (usually in human resources) and informing him or her of your experience. You also have the right to contact your state's department of labor and file a complaint. Naturally, as a vulnerable person on a job search, it is wise to consider the ramifications of reporting versus not reporting. Consider the potential risks versus the rewards. Just as important for you, ask yourself what type of school, agency, or academic department you want to work in. If the potential job site does not seem a good fit for your personal values, you will likely be unhappy working there. As a counselor who spent more than 20 years providing career counseling and career advising, I have heard many sad stories from employees whose values are not a good fit for their place of work. Accepting a job is a bit like a marriage; you can get out of it (thankfully!) but the getting out is emotionally expensive.

DEALING WITH REJECTION

On the path to career success, you will experience some rejection. This section of the chapter will offer concrete suggestions to manage your disappointment if you do not get a position that you wanted. Fortunately, such rejection is not personal (except in rare cases), will pass, and does not have to keep you from landing another viable job. Rejection is also universally experienced; everyone has been rejected for something he or she desired.

Therefore, you have just suffered a setback in your job search. That dream job—the one you seemed perfect for—was given to someone else. Perhaps you had a great interview where the search committee seemed to hang on your every word (or so you thought). You left the interview convinced you would soon be getting a call with a job offer. Then, with a brief and stilted phone call, your dreams burst into flames of disappointment. You hang up the phone stunned and numb from the shock of rejection. You try to make sense of it, but your mind cannot seem to accommodate the unexpected setback.

This scenario has been experienced by just about every job seeker in history. The critical factor is to acknowledge that you will have failures. For each job advertised, usually only one person will be selected. This means, of course, that if 30 applicants apply for a school counseling opening, 29 will be disappointed.

There are several reasonable reasons for job rejection:

1. A more qualified candidate was selected. Or, the committee thought the successful candidate was more qualified.
2. The successful candidate seemed a better fit for the position. A candidate with less experience might be hired because she has a counseling specialty area other candidates lack (e.g., trauma counseling, play therapy experience, mediation training, etc.) or she simply seemed to connect better with the search committee.
3. Fit has cultural and gender implications. For example, if all the current school counseling staff is female, a male candidate may have a better chance at the job.
4. The successful candidate was simply better prepared than the other finalists. Bolles (2009) makes the point that the most prepared applicant will likely be hired over a more qualified one. Preparation includes a well-crafted résumé or CV, succinct and error-free cover letters, and good interviews. A more qualified candidate could torpedo his or her candidacy by lack of preparation in of these areas.
5. A candidate's behavior was inappropriate during the interview. Inappropriate behavior could be excessive drinking, making racist or sexist jokes, rudeness to committee members, or raising inappropriate topics during the interview.
6. A candidate displayed a lack of confidence at the interview. You might be the most qualified candidate, but if you do not present as such, someone else will get the job offer. Self-critical comments such as "It's nothing," or "Anyone could have done it," or, "My colleagues actually did most of the work," send the wrong message. Be confident, not cocky, but confident.
7. A candidate was dishonest. Were you caught in a lie on your résumé or CV? Did you overly embellish your credentials during the interview phase?
8. A candidate's appearance was unprofessional. Granted, the counseling profession is not as formal as that of, say, banking or finance. Nevertheless, play it conservative; women should wear dress slacks, skirt, or dress. Men should wear a tie or sport coat. Do not go overboard with cologne or perfume.
9. The search was a failed one. Sometimes a committee will not hire because of a shallow applicant pool or a general dissatisfaction with the finalists.
10. There was behind-the-scenes politicking. You can never really know what goes on behind closed doors. Politics can play a role. You never know.

11. A candidate posted inappropriate content on the Internet. Social networking sites have created a medium for sharing information and meeting new people. They also contain and chronicle much outlandish behavior. Make sure your online persona matches what you wish to convey in your job search. (Hodges & Connelly, 2010, pp. 88–91)

Transforming Your Disappointment

Fortunately, most applicants are resilient and understand there will be other job opportunities. The important point is to learn from disappointment and adapt that knowledge to new opportunities. When you get the disappointing phone call, e-mail, or thin envelope, here are some suggestions for dealing with job rejection:

1. Allow yourself some time to adjust to the situation. Do not push yourself to feel "okay." Talk the situation over with a trusted friend or colleague. Be honest with yourself about the disappointment and pain.
2. Stay physically active. Activity routines are a staple of health, especially during a job search. Physical activity works off anxiety and promotes relaxation.
3. When you have a little distance from the disappointment, reflect back on the experience. What went wrong? What seemed to go well? How could you improve for the next application or interview? This aspect of self-reflection is a critical task in the job search process.
4. Get feedback from someone in the professional field. If you are seeking a school counseling position, ask a professional school counselor to look over your résumé or CV and for tips. Practice interviewing with a career counselor or a professional counselor and have them grade you.

Professional Self-Reflection

1. How would you describe your current job search?
2. Ideally, where would you like to be in your professional life? Describe the job, geographic location, salary, and anything else that seems pertinent.
3. How can you begin to create the professional life you described in the previous question? Cite anything that could help you accomplish your professional goals.
4. If you were recently rejected for a job (or jobs) you wanted, what did you learn that could help you in future job searches?
5. What supports do you have for this transitional time? Examples of support can be family members, friends, a spiritual community, fellow graduate students, support groups, and the like.
6. What personal strengths do you have that will assist you in coping with this transition time? Examples of personal strengths are a positive outlook, good work ethic, fitness routine, and the like.

Continued

7. Think of when you were faced with previous challenges. How have you coped with previous disappointments? How can previous experience assist you now?
8. Think of someone who has been successfully transitioned through job rejection and then found success. Ask them for tips on how you can do the same.
9. Ask yourself, "What else can I do to become the strongest candidate possible?"
10. When you do land a professional counseling position, how will your life be different?
11. What would potential employers find attractive about you? What criticisms might they have? What is your ratio of strength to criticisms?
12. Networking is an essential component of a successful job search. What can you do to create an effective supportive network?
13. When writing cover letters, résumés or CVs, interviewing, and so forth, what message would you like to convey? How can you create that desired message?
14. If you were looking to hire a counselor or counselor educator, what qualities would you be looking for? Now, how well do you match up to those qualities? If you do not match up to the desired qualities, what do you need to do to meet them?
15. If a potential employer were to say, "Tell me five reasons why I should hire you." How would you answer? (Hodges & Connelly, 2010, pp. 94–96)

EVALUATING A JOB OFFER

Congratulations, you have a job offer! This is a big deal even if you are not interested in the job. When you receive an offer, it may be tempting to accept on the spot, especially during tough economic times. Be aware that if you accept the job unconditionally, you may be losing any leverage you might have in the negotiation process. Certainly, you want to express excitement and gratitude on receiving the offer and you may even feel the salary and benefits are very good. Still, as this is a big step, ask for a few days to think it over. Most employers, reasonable ones anyway, will respect this request.

Be thorough in your decision-making process, because you do not want to hastily accept a job only to find there is something you missed in the process (e.g., moving expense reimbursement, annual raises, etc.). There are many issues to consider:

■ What life changes would accepting this job entail?
■ What expenses would I incur by accepting the job (e.g., moving expenses, selling or buying a home, uprooting children from school and friends, moving away from family, etc.)?
■ What would I be gaining by accepting this offer (other than a paycheck)?
■ What would I be giving up by accepting this job?
■ Does the salary range seem equitable compared to other jobs of this type? Will it be enough to live on? Additionally, what will my counter offer be?
■ How excited am I about this offer? Would I want to work with the staff? Does this position offer good potential for professional growth?

If you are still unsure about accepting the job, a simple and common technique to try is a pro–con exercise. Using a pen, split a sheet of paper down the center. Label the left side "pro" and the right side "con." Then, list all the pros and cons you can think of. Naturally, you want the pro list to be longer than the con list. If the con list is longer or the lists are of about equal length, this should give you pause before accepting the offer. Let us examine this list:

Pro	**Con**
1. It is a job.	*1.* It is an expensive area.
2. It includes good salary and benefits.	2. It requires an expensive move.
3. It is in a desirable area of the country.	3. It is far from friends and family.
4. It has good potential for promotion.	*4.* I might get other offers.
5. I would have likable colleagues.	
6. The area has job potential for partner.	
7. I am excited about the job!	

In this case, the pros outnumber the cons, although there are significant cons in the list. Thus, this candidate has a difficult decision to make. There are some significant pros as well, and the most significant one may be item number 7—excitement about the job. Some readers may be in the enviable position of entertaining several offers at once, and the pro–con lists would be longer than a list for one offer. Regardless, the ultimate decision to accept or reject the offer can be a difficult one.

Here is another example of a counselor weighing an offer:

Pro	**Con**
1. It is a very good job.	*1.* It is a 500-mile move.
2. We love the location!	2. I will be leaving friends.
3. They will help my partner search for a job.	3. My partner will need to find a job.
4. Excellent potential for promotion.	
5. I like the staff/faculty.	
6. The salary and benefits are very good.	
7. They will pay $3,000 for the move.	
8. We are close to family.	
9. I am very excited about the job!	

In this example, the pros seem to far outnumber the cons. It is likely this counselor would have an easier time making a decision of whether to accept than the one in the previous scenario.

Another method of assessing whether or not to accept a job involves a decision tree. In the following example, continue down the list until you arrive at a "no" answer. A "no" answer would suggest that you seriously consider whether accepting this job is a wise decision.

Step 1: Do I want really this job? Yes or no?

Step 2: Does this job fit my needs or my family's needs regarding professional challenge, financial security, benefits, stability, and lifestyle? Yes or no?

Step 3: If taking this job necessitates a move, would I or my family be willing to relocate? Yes or no?

Step 4: Would the relocation be worth the disruption in our lives (distance from family, friends, school change, spouse or partner's job change, etc.)? Yes or no?

Step 5: Are the administration and staff (or faculty) at this position actually supportive of diversity? Yes or no?

Step 6: Do I feel committed to this job for 3–5 years? Yes or no?

Step 7: Does the job environment seem healthy (e.g., healthy collegial relations, small annual turnover rate, supportive supervisor, etc.)? Yes or no?

Step 8: Can I say, "This is the type of job I'm excited about?" Yes or no?

Step 9: Do the pros of accepting this job outweigh the cons? Yes or no?

If you answered "yes" to the question, do the pros significantly outweigh the cons? Yes or no?

(Hodges & Connelly, 2010, p. 81)

If You Reject the Offer

Be professional. Thank whoever has offered you the position. If the person asks why you are turning down the offer, be as honest as you feel comfortable. For example, if the staff seemed rude, you might want to consider whether you would actually disclose that. If you are rejecting the offer because of salary, because you found a job that offers a better fit with your goals, or because you have found one in a preferred geographic location, that likely will not be as difficult to mention. Remember, the counseling profession can be very small, so do not burn any bridges.

If You Accept the Offer

This is the place all job seekers want to be; they have an offer and have decided to accept it. Now, your work is still not done. Anyone extending a job offer understands that a savvy candidate will attempt to negotiate the best possible terms. Many people, and this may especially be true of counselors fresh out of graduate school, may be uncomfortable with negotiation, especially during tough economic times. Determine what salary you and your family need, then practice negotiating with a career counselor or friend. Now, here are some things to keep in mind regarding negotiation:

- You may have been given a specific salary figure (likely). Your ability to move that figure upward will depend on what you have to offer (e.g., special training, related experience, publications, etc.), your apparent skill level, and how much the employer wants you.

- Beyond salary, what are the other negotiables? Is a costly move involved? Are you a dual-income family and losing one income with the move? Can the employer assist your spouse or partner in finding a job?
- How good are the benefits? What and *who* does the health plan include (e.g., domestic partners, stepchildren, etc.)? What about the retirement package. If you are young do not discount this issue because it will become increasingly important over time.
- How many vacation days do you receive per year? How many sick days?
- What type of annual salary increase or merit increase is offered? Will you have a probationary period? Does the job involve tenure, and, if so, what is the length of time before you can apply for tenure?
- What opportunity is there for advancement?
- Will the employer pay for you to receive additional training (e.g., attending conferences, workshops, etc.)?
- Regardless of what transpires, be courteous during the negotiation phase. Do not become rigid and make statements such as "This is my final offer!" Be flexible when necessary without giving in on everything. For example, you might be more flexible on salary, but hold the line on moving expenses.
- When you agree to a package, get the agreement in writing.

Your new employer will expect you to be enthusiastic when you begin. Be realistic and give yourself time to adjust to a new place, new colleagues, and new challenges. Remember that most people struggle in their jobs not because they lack the skill, but because of conflicts with coworkers (Bolles, 2009). Therefore, extend yourself to your new colleagues by asking for their input, ideas, and critique. Be respectful when you disagree in staff meetings, and learn to listen to people you find difficult.

FINAL THOUGHTS ON CONCLUDING YOUR PRACTICUM/INTERNSHIP AND BEGINNING YOUR CAREER

- Remember, your career is in transition. The work setting you begin with is unlikely to be the one you finish your career with.
- Because you are new in the profession and lack licensure, your initial job out of graduate school may not be one you stay with for the long term. However, remember, although the initial job after graduation may not be ideal, it provides you the opportunity for professional growth and to receive supervision for licensure. State licensure and 3–5 years experience gives you professional mobility.
- Although graduate school experiences vary, many graduate students experience their counseling programs as nurturing environments. Do not expect your first professional job to be like your graduate program.
- Make sure to keep your résumé or CV current so that when more desirable positions become available, you are ready to apply.

- Take advantage of all trainings your school, agency, college, and so forth, has to offer. As a professional counselor, you should be a lifelong learner. Certificate trainings in specific clinical, legal, or professional issues are great ways to upgrade and expand your skills. Take advantage of these.
- If the agency, school, or college counseling center has a preferred treatment approach (e.g., DBT, Cognitive–Behavioral Therapy [CBT], Solution-Focused Therapy [SFT], etc.) keep an open mind about it, even if you prefer a different theoretical approach. Working from a new theoretical modality also broadens your experience and enhances your clinical skills.
- Keep in mind that this is simply your first professional (post-master's) experience. It is likely, in fact almost a certainty, that you will change jobs in the future. However, remember, you will be more marketable when you are licensed and have a few years of post-master's experience under your belt.
- Set some professional goals for yourself, such as to develop expertise in the treatment model you are learning (e.g., CBT, DBT, etc.), to develop harmonious relationships with the staff, to stay in the job for 2 years, to receive training in a new skill area, and so forth.
- Keep a folder of the applications you make for employment. Many students, especially doctoral students looking for an academic job, may make 20–30 applications. You want to keep the positions you apply for from merging together in your mind and a file of all applications filed can assist with organization. In addition, some search committees work slower than others do. I once applied for a job and did not hear from the search committee until 6 months later.
- Anytime you apply for a counseling position, be sure to examine the Web site of the organization.

RECOMMENDED READING

Here are a number of texts I have used and found helpful in counseling students regarding résumé and cover letter writing, self-exploration, visioning career goals, and the job search process in general:

Bolles, R. N. (2009). *What color is your parachute?* Berkeley, CA: Ten Speed Pres. (updated annually)

Capacchione, L. (2000). *Visioning: Ten steps to designing the life of your dreams.* New York: Tarcher/ Putnam.

Enelow, W. S., & Kursmark, L. M. (2007). *Cover letters: Trade secrets of professional resume writers.* Indianapolis, IN: JIST Works.

Hodges, S., & Connelly, A. R. (2010). *A job search manual for counselors and counselor educators: How to navigate and promote your counseling career.* Alexandria, VA: American Counseling Association.

Parker, Y. (2002). *The damn good resume guide: A crash course in resume writing.* Berkeley, CA: Ten Speed Press.

Yate, M. (2007). *Knock' em dead 2007: The ultimate job seekers guide.* Avon, MA: Adams Media.

List of Professional Counseling Organizations

AMERICAN COUNSELING ASSOCIATION (ACA)

ACA is the flagship organization for counselors and the world's largest organization representing the counseling profession. All counselors should hold a membership in the ACA. Membership in the ACA also includes a subscription to the *Journal of Counseling and Development*, the monthly magazine *Counseling Today*, and numerous other tools for professional development.

http://www.counseling.org

ACA also includes 19 affiliate divisions representing various counseling specialties:

- **American College Counseling Association (ACCA)**
  ACCA is the primary professional organization for college, university, and community college counseling professionals. ACCA membership is also open to psychologists, social workers, and so forth.
  http://www.collegecounseling.org

- **American Mental Health Counselors Association (AMHCA)**
  AMHCA is the professional division representing clinical mental health counseling.
  http://www.amhca.org

- **American Rehabilitation Counseling Association (ARCA)**
  ARCA represents the profession of rehabilitation, rehabilitation counseling faculty, and graduate students in rehabilitation counseling.
  http://www.arcaweb.org

- **American School Counselor Association (ASCA)**
  ASCA promotes the profession of school counseling.
  http://www.schoolcounselor.org

- **Association for Adult Development and Aging (AADA)**
  AADA serves as the professional organization devoted to supporting counselors serving senior populations.
  http://www.aadaweb.org/

- **Association for Assessment in Counseling and Education (AACE)**
AACE promotes the ethical and effective use of assessment (testing) in counseling and education.
http://www.theaaceonline.com/

- **Association for Counselor Education and Supervision (ACES)**
ACES is an umbrella organization for counselor educators in all counseling affiliates (Clinical Mental Health Counseling, School Counseling, Marriage and Family Counseling, etc.), as well as counseling supervisors out in the field. ACES membership is also open to counseling psychologists and members in related mental health professions.
http://www.acesonline.net

- **Association for Counselors and Educators in Government (ACEG)**
ACEG is dedicated to exploring counseling issues and concerns in municipal, state, federal, and military settings.
http://www.dantes.doded.mil/dantes_web/organizations/aceg/index.htm

- **Association for Creativity in Counseling (ACC)**
ACC is a professional affiliate organization for creative arts counseling (e.g., art, music, dance, drama therapy, etc.) as well as novel counseling approaches. ACC also encourages creative expression in the manner of poetry, prose, musical performance, and so forth by individual counselors.
http://www.creativecounselor.org

- **Association for Lesbian, Gay, Bisexual, and Transgender Issues in Counseling (ALGBTIC)**
ALGBTIC educates counselors on concerns regarding the needs of lesbian, gay, bisexual, and transgender clients. ALGBTIC also serves as an advocacy organization both within and beyond the counseling profession.
http://www.algbtic.org

- **Association for Multicultural Counseling and Development (AMCD)**
AMCD strives to improve the understanding of multicultural issues in counseling. Multicultural issues could be related to race, sexual orientation, class, disability, culture, religion or spirituality, and many other issues.
http://www.amcdaca.org/amcd/default.cfm

- **Association for Specialists in Group Work (ASGW)**
ASGW provides professional leadership and promotes research in the field of group counseling in schools, colleges/universities, correctional facilities, hospitals, and so forth.
http://www.asgw.org

- **Association for Spiritual, Ethical, and Religious Values in Counseling (ASERVIC)**
ASERVIC is devoted to exploring and addressing spiritual, religious, and ethical issues in counseling.
http://www.aservic.org

■ **Counseling Association for Humanistic Education and Development (C-AHEAD)**
C-AHEAD provides a professional forum for information on humanistic-oriented counseling practices.
http://www.c-ahead.org

■ **Counselors for Social Justice (CSJ)**
CSJ is one of the newest ACA divisions and is committed to plurality on a broad array of social justice issues.
http://www.counselorsforsocialjustice.com

■ **International Association of Addictions and Offender Counselors (IAAOC)**
IAAOC advocates for the development of effective practice in substance abuse treatment, counseling juvenile offenders, and counselors working in correctional facilities.
http://www.iaaoc.org

■ **International Association of Marriage and Family Counselors (IAMFC)**
IAMFC is the ACA division devoted to studying and promoting the field of couples and family counseling.
http://www.iamfc.com

■ **National Career Development Association (NCDA)**
NCDA's mission is to promote career and vocational counseling and development.
http://www.associationdatabase.com/aws/NCDA/pt/sp/Home_Page

■ **National Employment Counseling Association (NECA)**
NECA's charge is professional leadership and development for counselors working in employment settings.
http://www.employmentcounseling.org/

ADDITIONAL PROFESSIONAL ASSOCIATIONS (INDEPENDENT OF THE AMERICAN COUNSELING ASSOCIATION)

■ **American Association of State Boards of Counseling (AACSB)**
AACSB promotes unification and reciprocity among U.S. state counseling licensure requirements.
http://www.aacsb.org

■ **International Association for Counselling (IAC)**
IAC is the professional counseling organization promoting the international counseling profession.
http://www.iac.coe.uga.edu/index.html

■ **International Association for Counseling Services (IACS)**
IACS accredits counseling centers, clinics, and so forth.
http://www.iacs.org

PROFESSIONAL ACCREDITING ORGANIZATIONS

- **Council for Accreditation of Counseling and Related Educational Programs (CACREP)**
  CACREP, an ACA organizational affiliate, is the international accrediting organization for counseling programs. CACREP accredits graduate programs in colleges and universities. The types of graduate counseling programs accredited by CACREP are: doctoral programs in Counselor Education, and master's degree programs in Clinical Mental Health Counseling, Marriage and Family Counseling, School Counseling, Student Affairs and Counseling, and College Counseling. (Note: CACREP does not accredit Rehabilitation Counseling [see the Commission on Rehabilitation Education].)
  http://www.cacrep.org
  E-mail: cacrep@cacrep.org

- **Commission on Rehabilitation Education (CORE)**
  CORE accredits graduate programs in Rehabilitation Counseling.
  http://www.core-rehab.org
  E-mail: core@core.org

- **Commission on Rehabilitation Counselor Certification (CRCC)**
  CRCC, like NBCC, provides certification for individual rehabilitation counselors. Certification, unlike licensure, is usually a voluntary credential for counselors. Licensure, often a mandatory credential, is overseen by state licensure boards (see State Licensure Boards).

- **National Board for Certified Counselors (NBCC)**
  NBCC serves as an independent credentialing organization for the counseling profession. Although U.S. states and territories are responsible for licensing counselors, NBCC provides certification for specialty areas. Examples of NBCC specialty area certification are: National Certified Counselor (NCC), National Certified Clinical Mental Health Counselor (NCCMHC), National Certified Career Counselor (NCCC), and Approved Clinical Supervisor (ACS).
  http://www.nbcc.org
  E-mail: nbcc@nbcc.org

ACA Code of Ethics*

ACA CODE OF ETHICS PREAMBLE

The American Counseling Association is an educational, scientific, and professional organization whose members work in a variety of settings and serve in multiple capacities. ACA members are dedicated to the enhancement of human development throughout the life span. Association members recognize diversity and embrace a cross-cultural approach in support of the worth, dignity, potential, and uniqueness of people within their social and cultural contexts.

Professional values are an important way of living out an ethical commitment. Values inform principles. Inherently held values that guide our behaviors or exceed prescribed behaviors are deeply ingrained in the counselor and developed out of personal dedication, rather than the mandatory requirement of an external organization.

ACA CODE OF ETHICS PURPOSE

The *ACA Code of Ethics* serves five main purposes:

1. The *Code* enables the association to clarify to current and future members, and to those served by members, the nature of the ethical responsibilities held in common by its members.
2. The *Code* helps support the mission of the association.
3. The *Code* establishes principles that define ethical behavior and best practices of association members.
4. The *Code* serves as an ethical guide designed to assist members in constructing a professional course of action that best serves those utilizing counseling services and best promotes the values of the counseling profession.
5. The *Code* serves as the basis for processing of ethical complaints and inquiries initiated against members of the association.

The *ACA Code of Ethics* contains eight main sections that address the following areas:

Section A: The Counseling Relationship
Section B: Confidentiality, Privileged Communication, and Privacy

---

*Because of space limitations, I have included only the ethical codes of the American Counseling Association and the American School Counselors Association. Naturally, know the ethical code of the particular counseling affiliate organization to which you belong (e.g., AMHCA, ARCA, etc.). Reprinted by permission of the American Counseling Association.

Section C: Professional Responsibility
Section D: Relationships With Other Professionals
Section E: Evaluation, Assessment, and Interpretation
Section F: Supervision, Training, and Teaching
Section G: Research and Publication
Section H: Resolving Ethical Issues

Each section of the *ACA Code of Ethics* begins with an Introduction. The introductions to each section discuss what counselors should aspire to with regard to ethical behavior and responsibility. The Introduction helps set the tone for that particular section and provides a starting point that invites reflection on the ethical mandates contained in each part of the *ACA Code of Ethics*.

When counselors are faced with ethical dilemmas that are difficult to resolve, they are expected to engage in a carefully considered ethical decision-making process. Reasonable differences of opinion can and do exist among counselors with respect to the ways in which values, ethical principles, and ethical standards would be applied when they conflict. While there is no specific ethical decision-making model that is most effective, counselors are expected to be familiar with a credible model of decision making that can bear public scrutiny and its application.

Through a chosen ethical decision-making process and evaluation of the context of the situation, counselors are empowered to make decisions that help expand the capacity of people to grow and develop.

A brief glossary is given to provide readers with a concise description of some of the terms used in the *ACA Code of Ethics*.

SECTION A

The Counseling Relationship

Introduction

Counselors encourage client growth and development in ways that foster the interest and welfare of clients and promote formation of healthy relationships. Counselors actively attempt to understand the diverse cultural backgrounds of the clients they serve.

Counselors also explore their own cultural identities and how these affect their values and beliefs about the counseling process.

Counselors are encouraged to contribute to society by devoting a portion of their professional activity to services for which there is little or no financial return (pro bono publico).

A.1. Welfare of Those Served by Counselors

A.1.a. Primary Responsibility

The primary responsibility of counselors is to respect the dignity and to promote the welfare of clients.

A.1.b. Records

Counselors maintain records necessary for rendering professional services to their clients and as required by laws, regulations, or agency or institution procedures. Counselors include sufficient and timely documentation in their client records to facilitate the delivery and continuity of needed services. Counselors take reasonable steps to ensure that documentation in records accurately reflects client progress and services provided. If errors are made in client records, counselors take steps to properly note the correction of such errors according to agency or institutional policies. *(See A.12.g.7., B.6., B.6.g., G.2.j.)*

A.1.c. Counseling Plans

Counselors and their clients work jointly in devising integrated counseling plans that offer reasonable promise of success and are consistent with abilities and circumstances of clients. Counselors and clients regularly review counseling plans to assess their continued viability and effectiveness, respecting the freedom of choice of clients. *(See A.2.a., A.2.d., A.12.g.)*

A.1.d. Support Network Involvement

Counselors recognize that support networks hold various meanings in the lives of clients and consider enlisting the support, understanding, and involvement of others (e.g., religious/spiritual/community leaders, family members, and friends) as positive resources, when appropriate, with client consent.

A.1.e. Employment Needs

Counselors work with their clients considering employment in jobs that are consistent with the overall abilities, vocational limitations, physical restrictions, general temperament, interest and aptitude patterns, social skills, education, general qualifications, and other relevant characteristics and needs of clients. When appropriate, counselors appropriately trained in career development will assist in the placement of clients in positions that are consistent with the interest, culture, and the welfare of clients, employers, and/or the public.

A.2. Informed Consent in the Counseling Relationship

(See A.12.g., B.5., B.6.b., E.3., E.13.b., F.1.c., G.2.a.)

A.2.a. Informed Consent

Clients have the freedom to choose whether to enter into or remain in a counseling relationship and need adequate information about the counseling process and the counselor. Counselors have an obligation to review in writing and verbally with clients the rights and responsibilities of both the counselor and the client. Informed consent is an ongoing part of the counseling process, and counselors appropriately document discussions of informed consent throughout the counseling relationship.

A.2.b. Types of Information Needed

Counselors explicitly explain to clients the nature of all services provided. They inform clients about issues such as, but not limited to, the following: the purposes, goals, techniques, procedures, limitations, potential risks, and benefits of services; the counselor's qualifications, credentials, and relevant experience; continuation of services upon the incapacitation or death of a counselor; and other pertinent information. Counselors take steps to ensure that clients understand the implications of diagnosis, the intended use of tests and reports, fees, and billing arrangements. Clients have the right to confidentiality and to be provided with an explanation of its limitations (including how supervisors and/or treatment team professionals are involved); to obtain clear information about their records to participate in the ongoing counseling plans; and to refuse any services or modality change and to be advised of the consequences of such refusal.

A.2.c. Developmental and Cultural Sensitivity

Counselors communicate information in ways that are both developmentally and culturally appropriate. Counselors use clear and understandable language when discussing issues related to informed consent. When clients have difficulty understanding the language used by counselors, they provide necessary services (e.g., arranging for a qualified interpreter or translator) to ensure comprehension by clients. In collaboration with clients, counselors consider cultural implications of informed consent procedures and, where possible, counselors adjust their practices accordingly.

A.2.d. Inability to Give Consent

When counseling minors or persons unable to give voluntary consent, counselors seek the assent of clients to services, and include them in decision making as appropriate. Counselors recognize the need to balance the ethical rights of clients to make choices, their capacity to give consent or assent to receive services, and parental or familial legal rights and responsibilities to protect these clients and make decisions on their behalf.

A.3. Clients Served by Others

When counselors learn that their clients are in a professional relationship with another mental health professional, they request release from clients to inform the other professionals and strive to establish positive and collaborative professional relationships.

A.4. Avoiding Harm and Imposing Values

A.4.a. Avoiding Harm

Counselors act to avoid harming their clients, trainees, and research participants and to minimize or to remedy unavoidable or unanticipated harm.

A.4.b. Personal Values

Counselors are aware of their own values, attitudes, beliefs, and behaviors and avoid imposing values that are inconsistent with counseling goals. Counselors respect the diversity of clients, trainees, and research participants.

A.5. Roles and Relationships With Clients

(See F.3., F.10., G.3.)

A.5.a. Current Clients

Sexual or romantic counselor–client interactions or relationships with current clients, their romantic partners, or their family members are prohibited.

A.5.b. Former Clients

Sexual or romantic counselor–client interactions or relationships with former clients, their romantic partners, or their family members are prohibited for a period of 5 years following the last professional contact. Counselors, before engaging in sexual or romantic interactions or relationships with clients, their romantic partners, or client family members after 5 years following the last professional contact, demonstrate forethought and document (in written form) whether the interactions or relationship can be viewed as exploitive in some way and/or whether there is still potential to harm the former client; in cases of potential exploitation and/or harm, the counselor avoids entering such an interaction or relationship.

A.5.c. Nonprofessional Interactions or Relationships (Other Than Sexual or Romantic Interactions or Relationships)

Counselor–client nonprofessional relationships with clients, former clients, their romantic partners, or their family members should be avoided, except when the interaction is potentially beneficial to the client. *(See A.5.d.)*

A.5.d. Potentially Beneficial Interactions

When a counselor–client nonprofessional interaction with a client or former client may be potentially beneficial to the client or former client, the counselor must document in case records, prior to the interaction (when feasible), the rationale for such an interaction, the potential benefit, and anticipated consequences for the client or former client and other individuals significantly involved with the client or former client. Such interactions should be initiated with appropriate client consent. Where unintentional harm occurs to the client or former client, or to an individual significantly involved with the client or former client, due to the nonprofessional interaction, the counselor must show evidence of an attempt to remedy such harm. Examples of potentially beneficial interactions include, but are not limited to, attending a formal ceremony (e.g., a wedding/commitment ceremony or graduation); purchasing a service or product provided by a client or former client (excepting unrestricted bartering); hospital visits to an ill family member; mutual membership in a professional association, organization, or community. *(See A.5.c.)*

A.5.e. Role Changes in the Professional Relationship

When a counselor changes a role from the original or most recent contracted relationship, he or she obtains informed consent from the client and explains the right of the client to refuse services related to the change. Examples of role changes include

1. changing from individual to relationship or family counseling, or vice versa;
2. changing from a nonforensic evaluative role to a therapeutic role, or vice versa;
3. changing from a counselor to a researcher role (i.e., enlisting clients as research participants), or vice versa; and
4. changing from a counselor to a mediator role, or vice versa.

Clients must be fully informed of any anticipated consequences (e.g., financial, legal, personal, or therapeutic) of counselor role changes.

A.6. Roles and Relationships at Individual, Group, Institutional, and Societal Levels

A.6.a. Advocacy

When appropriate, counselors advocate at individual, group, institutional, and societal levels to examine potential barriers and obstacles that inhibit access and/or the growth and development of clients.

A.6.b. Confidentiality and Advocacy

Counselors obtain client consent prior to engaging in advocacy efforts on behalf of an identifiable client to improve the provision of services and to work toward removal of systemic barriers or obstacles that inhibit client access, growth, and development.

A.7. Multiple Clients

When a counselor agrees to provide counseling services to two or more persons who have a relationship, the counselor clarifies at the outset which person or persons are clients and the nature of the relationships the counselor will have with each involved person. If it becomes apparent that the counselor may be called upon to perform potentially conflicting roles, the counselor will clarify, adjust, or withdraw from roles appropriately. *(See A.8.a., B.4.)*

A.8. Group Work

(See B.4.a.)

A.8.a. Screening

Counselors screen prospective group counseling/therapy participants. To the extent possible, counselors select members whose needs and goals are compatible with goals of the group, who will not impede the group process, and whose well-being will not be jeopardized by the group experience.

A.8.b. Protecting Clients

In a group setting, counselors take reasonable precautions to protect clients from physical, emotional, or psychological trauma.

A.9. End-of-Life Care for Terminally Ill Clients

A.9.a. Quality of Care

Counselors strive to take measures that enable clients

1. to obtain high-quality end-of-life care for their physical, emotional, social, and spiritual needs;
2. to exercise the highest degree of self-determination possible;
3. to be given every opportunity possible to engage in informed decision making regarding their end-of-life care; and
4. to receive complete and adequate assessment regarding their ability to make competent, rational decisions on their own behalf from a mental health professional who is experienced in end-of-life care practice.

A.9.b. Counselor Competence, Choice, and Referral

Recognizing the personal, moral, and competence issues related to end-of-life decisions, counselors may choose to work or not work with terminally ill clients who wish to explore their end-of-life options. Counselors provide appropriate referral information to ensure that clients receive the necessary help.

A.9.c. Confidentiality

Counselors who provide services to terminally ill individuals who are considering hastening their own deaths have the option of breaking or not breaking confidentiality, depending on applicable laws and the specific circumstances of the situation and after seeking consultation or supervision from appropriate professional and legal parties. *(See B.5.c., B.7.c.)*

A.10. Fees and Bartering

A.10.a. Accepting Fees From Agency Clients

Counselors refuse a private fee or other remuneration for rendering services to persons who are entitled to such services through the counselor's employing agency or institution. The policies of a particular agency may make explicit provisions for agency clients to receive counseling services from members of its staff in private practice. In such instances, the clients must be informed of other options open to them should they seek private counseling services.

A.10.b. Establishing Fees

In establishing fees for professional counseling services, counselors consider the financial status of clients and locality. In the event that the established fee structure is inappropriate for a client, counselors assist clients in attempting to find comparable services of acceptable cost.

A.10.c. Nonpayment of Fees

If counselors intend to use collection agencies or take legal measures to collect fees from clients who do not pay for services as agreed upon, they first inform clients of intended actions and offer clients the opportunity to make payment.

A.10.d. Bartering

Counselors may barter only if the relationship is not exploitive or harmful and does not place the counselor in an unfair advantage, if the client requests it, and if such arrangements are an accepted practice among professionals in the community. Counselors consider the cultural implications of bartering and discuss relevant concerns with clients and document such agreements in a clear written contract.

A.10.e. Receiving Gifts

Counselors understand the challenges of accepting gifts from clients and recognize that in some cultures, small gifts are a token of respect and showing gratitude. When determining whether or not to accept a gift from clients, counselors take into account the therapeutic relationship, the monetary value of the gift, a client's motivation for giving the gift, and the counselor's motivation for wanting or declining the gift.

A.11. Termination and Referral

A.11.a. Abandonment Prohibited

Counselors do not abandon or neglect clients in counseling. Counselors assist in making appropriate arrangements for the continuation of treatment, when necessary, during interruptions such as vacations, illness, and following termination.

A.11.b. Inability to Assist Clients

If counselors determine an inability to be of professional assistance to clients, they avoid entering or continuing counseling relationships. Counselors are knowledgeable about culturally and clinically appropriate referral resources and suggest these alternatives. If clients decline the suggested referrals, counselors should discontinue the relationship.

A.11.c. Appropriate Termination

Counselors terminate a counseling relationship when it becomes reasonably apparent that the client no longer needs assistance, is not likely to benefit, or is being harmed by continued counseling. Counselors may terminate counseling when in jeopardy of harm by the client, or another person with whom the client has a relationship, or when clients do not pay fees as agreed upon. Counselors provide pretermination counseling and recommend other service providers when necessary.

A.11.d. Appropriate Transfer of Services

When counselors transfer or refer clients to other practitioners, they ensure that appropriate clinical and administrative processes are completed and open communication is maintained with both clients and practitioners.

A.12. Technology Applications

A.12.a. Benefits and Limitations

Counselors inform clients of the benefits and limitations of using information technology applications in the counseling process and in business/billing procedures. Such technologies include but are not limited to computer hardware and software, telephones, the World Wide Web, the Internet, online assessment instruments, and other communication devices.

A.12.b. Technology-Assisted Services

When providing technology-assisted distance counseling services, counselors determine that clients are intellectually, emotionally, and physically capable of using the application and that the application is appropriate for the needs of clients.

A.12.c. Inappropriate Services

When technology-assisted distance counseling services are deemed inappropriate by the counselor or client, counselors consider delivering services face to face.

A.12.d. Access

Counselors provide reasonable access to computer applications when providing technology-assisted distance counseling services.

A.12.e. Laws and Statutes

Counselors ensure that the use of technology does not violate the laws of any local, state, national, or international entity and observe all relevant statutes.

A.12.f. Assistance

Counselors seek business, legal, and technical assistance when using technology applications, particularly when the use of such applications crosses state or national boundaries.

A.12.g. Technology and Informed Consent

As part of the process of establishing informed consent, counselors do the following:

1. Address issues related to the difficulty of maintaining the confidentiality of electronically transmitted communications.
2. Inform clients of all colleagues, supervisors, and employees, such as Informational Technology (IT) administrators, who might have authorized or unauthorized access to electronic transmissions.
3. Urge clients to be aware of all authorized or unauthorized users including family members and fellow employees who have access to any technology clients may use in the counseling process.
4. Inform clients of pertinent legal rights and limitations governing the practice of a profession over state lines or international boundaries.
5. Use encrypted Web sites and e-mail communications to help ensure confidentiality when possible.
6. When the use of encryption is not possible, counselors notify clients of this fact and limit electronic transmissions to general communications that are not client specific.
7. Inform clients if and for how long archival storage of transaction records are maintained.
8. Discuss the possibility of technology failure and alternate methods of service delivery.
9. Inform clients of emergency procedures, such as calling 911 or a local crisis hotline, when the counselor is not available.
10. Discuss time zone differences, local customs, and cultural or language differences that might impact service delivery.
11. Inform clients when technology-assisted distance counseling services are not covered by insurance. *(See A.2.)*

A.12.h. Sites on the World Wide Web

Counselors maintaining sites on the World Wide Web (the Internet) do the following:

1. Regularly check that electronic links are working and professionally appropriate.
2. Establish ways clients can contact the counselor in case of technology failure.

3. Provide electronic links to relevant state licensure and professional certification boards to protect consumer rights and facilitate addressing ethical concerns.
4. Establish a method for verifying client identity.
5. Obtain the written consent of the legal guardian or other authorized legal representative prior to rendering services in the event the client is a minor child, an adult who is legally incompetent, or an adult incapable of giving informed consent.
6. Strive to provide a site that is accessible to persons with disabilities.
7. Strive to provide translation capabilities for clients who have a different primary language while also addressing the imperfect nature of such translations.
8. Assist clients in determining the validity and reliability of information found on the World Wide Web and other technology applications.

SECTION B

Confidentiality, Privileged Communication, and Privacy

Introduction

Counselors recognize that trust is a cornerstone of the counseling relationship. Counselors aspire to earn the trust of clients by creating an ongoing partnership, establishing and upholding appropriate boundaries, and maintaining confidentiality. Counselors communicate the parameters of confidentiality in a culturally competent manner.

B.1. Respecting Client Rights

B.1.a. Multicultural/Diversity Considerations

Counselors maintain awareness and sensitivity regarding cultural meanings of confidentiality and privacy. Counselors respect differing views toward disclosure of information. Counselors hold ongoing discussions with clients as to how, when, and with whom information is to be shared.

B.1.b. Respect for Privacy

Counselors respect client rights to privacy. Counselors solicit private information from clients only when it is beneficial to the counseling process.

B.1.c. Respect for Confidentiality

Counselors do not share confidential information without client consent or without sound legal or ethical justification.

B.1.d. Explanation of Limitations

At initiation and throughout the counseling process, counselors inform clients of the limitations of confidentiality and seek to identify foreseeable situations in which confidentiality must be breached. *(See A.2.b.)*

B.2. Exceptions

B.2.a. Danger and Legal Requirements

The general requirement that counselors keep information confidential does not apply when disclosure is required to protect clients or identified others from serious and foreseeable harm or when legal requirements demand that confidential information must be revealed. Counselors consult with other professionals when in doubt as to the validity of an exception. Additional considerations apply when addressing end-of-life issues. *(See A.9.c.)*

B.2.b. Contagious, Life-Threatening Diseases

When clients disclose that they have a disease commonly known to be both communicable and life threatening, counselors may be justified in disclosing information to identifiable third parties, if they are known to be at demonstrable and high risk of contracting the disease. Prior to making a disclosure, counselors confirm that there is such a diagnosis and assess the intent of clients to inform the third parties about their disease or to engage in any behaviors that may be harmful to an identifiable third party.

B.2.c. Court-Ordered Disclosure

When subpoenaed to release confidential or privileged information without a client's permission, counselors obtain written, informed consent from the client or take steps to prohibit the disclosure or have it limited as narrowly as possible due to potential harm to the client or counseling relationship.

B.2.d. Minimal Disclosure

To the extent possible, clients are informed before confidential information is disclosed and are involved in the disclosure decision-making process. When circumstances require the disclosure of confidential information, only essential information is revealed.

B.3. Information Shared With Others

B.3.a. Subordinates

Counselors make every effort to ensure that privacy and confidentiality of clients are maintained by subordinates, including employees, supervisees, students, clerical assistants, and volunteers. *(See F.1.c.)*

B.3.b. Treatment Teams

When client treatment involves a continued review or participation by a treatment team, the client will be informed of the team's existence and composition, information being shared, and the purposes of sharing such information.

B.3.c. Confidential Settings

Counselors discuss confidential information only in settings in which they can reasonably ensure client privacy.

B.3.d. Third-Party Payers

Counselors disclose information to third-party payers only when clients have authorized such disclosure.

B.3.e. Transmitting Confidential Information

Counselors take precautions to ensure the confidentiality of information transmitted through the use of computers, electronic mail, facsimile machines, telephones, voicemail, answering machines, and other electronic or computer technology. *(See A.12.g.)*

B.3.f. Deceased Clients

Counselors protect the confidentiality of deceased clients, consistent with legal requirements and agency or setting policies.

B.4. Groups and Families

B.4.a. Group Work

In group work, counselors clearly explain the importance and parameters of confidentiality for the specific group being entered.

B.4.b. Couples and Family Counseling

In couples and family counseling, counselors clearly define who is considered "the client" and discuss expectations and limitations of confidentiality. Counselors seek agreement and document in writing such agreement among all involved parties having capacity to give consent concerning each individual's right to confidentiality and any obligation to preserve the confidentiality of information known.

B.5. Clients Lacking Capacity to Give Informed Consent

B.5.a. Responsibility to Clients

When counseling minor clients or adult clients who lack the capacity to give voluntary, informed consent, counselors protect the confidentiality of information received in the counseling relationship as specified by federal and state laws, written policies, and applicable ethical standards.

B.5.b. Responsibility to Parents and Legal Guardians

Counselors inform parents and legal guardians about the role of counselors and the confidential nature of the counseling relationship. Counselors are sensitive to the cultural diversity of families and respect the inherent rights and responsibilities of parents/guardians over the welfare of their children/ charges according to law. Counselors work to establish, as appropriate, collaborative relationships with parents/guardians to best serve clients.

B.5.c. Release of Confidential Information

When counseling minor clients or adult clients who lack the capacity to give voluntary consent to release confidential information, counselors seek permission from an appropriate third party to disclose information. In such instances, counselors inform clients consistent with their level of understanding and take culturally appropriate measures to safeguard client confidentiality.

B.6. Records

B.6.a. Confidentiality of Records

Counselors ensure that records are kept in a secure location and that only authorized persons have access to records.

B.6.b. Permission to Record

Counselors obtain permission from clients prior to recording sessions through electronic or other means.

B.6.c. Permission to Observe

Counselors obtain permission from clients prior to observing counseling sessions, reviewing session transcripts, or viewing recordings of sessions with supervisors, faculty, peers, or others within the training environment.

B.6.d. Client Access

Counselors provide reasonable access to records and copies of records when requested by competent clients. Counselors limit the access of clients to their records, or portions of their records, only when there is compelling evidence that such access would cause harm to the client. Counselors document the request of clients and the rationales for withholding some or all of the record in the files of clients. In situations involving multiple clients, counselors provide individual clients with only those parts of records that related directly to them and do not include confidential information related to any other client.

B.6.e. Assistance With Records

When clients request access to their records, counselors provide assistance and consultation in interpreting counseling records.

B.6.f. Disclosure or Transfer

Unless exceptions to confidentiality exist, counselors obtain written permission from clients to disclose or transfer records to legitimate third parties. Steps are taken to ensure that receivers of counseling records are sensitive to their confidential nature. *(See A.3., E.4.)*

B.6.g. Storage and Disposal After Termination

Counselors store records following termination of services to ensure reasonable future access, maintain records in accordance with state and federal statutes governing records, and dispose of client records and other sensitive materials in a manner that protects client confidentiality. When records are of an artistic nature, counselors obtain client (or guardian) consent with regard to handling of such records or documents. *(See A.1.b.)*

B.6.h. Reasonable Precautions

Counselors take reasonable precautions to protect client confidentiality in the event of the counselor's termination of practice, incapacity, or death. *(See C.2.h.)*

B.7. Research and Training

B.7.a. Institutional Approval

When institutional approval is required, counselors provide accurate information about their research proposals and obtain approval prior to conducting their research. They conduct research in accordance with the approved research protocol.

B.7.b. Adherence to Guidelines

Counselors are responsible for understanding and adhering to state, federal, agency, or institutional policies or applicable guidelines regarding confidentiality in their research practices.

B.7.c. Confidentiality of Information Obtained in Research

Violations of participant privacy and confidentiality are risks of participation in research involving human participants. Investigators maintain all research records in a secure manner. They explain to participants the risks of violations of privacy and confidentiality and disclose to participants any limits of confidentiality that reasonably can be expected. Regardless of the degree to which confidentiality will be maintained, investigators must disclose to participants any limits of confidentiality that reasonably can be expected. *(See G.2.e.)*

B.7.d. Disclosure of Research Information

Counselors do not disclose confidential information that reasonably could lead to the identification of a research participant unless they have obtained the prior consent of the person. Use of data derived from counseling relationships for purposes of training, research, or publication is confined to content that is disguised to ensure the anonymity of the individuals involved. *(See G.2.a., G.2.d.)*

B.7.e. Agreement for Identification

Identification of clients, students, or supervisees in a presentation or publication is permissible only when they have reviewed the material and agreed to its presentation or publication. *(See G.4.d.)*

B.8. Consultation

B.8.a. Agreements

When acting as consultants, counselors seek agreements among all parties involved concerning each individual's rights to confidentiality, the obligation of each individual to preserve confidential information, and the limits of confidentiality of information shared by others.

B.8.b. Respect for Privacy

Information obtained in a consulting relationship is discussed for professional purposes only with persons directly involved with the case. Written and oral reports present only data germane to the purposes of the consultation, and every effort is made to protect client identity and to avoid undue invasion of privacy.

B.8.c. Disclosure of Confidential Information

When consulting with colleagues, counselors do not disclose confidential information that reasonably could lead to the identification of a client or other person or organization with whom they have a confidential relationship unless they have obtained the prior consent of the person or organization or the disclosure cannot be avoided. They disclose information only to the extent necessary to achieve the purposes of the consultation. *(See D.2.d.)*

SECTION C

Professional Responsibility

Introduction

Counselors aspire to open, honest, and accurate communication in dealing with the public and other professionals. They practice in a non-discriminatory manner within the boundaries of professional and personal competence and have a responsibility to abide by the *ACA Code of Ethics*. Counselors actively participate in local, state, and national associations that foster the development and improvement of counseling. Counselors advocate to promote change at the individual, group, institutional, and societal levels that improves the quality of life for individuals and groups and removes potential barriers to the provision or access of appropriate services being offered. Counselors have a responsibility to the public to engage in counseling practices that are based on rigorous research methodologies. In addition, counselors engage in self-care activities to maintain and promote their emotional, physical, mental, and spiritual well-being to best meet their professional responsibilities.

C.1. Knowledge of Standards

Counselors have a responsibility to read, understand, and follow the *ACA Code of Ethics* and adhere to applicable laws and regulations.

C.2. Professional Competence

C.2.a. Boundaries of Competence

Counselors practice only within the boundaries of their competence, based on their education, training, supervised experience, state and national professional credentials, and appropriate professional experience. Counselors gain knowledge, personal awareness, sensitivity, and skills pertinent to working with a diverse client population. *(See A.9.b., C.4.e., E.2., F.2., F.11.b.)*

C.2.b. New Specialty Areas of Practice

Counselors practice in specialty areas new to them only after appropriate education, training, and supervised experience. While developing skills in new specialty areas, counselors take steps to ensure the competence of their work and to protect others from possible harm. *(See F.6.f.)*

C.2.c. Qualified for Employment

Counselors accept employment only for positions for which they are qualified by education, training, supervised experience, state and national professional credentials, and appropriate professional experience. Counselors hire for professional counseling positions only individuals who are qualified and competent for those positions.

C.2.d. Monitor Effectiveness

Counselors continually monitor their effectiveness as professionals and take steps to improve when necessary. Counselors in private practice take reasonable steps to seek peer supervision as needed to evaluate their efficacy as counselors.

C.2.e. Consultation on Ethical Obligations

Counselors take reasonable steps to consult with other counselors or related professionals when they have questions regarding their ethical obligations or professional practice.

C.2.f. Continuing Education

Counselors recognize the need for continuing education to acquire and maintain a reasonable level of awareness of current scientific and professional information in their fields of activity. They take steps to maintain competence in the skills they use, are open to new procedures, and keep current with the diverse populations and specific populations with whom they work.

C.2.g. Impairment

Counselors are alert to the signs of impairment from their own physical, mental, or emotional problems and refrain from offering or providing professional services when such impairment is likely to harm a client or others. They seek assistance for problems that reach the level of professional impairment, and, if necessary, they limit, suspend, or terminate their professional responsibilities until such time it is determined that they may safely resume their work. Counselors assist colleagues or supervisors in recognizing their own professional impairment and provide consultation and assistance when warranted with colleagues or supervisors showing signs of impairment and intervene as appropriate to prevent imminent harm to clients. *(See A.11.b., F.8.b.)*

C.2.h. Counselor Incapacitation or Termination of Practice

When counselors leave a practice, they follow a prepared plan for transfer of clients and files. Counselors prepare and disseminate to an identified colleague or "records custodian" a plan for the transfer of clients and files in the case of their incapacitation, death, or termination of practice.

C.3. Advertising and Soliciting Clients

C.3.a. Accurate Advertising

When advertising or otherwise representing their services to the public, counselors identify their credentials in an accurate manner that is not false, misleading, deceptive, or fraudulent.

C.3.b. Testimonials

Counselors who use testimonials do not solicit them from current clients nor former clients nor any other persons who may be vulnerable to undue influence.

C.3.c. Statements by Others

Counselors make reasonable efforts to ensure that statements made by others about them or the profession of counseling are accurate.

C.3.d. Recruiting Through Employment

Counselors do not use their places of employment or institutional affiliation to recruit or gain clients, supervisees, or consultees for their private practices.

C.3.e. Products and Training Advertisements

Counselors who develop products related to their profession or conduct work-shops or training events ensure that the advertisements concerning these prod-ucts or events are accurate and disclose adequate information for consumers to make informed choices. *(See C.6.d.)*

C.3.f. Promoting to Those Served

Counselors do not use counseling, teaching, training, or supervisory relationships to promote their products or training events in a manner that is deceptive or would exert undue influence on individuals who may be vulnerable. However, counselor educators may adopt textbooks they have authored for instructional purposes.

C.4. Professional Qualifications

C.4.a. Accurate Representation

Counselors claim or imply only professional qualifications actually completed and correct any known misrepresentations of their qualifications by others. Counselors truthfully represent the qualifications of their professional colleagues. Counselors clearly distinguish between paid and volunteer work experience and accurately describe their continuing education and specialized training. *(See C.2.a.)*

C.4.b. Credentials

Counselors claim only licenses or certifications that are current and in good standing.

C.4.c. Educational Degrees

Counselors clearly differentiate between earned and honorary degrees.

C.4.d. Implying Doctoral-Level Competence

Counselors clearly state their highest earned degree in counseling or closely related field. Counselors do not imply doctoral-level competence when only possessing a master's degree in counseling or a related field by referring to themselves as "Dr." in a counseling context when their doctorate is not in counseling or a related field.

C.4.e. Program Accreditation Status

Counselors clearly state the accreditation status of their degree programs at the time the degree was earned.

C.4.f. Professional Membership

Counselors clearly differentiate between current, active memberships and former memberships in associations. Members of the American Counseling Association must clearly differentiate between professional membership, which implies the possession of at least a master's degree in counseling, and regular membership, which is open to individuals whose interests and activities are consistent with those of ACA but are not qualified for professional membership.

C.5. Nondiscrimination

Counselors do not condone or engage in discrimination based on age, culture, disability, ethnicity, race, religion/spirituality, gender, gender identity, sexual orientation, marital status/partnership, language preference, socioeconomic status, or any basis proscribed by law. Counselors do not discriminate against clients, students, employees, supervisees, or research participants in a manner that has a negative impact on these persons.

C.6.Public Responsibility

C.6.a. Sexual Harassment

Counselors do not engage in or condone sexual harassment. Sexual harassment is defined as sexual solicitation, physical advances, or verbal or nonverbal conduct that is sexual in nature, that occurs in connection with professional activities or roles, and that either

1. is unwelcome, is offensive, or creates a hostile workplace or learning environment, and counselors know or are told this; or
2. is sufficiently severe or intense to be perceived as harassment to a reasonable person in the context in which the behavior occurred.

Sexual harassment can consist of a single intense or severe act or multiple persistent or pervasive acts.

C.6.b. Reports to Third Parties

Counselors are accurate, honest, and objective in reporting their professional activities and judgments to appropriate third parties, including courts, health insurance companies, those who are the recipients of evaluation reports, and others. *(See B.3., E.4.)*

C.6.c. Media Presentations

When counselors provide advice or comment by means of public lectures, demonstrations, radio or television programs, prerecorded tapes, technology-based applications, printed articles, mailed material, or other media, they take reasonable precautions to ensure that

1. the statements are based on appropriate professional counseling literature and practice,
2. the statements are otherwise consistent with the *ACA Code of Ethics*, and
3. the recipients of the information are not encouraged to infer that a professional counseling relationship has been established.

C.6.d. Exploitation of Others

Counselors do not exploit others in their professional relationships. *(See C.3.e.)*

C.6.e. Scientific Bases for Treatment Modalities

Counselors use techniques/ procedures/modalities that are grounded in theory and/or have an empirical or scientific foundation. Counselors who do not must define the techniques/procedures as "unproven" or "developing" and explain the potential risks and ethical considerations of using such techniques/procedures and take steps to protect clients from possible harm. *(See A.4.a., E.5.c., E.5.d.)*

C.7. Responsibility to Other Professionals

C.7.a. Personal Public Statements

When making personal statements in a public context, counselors clarify that they are speaking from their personal perspectives and that they are not speaking on behalf of all counselors or the profession.

SECTION D

Relationships With Other Professionals

Introduction

Professional counselors recognize that the quality of their interactions with colleagues can influence the quality of services provided to clients. They work to become knowledgeable about colleagues within and outside the field of counseling. Counselors develop positive working relationships and systems of communication with colleagues to enhance services to clients.

D.1. Relationships With Colleagues, Employers, and Employees

D.1.a. Different Approaches

Counselors are respectful of approaches to counseling services that differ from their own. Counselors are respectful of traditions and practices of other professional groups with which they work.

D.1.b. Forming Relationships

Counselors work to develop and strengthen interdisciplinary relations with colleagues from other disciplines to best serve clients.

D.1.c. Interdisciplinary Teamwork

Counselors who are members of interdisciplinary teams delivering multifaceted services to clients keep the focus on how to best serve the clients. They participate in and contribute to decisions that affect the well-being of clients by drawing on the perspectives, values, and experiences of the counseling profession and those of colleagues from other disciplines. *(See A.1.a.)*

D.1.d. Confidentiality

When counselors are required by law, institutional policy, or extraordinary circumstances to serve in more than one role in judicial or administrative proceedings, they clarify role expectations and the parameters of confidentiality with their colleagues. *(See B.1.c., B.1.d., B.2.c., B.2.d., B.3.b.)*

D.1.e. Establishing Professional and Ethical Obligations

Counselors who are members of interdisciplinary teams clarify professional and ethical obligations of the team as a whole and of its individual members. When a team decision raises ethical concerns, counselors first attempt to resolve the concern within the team. If they cannot reach resolution among team members, counselors pursue other avenues to address their concerns consistent with client well-being.

D.1.f. Personnel Selection and Assignment

Counselors select competent staff and assign responsibilities compatible with their skills and experiences.

D.1.g. Employer Policies

The acceptance of employment in an agency or institution implies that counselors are in agreement with its general policies and principles. Counselors strive to reach agreement with employers as to acceptable standards of conduct that allow for changes in institutional policy conducive to the growth and development of clients.

D.1.h. Negative Conditions

Counselors alert their employers of inappropriate policies and practices. They attempt to effect changes in such policies or procedures through constructive action within the organization. When such policies are potentially disruptive or damaging to clients or may limit the effectiveness of services provided and change cannot be effected, counselors take appropriate further action. Such action may include referral to appropriate certification, accreditation, or state licensure organizations, or voluntary termination of employment.

D.1.i. Protection From Punitive Action

Counselors take care not to harass or dismiss an employee who has acted in a responsible and ethical manner to expose inappropriate employer policies or practices.

D.2. Consultation

D.2.a. Consultant Competency

Counselors take reasonable steps to ensure that they have the appropriate resources and competencies when providing consultation services. Counselors provide appropriate referral resources when requested or needed. *(See C.2.a.)*

D.2.b. Understanding Consultees

When providing consultation, counselors attempt to develop with their consultees a clear understanding of problem definition, goals for change, and predicted consequences of interventions selected.

D.2.c. Consultant Goals

The consulting relationship is one in which consultee adaptability and growth toward self-direction are consistently encouraged and cultivated.

D.2.d. Informed Consent in Consultation

When providing consultation, counselors have an obligation to review, in writing and verbally, the rights and responsibilities of both counselors and consultees. Counselors use clear and understandable language to inform all parties involved about the purpose of the services to be provided, relevant costs, potential risks and benefits, and the limits of confidentiality. Working in conjunction with the consultee, counselors attempt to develop a clear definition of the problem, goals for change, and predicted consequences of interventions that are culturally responsive and appropriate to the needs of consultees. *(See A.2.a., A.2.b.)*

SECTION E

Evaluation, Assessment, and Interpretation

Introduction

Counselors use assessment instruments as one component of the counseling process, taking into account the client personal and cultural context. Counselors promote the well-being of individual clients or groups of clients by developing and using appropriate educational, psychological, and career assessment instruments.

E.1. General

E.1.a. Assessment

The primary purpose of educational, psychological, and career assessment is to provide measurements that are valid and reliable in either comparative or absolute terms. These include, but are not limited to, measurements of ability, personality, interest, intelligence, achievement, and performance. Counselors recognize the need to interpret the statements in this section as applying to both quantitative and qualitative assessments.

E.1.b. Client Welfare

Counselors do not misuse assessment results and interpretations, and they take reasonable steps to prevent others from misusing the information these techniques provide. They respect the client's right to know the results, the interpretations made, and the bases for counselors' conclusions and recommendations.

E.2. Competence to Use and Interpret Assessment Instruments

E.2.a. Limits of Competence

Counselors utilize only those testing and assessment services for which they have been trained and are competent. Counselors using technology-assisted test interpretations are trained in the construct being measured and the specific instrument being used prior to using its technology-based application. Counselors take reasonable measures to ensure the proper use of psychological and career assessment techniques by persons under their supervision. *(See A.12.)*

E.2.b. Appropriate Use

Counselors are responsible for the appropriate application, scoring, interpretation, and use of assessment instruments relevant to the needs of the client, whether they score and interpret such assessments themselves or use technology or other services.

E.2.c. Decisions Based on Results

Counselors responsible for decisions involving individuals or policies that are based on assessment results have a thorough understanding of educational, psychological, and career measurement, including validation criteria, assessment research, and guidelines for assessment development and use.

E.3. Informed Consent in Assessment

E.3.a. Explanation to Clients

Prior to assessment, counselors explain the nature and purposes of assessment and the specific use of results by potential recipients. The explanation will be given in the language of the client (or other legally authorized person on behalf of the client), unless an explicit exception has been agreed upon in advance. Counselors consider the client's personal or cultural context, the level of the client's understanding of the results, and the impact of the results on the client. *(See A.2., A.12.g., F.1.c.)*

E.3.b. Recipients of Results

Counselors consider the examinee's welfare, explicit understandings, and prior agreements in determining who receives the assessment results. Counselors include accurate and appropriate interpretations with any release of individual or group assessment results. *(See B.2.c., B.5.)*

E.4. Release of Data to Qualified Professionals

Counselors release assessment data in which the client is identified only with the consent of the client or the client's legal representative. Such data are released only to persons recognized by counselors as qualified to interpret the data. *(See B.1., B.3., B.6.b.)*

E.5. Diagnosis of Mental Disorders

E.5.a. Proper Diagnosis

Counselors take special care to provide proper diagnosis of mental disorders. Assessment techniques (including personal interview) used to determine client care (e.g., locus of treatment, type of treatment, or recommended follow-up) are carefully selected and appropriately used.

E.5.b. Cultural Sensitivity

Counselors recognize that culture affects the manner in which clients' problems are defined. Clients' socioeconomic and cultural experiences are considered when diagnosing mental disorders. *(See A.2.c.)*

E.5.c. Historical and Social Prejudices in the Diagnosis of Pathology

Counselors recognize historical and social prejudices in the misdiagnosis and pathologizing of certain individuals and groups and the role of mental health professionals in perpetuating these prejudices through diagnosis and treatment.

E.5.d. Refraining From Diagnosis

Counselors may refrain from making and/or reporting a diagnosis if they believe it would cause harm to the client or others.

E.6. Instrument Selection

E.6.a. Appropriateness of Instruments

Counselors carefully consider the validity, reliability, psychometric limitations, and appropriateness of instruments when selecting assessments.

E.6.b. Referral Information

If a client is referred to a third party for assessment, the counselor provides specific referral questions and sufficient objective data about the client to ensure that appropriate assessment instruments are utilized. *(See A.9.b., B.3.)*

E.6.c. Culturally Diverse Populations

Counselors are cautious when selecting assessments for culturally diverse populations to avoid the use of instruments that lack appropriate psychometric properties for the client population. *(See A.2.c., E.5.b.)*

E.7. Conditions of Assessment Administration

(See A.12.b, A.12.d.)

E.7.a. Administration Conditions

Counselors administer assessments under the same conditions that were established in their standardization. When assessments are not administered under standard conditions, as may be necessary to accommodate clients with disabilities, or when unusual behavior or irregularities occur during the administration, those conditions are noted in interpretation, and the results may be designated as invalid or of questionable validity.

E.7.b. Technological Administration

Counselors ensure that administration programs function properly and provide clients with accurate results when technological or other electronic methods are used for assessment administration.

E.7.c. Unsupervised Assessments

Unless the assessment instrument is designed, intended, and validated for self-administration and/or scoring, counselors do not permit inadequately supervised use.

E.7.d. Disclosure of Favorable Conditions

Prior to administration of assessments, conditions that produce most favorable assessment results are made known to the examinee.

E.8. Multicultural Issues/Diversity in Assessment

Counselors use with caution assessment techniques that were normed on populations other than that of the client. Counselors recognize the effects of age, color, culture, disability, ethnic group, gender, race, language preference, religion, spirituality, sexual orientation, and socioeconomic status on test administration and interpretation, and place test results in proper perspective with other relevant factors. *(See A.2.c., E.5.b.)*

E.9. Scoring and Interpretation of Assessments

E.9.a. Reporting

In reporting assessment results, counselors indicate reservations that exist regarding validity or reliability due to circumstances of the assessment or the inappropriateness of the norms for the person tested.

E.9.b. Research Instruments

Counselors exercise caution when interpreting the results of research instruments not having sufficient technical data to support respondent results. The specific purposes for the use of such instruments are stated explicitly to the examinee.

E.9.c. Assessment Services

Counselors who provide assessment scoring and interpretation services to support the assessment process confirm the validity of such interpretations. They accurately describe the purpose, norms, validity, reliability, and applications of the procedures and any special qualifications applicable to their use. The public offering of an automated test interpretations service is considered a profession-al-to-professional consultation. The formal responsibility of the consultant is to the consultee, but the ultimate and overriding responsibility is to the client. *(See D.2.)*

E.10. Assessment Security

Counselors maintain the integrity and security of tests and other assessment techniques consistent with legal and contractual obligations. Counselors do not appropriate, reproduce, or modify published assessments or parts thereof without acknowledgment and permission from the publisher.

E.11. Obsolete Assessments and Outdated Results

Counselors do not use data or results from assessments that are obsolete or outdated for the current purpose. Counselors make every effort to prevent the misuse of obsolete measures and assessment data by others.

E.12. Assessment Construction

Counselors use established scientific procedures, relevant standards, and current professional knowledge for assessment design in the development, publication, and utilization of educational and psychological assessment techniques.

E.13. Forensic Evaluation: Evaluation for Legal Proceedings

E.13.a. Primary Obligations

When providing forensic evaluations, the primary obligation of counselors is to produce objective findings that can be substantiated based on information and techniques appropriate to the evaluation, which may include examination of the individual and/or review of records. Counselors are entitled to form professional opinions based on their professional knowledge and expertise that can be supported by the data gathered in evaluations. Counselors will define the limits of their reports or testimony, especially when an examination of the individual has not been conducted.

E.13.b. Consent for Evaluation

Individuals being evaluated are informed in writing that the relationship is for the purposes of an evaluation and is not counseling in nature, and entities or individuals who will receive the evaluation report are identified. Written consent to be evaluated is obtained from those being evaluated unless a court orders the evaluation to be conducted without the written consent of individuals being evaluated. When children or vulnerable adults are being evaluated, informed written consent is obtained from a parent or guardian.

E.13.c. Client Evaluation Prohibited

Counselors do not evaluate individuals for forensic purposes they currently counsel or individuals they have counseled in the past. Counselors do not accept as counseling clients individuals they are evaluating or individuals they have evaluated in the past for forensic purposes.

E.13.d. Avoid Potentially Harmful Relationships

Counselors who provide forensic evaluations avoid potentially harmful professional or personal relationships with family members, romantic partners, and close friends of individuals they are evaluating or have evaluated in the past.

SECTION F

Supervision, Training, and Teaching

Introduction

Counselors aspire to foster meaningful and respectful professional relationships and to maintain appropriate boundaries with supervisees and students. Counselors have theoretical and pedagogical foundations for their work and aim to be fair, accurate, and honest in their assessments of counselors-in-training.

F.1. Counselor Supervision and Client Welfare

F.1.a. Client Welfare

A primary obligation of counseling supervisors is to monitor the services provided by other counselors or counselors-in-training. Counseling supervisors monitor client welfare and supervisee clinical performance and professional development. To fulfill these obligations, supervisors meet regularly with supervisees to review case notes, samples of clinical work, or live observations. Supervisees have a responsibility to understand and follow the *ACA Code of Ethics.*

F.1.b. Counselor Credentials

Counseling supervisors work to ensure that clients are aware of the qualifications of the supervisees who render services to the clients. *(See A.2.b.)*

F.1.c. Informed Consent and Client Rights

Supervisors make supervisees aware of client rights including the protection of client privacy and confidentiality in the counseling relationship. Supervisees provide clients with professional disclosure information and inform them of how the supervision process influences the limits of confidentiality. Supervisees make clients aware of who will have access to records of the counseling relationship and how these records will be used. *(See A.2.b., B.1.d.)*

F.2. Counselor Supervision Competence

F.2.a. Supervisor Preparation

Prior to offering clinical supervision services, counselors are trained in supervision methods and techniques. Counselors who offer clinical supervision services regularly pursue continuing education activities including both counseling and supervision topics and skills. *(See C.2.a., C.2.f.)*

F.2.b. Multicultural Issues/Diversity in Supervision

Counseling supervisors are aware of and address the role of multiculturalism/diversity in the supervisory relationship.

F.3. Supervisory Relationships

F.3.a. Relationship Boundaries With Supervisees

Counseling supervisors clearly define and maintain ethical professional, personal, and social relationships with their supervisees. Counseling supervisors avoid nonprofessional relationships with current supervisees. If supervisors must assume other professional roles (e.g., clinical and administrative supervisor, instructor) with supervisees, they work to minimize potential conflicts and explain to supervisees the expectations and responsibilities associated with each role. They do not engage in any form of nonprofessional interaction that may compromise the supervisory relationship.

F.3.b. Sexual Relationships

Sexual or romantic interactions or relationships with current supervisees are prohibited.

F.3.c. Sexual Harassment

Counseling supervisors do not condone or subject supervisees to sexual harassment. *(See C.6.a.)*

F.3.d. Close Relatives and Friends

Counseling supervisors avoid accepting close relatives, romantic partners, or friends as supervisees.

F.3.e. Potentially Beneficial Relationships

Counseling supervisors are aware of the power differential in their relationships with supervisees. If they believe nonprofessional relationships with a supervisee may be potentially beneficial to the supervisee, they take precautions similar to those taken by counselors when working with clients. Examples of potentially beneficial interactions or relationships include attending a formal ceremony; hospital visits; providing support during a stressful event; or mutual membership in a professional association, organization, or community. Counseling supervisors engage in open discussions with supervisees when they consider entering into relationships with them outside of their roles as clinical and/or administrative supervisors. Before engaging in nonprofessional relationships, supervisors discuss with supervisees and document the rationale for such interactions, potential benefits or drawbacks, and anticipated consequences for the supervisee. Supervisors clarify the specific nature and limitations of the additional role(s) they will have with the supervisee.

F.4. Supervisor Responsibilities

F.4.a. Informed Consent for Supervision

Supervisors are responsible for incorporating into their supervision the principles of informed consent and participation. Supervisors inform supervisees of the policies and procedures to which they are to adhere and the mechanisms for due process appeal of individual supervisory actions.

F.4.b. Emergencies and Absences

Supervisors establish and communicate to supervisees procedures for contacting them or, in their absence, alternative on-call supervisors to assist in handling crises.

F.4.c. Standards for Supervisees

Supervisors make their supervisees aware of professional and ethical standards and legal responsibilities. Supervisors of postdegree counselors encourage these counselors to adhere to professional standards of practice. *(See C.1.)*

F.4.d. Termination of the Supervisory Relationship

Supervisors or supervisees have the right to terminate the supervisory relationship with adequate notice. Reasons for withdrawal are provided to the other party. When cultural, clinical, or professional issues are crucial to the viability of the supervisory relationship, both parties make efforts to resolve differences. When termination is warranted, supervisors make appropriate referrals to possible alternative supervisors.

F.5. Counseling Supervision Evaluation, Remediation, and Endorsement

F.5.a. Evaluation

Supervisors document and provide supervisees with ongoing performance appraisal and evaluation feedback and schedule periodic formal evaluative sessions throughout the supervisory relationship.

F.5.b. Limitations

Through ongoing evaluation and appraisal, supervisors are aware of the limitations of supervisees that might impede performance. Supervisors assist supervisees in securing remedial assistance when needed. They recommend dismissal from training programs, applied counseling settings, or state or voluntary professional credentialing processes when those supervisees are unable to provide competent professional services. Supervisors seek consultation and document their decisions to dismiss or refer supervisees for assistance. They ensure that supervisees are aware of options available to them to address such decisions. *(See C.2.g.)*

F.5.c. Counseling for Supervisees

If supervisees request counseling, supervisors provide them with acceptable referrals. Counselors do not provide counseling services to supervisees. Supervisors address interpersonal competencies in terms of the impact of these issues on clients, the supervisory relationship, and professional functioning. *(See F.3.a.)*

F.5.d. Endorsement

Supervisors endorse supervisees for certification, licensure, employment, or completion of an academic or training program only when they believe supervisees are qualified for the endorsement. Regardless of qualifications, supervisors do not endorse supervisees whom they believe to be impaired in any way that would interfere with the performance of the duties associated with the endorsement.

F.6. Responsibilities of Counselor Educators

F.6.a. Counselor Educators

Counselor educators who are responsible for developing, implementing, and supervising educational programs are skilled as teachers and practitioners. They are knowledgeable regarding the ethical, legal, and regulatory aspects of the profession, are skilled in applying that knowledge, and make students and supervisees aware of their responsibilities. Counselor educators conduct counselor education and training programs in an ethical manner and serve as role models for professional behavior. *(See C.1., C.2.a., C.2.c.)*

F.6.b. Infusing Multicultural Issues/Diversity

Counselor educators infuse material related to multiculturalism/diversity into all courses and workshops for the development of professional counselors.

F.6.c. Integration of Study and Practice

Counselor educators establish education and training programs that integrate academic study and supervised practice.

F.6.d. Teaching Ethics

Counselor educators make students and supervisees aware of the ethical responsibilities and standards of the profession and the ethical responsibilities of students to the profession. Counselor educators infuse ethical considerations throughout the curriculum. *(See C.1.)*

F.6.e. Peer Relationships

Counselor educators make every effort to ensure that the rights of peers are not compromised when students or supervisees lead counseling groups or provide clinical supervision. Counselor educators take steps to ensure that students and supervisees understand they have the same ethical obligations as counselor educators, trainers, and supervisors.

F.6.f. Innovative Theories and Techniques

When counselor educators teach counseling techniques/procedures that are innovative, without an empirical foundation, or without a well-grounded theoretical foundation, they define the counseling techniques/procedures as "unproven" or "developing" and explain to students the potential risks and ethical considerations of using such techniques/procedures.

F.6.g. Field Placements

Counselor educators develop clear policies within their training programs regarding field placement and other clinical experiences. Counselor educators provide clearly stated roles and responsibilities for the student or supervisee, the site supervisor, and the program supervisor. They confirm that site supervisors are qualified to provide supervision and inform site supervisors of their professional and ethical responsibilities in this role.

F.6.h. Professional Disclosure

Before initiating counseling services, counselors-in-training disclose their status as students and explain how this status affects the limits of confidentiality. Counselor educators ensure that the clients at field placements are aware of the services rendered and the qualifications of the students and supervisees rendering those services. Students and supervisees obtain client permission before they use any information concerning the counseling relationship in the training process. *(See A.2.b.)*

F.7. Student Welfare

F.7.a. Orientation

Counselor educators recognize that orientation is a developmental process that continues throughout the educational and clinical training of students. Counseling faculty provide prospective students with information about the counselor education program's expectations:

1. the type and level of skill and knowledge acquisition required for successful completion of the training;
2. program training goals, objectives, and mission, and subject matter to be covered;
3. bases for evaluation;
4. training components that encourage self-growth or self-disclosure as part of the training process;
5. the type of supervision settings and requirements of the sites for required clinical field experiences;
6. student and supervisee evaluation and dismissal policies and procedures; and
7. up-to-date employment prospects for graduates.

F.7.b. Self-Growth Experiences

Counselor education programs delineate requirements for self-disclosure or self-growth experiences in their admission and program materials. Counselor educators use professional judgment when designing training experiences they conduct that require student and supervisee self-growth or self-disclosure. Students and supervisees are made aware of the ramifications their self-disclosure may have when counselors whose primary role as teacher, trainer, or supervisor requires acting on ethical obligations to the profession. Evaluative components of experiential training experiences explicitly delineate predetermined academic standards that are separate and do not depend on the student's level of self-disclosure. Counselor educators may require trainees to seek professional help to address any personal concerns that may be affecting their competency.

F.8. Student Responsibilities

F.8.a. Standards for Students

Counselors-in-training have a responsibility to understand and follow the *ACA Code of Ethics* and adhere to applicable laws, regulatory policies, and rules and policies governing professional staff behavior at the agency or placement setting. Students have the same obligation to clients as those required of professional counselors. *(See C.1., H.1.)*

F.8.b. Impairment

Counselors-in-training refrain from offering or providing counseling services when their physical, mental, or emotional problems are likely to harm a client or others. They are alert to the signs of impairment, seek assistance for problems, and notify their program supervisors when they are aware that they are unable to effectively provide services. In addition, they seek appropriate professional services for themselves to remediate the problems that are interfering with their ability to provide services to others. *(See A.1., C.2.d., C.2.g.)*

F.9. Evaluation and Remediation of Students

F.9.a. Evaluation

Counselors clearly state to students, prior to and throughout the training program, the levels of competency expected, appraisal methods, and timing of evaluations for both didactic and clinical competencies. Counselor educators provide students with ongoing performance appraisal and evaluation feedback throughout the training program.

F.9.b. Limitations

Counselor educators, throughout ongoing evaluation and appraisal, are aware of and address the inability of some students to achieve counseling competencies that might impede performance. Counselor educators

1. assist students in securing remedial assistance when needed,
2. seek professional consultation and document their decision to dismiss or refer students for assistance, and
3. ensure that students have recourse in a timely manner to address decisions to require them to seek assistance or to dismiss them and provide students with due process according to institutional policies and procedures. *(See C.2.g.)*

F.9.c. Counseling for Students

If students request counseling or if counseling services are required as part of a remediation process, counselor educators provide acceptable referrals.

F.10. Roles and Relationships Between Counselor Educators and Students

F.10.a. Sexual or Romantic Relationships

Sexual or romantic interactions or relationships with current students are prohibited.

F.10.b. Sexual Harassment

Counselor educators do not condone or subject students to sexual harassment. *(See C.6.a.)*

F.10.c. Relationships With Former Students

Counselor educators are aware of the power differential in the relationship between faculty and students. Faculty members foster open discussions with former students when considering engaging in a social, sexual, or other intimate relationship. Faculty members discuss with the former student how their former relationship may affect the change in relationship.

F.10.d. Nonprofessional Relationships

Counselor educators avoid nonprofessional or ongoing professional relationships with students in which there is a risk of potential harm to the student or that may compromise the training experience or grades assigned. In addition, counselor educators do not accept any form of professional services, fees, commissions, reimbursement, or remuneration from a site for student or supervisee placement.

F.10.e. Counseling Services

Counselor educators do not serve as counselors to current students unless this is a brief role associated with a training experience.

F.10.f. Potentially Beneficial Relationships

Counselor educators are aware of the power differential in the relationship between faculty and students. If they believe a nonprofessional relationship with a student may be potentially beneficial to the student, they take precautions similar to those taken by counselors when working with clients. Examples of potentially beneficial interactions or relationships include, but are not limited to, attending a formal ceremony; hospital visits; providing support during a stressful event; or mutual membership in a professional association, organization, or community. Counselor educators engage in open discussions with students when they consider entering into relationships with students outside of their roles as teachers and supervisors. They discuss with students the rationale for such interactions, the potential benefits and drawbacks, and the anticipated consequences for the student. Educators clarify the specific nature and limitations of the additional role(s) they will have with the student prior to engaging in a nonprofessional relationship. Nonprofessional relationships with students should be time-limited and initiated with student consent.

F.11. Multicultural/Diversity Competence in Counselor Education and Training Programs

F.11.a. Faculty Diversity

Counselor educators are committed to recruiting and retaining a diverse faculty.

F.11.b. Student Diversity

Counselor educators actively attempt to recruit and retain a diverse student body. Counselor educators demonstrate commitment to multicultural/diversity competence by recognizing and valuing diverse cultures and types of abilities students bring to the training experience. Counselor educators provide appropriate accommodations that enhance and support diverse student well-being and academic performance.

F.11.c. Multicultural/Diversity Competence

Counselor educators actively infuse multicultural/diversity competency in their training and supervision practices. They actively train students to gain awareness, knowledge, and skills in the competencies of multicultural practice. Counselor educators include case examples, role-plays, discussion questions, and other classroom activities that promote and represent various cultural perspectives.

SECTION G

Research and Publication

Introduction

Counselors who conduct research are encouraged to contribute to the knowledge base of the profession and promote a clearer understanding of the conditions that lead to a healthy and more just society. Counselors support efforts of researchers by participating fully and willingly whenever possible. Counselors minimize bias and respect diversity in designing and implementing research programs.

G.1. Research Responsibilities

G.1.a. Use of Human Research Participants

Counselors plan, design, conduct, and report research in a manner that is consistent with pertinent ethical principles, federal and state laws, host institutional regulations, and scientific standards governing research with human research participants.

G.1.b. Deviation From Standard Practice

Counselors seek consultation and observe stringent safeguards to protect the rights of research participants when a research problem suggests a deviation from standard or acceptable practices.

G. I .c. Independent Researchers

When independent researchers do not have access to an Institutional Review Board (IRB), they should consult with researchers who are familiar with IRB procedures to provide appropriate safeguards.

G. I .d. Precautions to Avoid Injury

Counselors who conduct research with human participants are responsible for the welfare of participants throughout the research process and should take reasonable precautions to avoid causing injurious psychological, emotional, physical, or social effects to participants.

G. I .e. Principal Researcher Responsibility

The ultimate responsibility for ethical research practice lies with the principal researcher. All others involved in the research activities share ethical obligations and responsibility for their own actions.

G. I .f. Minimal Interference

Counselors take reasonable precautions to avoid causing disruptions in the lives of research participants that could be caused by their involvement in research.

G. I .g. Multicultural/Diversity Considerations in Research

When appropriate to research goals, counselors are sensitive to incorporating research procedures that take into account cultural considerations. They seek consultation when appropriate.

G.2. Rights of Research Participants

(See A.2., A.7.)

G.2.a. Informed Consent in Research

Individuals have the right to consent to become research participants. In seeking consent, counselors use language that

1. accurately explains the purpose and procedures to be followed,
2. identifies any procedures that are experimental or relatively untried,
3. describes any attendant discomforts and risks,
4. describes any benefits or changes in individuals or organizations that might be reasonably expected,
5. discloses appropriate alternative procedures that would be advantageous for participants,
6. offers to answer any inquiries concerning the procedures,
7. describes any limitations on confidentiality,

8. describes the format and potential target audiences for the dissemination of research findings, and
9. instructs participants that they are free to withdraw their consent and to discontinue participation in the project at any time without penalty.

G.2.b. Deception

Counselors do not conduct research involving deception unless alternative procedures are not feasible and the prospective value of the research justifies the deception. If such deception has the potential to cause physical or emotional harm to research participants, the research is not conducted, regardless of prospective value. When the methodological requirements of a study necessitate concealment or deception, the investigator explains the reasons for this action as soon as possible during the debriefing.

G.2.c. Student/Supervisee Participation

Researchers who involve students or supervisees in research make clear to them that the decision regarding whether or not to participate in research activities does not affect one's academic standing or supervisory relationship. Students or supervisees who choose not to participate in educational research are provided with an appropriate alternative to fulfill their academic or clinical requirements.

G.2.d. Client Participation

Counselors conducting research involving clients make clear in the informed consent process that clients are free to choose whether or not to participate in research activities. Counselors take necessary precautions to protect clients from adverse consequences of declining or withdrawing from participation.

G.2.e. Confidentiality of Information

Information obtained about research participants during the course of an investigation is confidential. When the possibility exists that others may obtain access to such information, ethical research practice requires that the possibility, together with the plans for protecting confidentiality, be explained to participants as a part of the procedure for obtaining informed consent.

G.2.f. Persons Not Capable of Giving Informed Consent

When a person is not capable of giving informed consent, counselors provide an appropriate explanation to, obtain agreement for participation from, and obtain the appropriate consent of a legally authorized person.

G.2.g. Commitments to Participants

Counselors take reasonable measures to honor all commitments to research participants. *(See A.2.c.)*

G.2.h. Explanations After Data Collection

After data are collected, counselors provide participants with full clarification of the nature of the study to remove any misconceptions participants might have regarding the research. Where scientific or human values justify delaying or withholding information, counselors take reasonable measures to avoid causing harm.

G.2.i. Informing Sponsors

Counselors inform sponsors, institutions, and publication channels regarding research procedures and outcomes. Counselors ensure that appropriate bodies and authorities are given pertinent information and acknowledgment.

G.2.j. Disposal of Research Documents and Records

Within a reasonable period of time following the completion of a research project or study, counselors take steps to destroy records or documents (audio, video, digital, and written) containing confidential data or information that identifies research participants. When records are of an artistic nature, researchers obtain participant consent with regard to handling of such records or documents. *(See B.4.a., B.6.g.)*

G.3. Relationships With Research Participants (When Research Involves Intensive or Extended Interactions)

G.3.a. Nonprofessional Relationships

Nonprofessional relationships with research participants should be avoided.

G.3.b. Relationships With Research Participants

Sexual or romantic counselor–research participant interactions or relationships with current research participants are prohibited.

G.3.c. Sexual Harassment and Research Participants

Researchers do not condone or subject research participants to sexual harassment.

G.3.d. Potentially Beneficial Interactions

When a nonprofessional interaction between the researcher and the research participant may be potentially beneficial, the researcher must document, prior to the interaction (when feasible), the rationale for such an interaction, the potential benefit, and anticipated consequences for the research participant. Such interactions should be initiated with appropriate consent of the research participant. Where unintentional harm occurs to the research participant due to the nonprofessional interaction, the researcher must show evidence of an attempt to remedy such harm.

G.4. Reporting Results

G.4.a. Accurate Results

Counselors plan, conduct, and report research accurately. They provide thorough discussions of the limitations of their data and alternative hypotheses. Counselors do not engage in misleading or fraudulent research, distort data, misrepresent data, or deliberately bias their results. They explicitly mention all variables and conditions known to the investigator that may have affected the outcome of a study or the interpretation of data. They describe the extent to which results are applicable for diverse populations.

G.4.b. Obligation to Report Unfavorable Results

Counselors report the results of any research of professional value. Results that reflect unfavorably on institutions, programs, services, prevailing opinions, or vested interests are not withheld.

G.4.c. Reporting Errors

If counselors discover significant errors in their published research, they take reasonable steps to correct such errors in a correction erratum, or through other appropriate publication means.

G.4.d. Identity of Participants

Counselors who supply data, aid in the research of another person, report research results, or make original data available take due care to disguise the identity of respective participants in the absence of specific authorization from the participants to do otherwise. In situations where participants self-identify their involvement in research studies, researchers take active steps to ensure that data is adapted/changed to protect the identity and welfare of all parties and that discussion of results does not cause harm to participants.

G.4.e. Replication Studies

Counselors are obligated to make available sufficient original research data to qualified professionals who may wish to replicate the study.

G.5. Publication

G.5.a. Recognizing Contributions

When conducting and reporting research, counselors are familiar with and give recognition to previous work on the topic, observe copyright laws, and give full credit to those to whom credit is due.

G.5.b. Plagiarism

Counselors do not plagiarize; that is, they do not present another person's work as their own work.

G.5.c. Review/Republication of Data or Ideas

Counselors fully acknowledge and make editorial reviewers aware of prior publication of ideas or data where such ideas or data are submitted for review or publication.

G.5.d. Contributors

Counselors give credit through joint authorship, acknowledgment, footnote statements, or other appropriate means to those who have contributed significantly to research or concept development in accordance with such contributions. The principal contributor is listed first, and minor technical or professional contributions are acknowledged in notes or introductory statements.

G.5.e. Agreement of Contributors

Counselors who conduct joint research with colleagues or students/supervisees establish agreements in advance regarding allocation of tasks, publication credit, and types of acknowledgment that will be received.

G.5.f. Student Research

For articles that are substantially based on students' course papers, projects, dissertations or theses, and on which students have been the primary contributors, they are listed as principal authors.

G.5.g. Duplicate Submission

Counselors submit manuscripts for consideration to only one journal at a time. Manuscripts that are published in whole or in substantial part in another journal or published work are not submitted for publication without acknowledgment and permission from the previous publication.

G.5.h. Professional Review

Counselors who review material submitted for publication, research, or other scholarly purposes respect the confidentiality and proprietary rights of those who submitted it. Counselors use care to make publication decisions based on valid and defensible standards. Counselors review article submissions in a timely manner and based on their scope and competency in research methodologies. Counselors who serve as reviewers at the request of editors or publishers make every effort to only review materials that are within their scope of competency and use care to avoid personal biases.

SECTION H

Resolving Ethical Issues

Introduction

Counselors behave in a legal, ethical, and moral manner in the conduct of their professional work. They are aware that client protection and trust in the profession depend on a high level of professional conduct. They hold other counselors to the same standards and are willing to take appropriate action to ensure that these standards are upheld.

Counselors strive to resolve ethical dilemmas with direct and open communication among all parties involved and seek consultation with colleagues and supervisors when necessary. Counselors incorporate ethical practice into their daily professional work. They engage in ongoing professional development regarding current topics in ethical and legal issues in counseling.

H.1. Standards and the Law

(See F.9.a.)

H.1.a. Knowledge

Counselors understand the *ACA Code of Ethics* and other applicable ethics codes from other professional organizations or from certification and licensure bodies of which they are members. Lack of knowledge or misunderstanding of an ethical responsibility is not a defense against a charge of unethical conduct.

H.1.b. Conflicts Between Ethics and Laws

If ethical responsibilities conflict with law, regulations, or other governing legal authority, counselors make known their commitment to the *ACA Code of Ethics* and take steps to resolve the conflict. If the conflict cannot be resolved by such means, counselors may adhere to the requirements of law, regulations, or other governing legal authority.

H.2. Suspected Violations

H.2.a. Ethical Behavior Expected

Counselors expect colleagues to adhere to the *ACA Code of Ethics*. When counselors possess knowledge that raises doubts as to whether another counselor is acting in an ethical manner, they take appropriate action. *(See H.2.b., H.2.c.)*

H.2.b. Informal Resolution

When counselors have reason to believe that another counselor is violating or has violated an ethical standard, they attempt first to resolve the issue informally with the other counselor if feasible, provided such action does not violate confidentiality rights that may be involved.

H.2.c. Reporting Ethical Violations

If an apparent violation has substantially harmed or is likely to substantially harm a person or organization and is not appropriate for informal resolution or is not resolved properly, counselors take further action appropriate to the situation. Such action might include referral to state or national committees on professional ethics, voluntary national certification bodies, state licensing boards, or to the appropriate institutional authorities. This standard does not apply when an intervention would violate confidentiality rights or when counselors have been retained to review the work of another counselor whose professional conduct is in question.

H.2.d. Consultation

When uncertain as to whether a particular situation or course of action may be in violation of the *ACA Code of Ethics,* counselors consult with other counselors who are knowledgeable about ethics and the *ACA Code of Ethics,* with colleagues, or with appropriate authorities

H.2.e. Organizational Conflicts

If the demands of an organization with which counselors are affiliated pose a conflict with the *ACA Code of Ethics,* counselors specify the nature of such conflicts and express to their supervisors or other responsible officials their commitment to the *ACA Code of Ethics.* When possible, counselors work toward change within the organization to allow full adherence to the *ACA Code of Ethics.* In doing so, they address any confidentiality issues.

H.2.f. Unwarranted Complaints

Counselors do not initiate, participate in, or encourage the filing of ethics complaints that are made with reckless disregard or willful ignorance of facts that would disprove the allegation.

H.2.g. Unfair Discrimination Against Complainants and Respondents

Counselors do not deny persons employment, advancement, admission to academic or other programs, tenure, or promotion based solely upon their having made or their being the subject of an ethics complaint. This does not preclude taking action based upon the outcome of such proceedings or considering other appropriate information.

H.3. Cooperation With Ethics Committees

Counselors assist in the process of enforcing the *ACA Code of Ethics.* Counselors cooperate with investigations, proceedings, and requirements of the ACA Ethics Committee or ethics committees of other duly constituted associations or boards having jurisdiction over those charged with a violation. Counselors are familiar with the *ACA Policies and Procedures for Processing Complaints of Ethical Violations* and use it as a reference for assisting in the enforcement of the *ACA Code of Ethics.*

GLOSSARY OF TERMS

Advocacy – promotion of the well-being of individuals and groups, and the counseling profession within systems and organizations. Advocacy seeks to remove barriers and obstacles that inhibit access, growth, and development.

Assent – to demonstrate agreement, when a person is otherwise not capable or competent to give formal consent (e.g., informed consent) to a counseling service or plan.

Client – an individual seeking or referred to the professional services of a counselor for help with problem resolution or decision making.

Counselor – a professional (or a student who is a counselor-in-training) engaged in a counseling practice or other counseling-related services. Counselors fulfill many roles and responsibilities such as counselor educators, researchers, supervisors, practitioners, and consultants.

Counselor Educator – a professional counselor engaged primarily in developing, implementing, and supervising the educational preparation of counselors-in-training.

Counselor Supervisor – a professional counselor who engages in a formal relationship with a practicing counselor or counselor-in-training for the purpose of overseeing that individual's counseling work or clinical skill development.

Culture – membership in a socially constructed way of living, which incorporates collective values, beliefs, norms, boundaries, and lifestyles that are cocreated with others who share similar worldviews comprising biological, psychosocial, historical, psychological, and other factors.

Diversity – the similarities and differences that occur within and across cultures, and the intersection of cultural and social identities.

Documents – any written, digital, audio, visual, or artistic recording of the work within the counseling relationship between counselor and client.

Examinee – a recipient of any professional counseling service that includes educational, psychological, and career appraisal utilizing qualitative or quantitative techniques.

Forensic Evaluation – any formal assessment conducted for court or other legal proceedings.

Multicultural/Diversity Competence – a capacity whereby counselors possess cultural and diversity awareness and knowledge about self and others, and how this awareness and knowledge is applied effectively in practice with clients and client groups.

Multicultural/Diversity Counseling – counseling that recognizes diversity and embraces approaches that support the worth, dignity, potential, and uniqueness of individuals within their historical, cultural, economic, political, and psychosocial contexts.

Student – an individual engaged in formal educational preparation as a counselor-in-training.

Supervisee – a professional counselor or counselor-in-training whose counseling work or clinical skill development is being overseen in a formal supervisory relationship by a qualified trained professional.

Supervisor – counselors who are trained to oversee the professional clinical work of counselors and counselors-in-training.

Teaching – all activities engaged in as part of a formal educational program designed to lead to a graduate degree in counseling.

Training – the instruction and practice of skills related to the counseling profession. Training contributes to the ongoing proficiency of students and professional counselors.

ASCA Ethical Standards for School Counselors*

ETHICAL STANDARDS FOR SCHOOL COUNSELORS

Revised June 26, 2004
Ethical Standards for School Counselors was adopted by the ASCA Delegate Assembly, March 19, 1984, revised March 27, 1992, June 25, 1998, and June 26, 2004.

PREAMBLE

The American School Counselor Association (ASCA) is a professional organization whose members are certified/licensed in school counseling with unique qualifications and skills to address the academic, personal/social and career development needs of all students.

Professional school counselors are advocates, leaders, collaborators and consultants who create opportunities for equity in access and success in educational opportunities by connecting their programs to the mission of schools and subscribing to the following tenets of professional responsibility:

- Each person has the right to be respected, be treated with dignity and have access to a comprehensive school counseling program that advocates for and affirms all students from diverse populations regardless of ethnic/racial status, age, economic status, special needs, English as a second language or other language group, immigration status, sexual orientation, gender, gender identity/expression, family type, religious/spiritual identity and appearance.
- Each person has the right to receive the information and support needed to move toward self-direction and self-development and affirmation within one's group identities, with special care being given to students who have historically not received adequate educational services: students of color, low socioeconomic students, students with disabilities and students with nondominant language backgrounds.
- Each person has the right to understand the full magnitude and meaning of his/her educational choices and how those choices will affect future opportunities.

---

*Because of space limitations, I have included only the ethical codes of the American Counseling Association and the American School Counselors Association. Naturally, know the ethical code of the particular counseling affiliate organization to which you belong (e.g., AMHCA, ARCA, etc.). Reprinted by permission of the American School Counselor Association.

■ Each person has the right to privacy and thereby the right to expect the counselor-student relationship to comply with all laws, policies and ethical standards pertaining to confidentiality in the school setting.

In this document, ASCA specifies the principles of ethical behavior necessary to maintain the high standards of integrity, leadership and professionalism among its members. The Ethical Standards for School Counselors were developed to clarify the nature of ethical responsibilities held in common by school counseling professionals. The purposes of this document are to:

■ Serve as a guide for the ethical practices of all professional school counselors regardless of level, area, population served or membership in this professional association;
■ Provide self-appraisal and peer evaluations regarding counselor responsibilities to students, parents/guardians, colleagues and professional associates, schools, communities and the counseling profession; and
■ Inform those served by the school counselor of acceptable counselor practices and expected professional behavior.

A. RESPONSIBILITIES TO STUDENTS

A.I. Responsibilities to Students

The professional school counselor:

a. Has a primary obligation to the student, who is to be treated with respect as a unique individual.
b. Is concerned with the educational, academic, career, personal and social needs and encourages the maximum development of every student.
c. Respects the student's values and beliefs and does not impose the counselor's personal values.
d. Is knowledgeable of laws, regulations and policies relating to students and strives to protect and inform students regarding their rights.

A.2. Confidentiality

The professional school counselor:

a. Informs students of the purposes, goals, techniques and rules of procedure under which they may receive counseling at or before the time when the counseling relationship is entered. Disclosure notice includes the limits of confidentiality such as the possible necessity for consulting with other professionals, privileged communication, and legal or authoritative restraints. The meaning and limits of confidentiality are defined in developmentally appropriate terms to students.
b. Keeps information confidential unless disclosure is required to prevent clear and imminent danger to the student or others or when legal requirements

demand that confidential information be revealed. Counselors will consult with appropriate professionals when in doubt as to the validity of an exception.

c. In absence of state legislation expressly forbidding disclosure, considers the ethical responsibility to provide information to an identified third party who, by his/her relationship with the student, is at a high risk of contracting a disease that is commonly known to be communicable and fatal. Disclosure requires satisfaction of all of the following conditions:
   - Student identifies partner or the partner is highly identifiable
   - Counselor recommends the student notify partner and refrain from further high-risk behavior
   - Student refuses
   - Counselor informs the student of the intent to notify the partner
   - Counselor seeks legal consultation as to the legalities of informing the partner

d. Requests of the court that disclosure not be required when the release of confidential information may potentially harm a student or the counseling relationship.

e. Protects the confidentiality of students' records and releases personal data in accordance with prescribed laws and school policies. Student information stored and transmitted electronically is treated with the same care as traditional student records.

f. Protects the confidentiality of information received in the counseling relationship as specified by federal and state laws, written policies and applicable ethical standards. Such information is only to be revealed to others with the informed consent of the student, consistent with the counselor's ethical obligation.

g. Recognizes his/her primary obligation for confidentiality is to the student but balances that obligation with an understanding of the legal and inherent rights of parents/guardians to be the guiding voice in their children's lives.

A.3. Counseling Plans

The professional school counselor:

a. Provides students with a comprehensive school counseling program that includes a strong emphasis on working jointly with all students to develop academic and career goals.

b. Advocates for counseling plans supporting students right to choose from the wide array of options when they leave secondary education. Such plans will be regularly reviewed to update students regarding critical information they need to make informed decisions.

A.4. Dual Relationships

The professional school counselor:

a. Avoids dual relationships that might impair his/her objectivity and increase the risk of harm to the student (*e.g.*, counseling one's family members, close friends or associates). If a dual relationship is unavoidable, the counselor is responsible for taking action to eliminate or reduce the potential for harm. Such safeguards might include informed consent, consultation, supervision and documentation.

b. Avoids dual relationships with school personnel that might infringe on the integrity of the counselor/student relationship

A.5. Appropriate Referrals

The professional school counselor:

a. Makes referrals when necessary or appropriate to outside resources. Appropriate referrals may necessitate informing both parents/guardians and students of applicable resources and making proper plans for transitions with minimal interruption of services. Students retain the right to discontinue the counseling relationship at any time.

A.6. Group Work

The professional school counselor:

a. Screens prospective group members and maintains an awareness of participants' needs and goals in relation to the goals of the group. The counselor takes reasonable precautions to protect members from physical and psychological harm resulting from interaction within the group.

b. Notifies parents/guardians and staff of group participation if the counselor deems it appropriate and if consistent with school board policy or practice.

c. Establishes clear expectations in the group setting and clearly states that confidentiality in group counseling cannot be guaranteed. Given the developmental and chronological ages of minors in schools, the counselor recognizes the tenuous nature of confidentiality for minors renders some topics inappropriate for group work in a school setting.

d. Follows up with group members and documents proceedings as appropriate.

A.7. Danger to Self or Others

The professional school counselor:

a. Informs parents/guardians or appropriate authorities when the student's condition indicates a clear and imminent danger to the student or others. This is to be done after careful deliberation and, where possible, after consultation with other counseling professionals.

b. Will attempt to minimize threat to a student and may choose to 1) inform the student of actions to be taken, 2) involve the student in a three-way communication with parents/guardians when breaching confidentiality or 3) allow the student to have input as to how and to whom the breach will be made.

A.8. Student Records

The professional school counselor:

a. Maintains and secures records necessary for rendering professional services to the student as required by laws, regulations, institutional procedures and confidentiality guidelines.
b. Keeps sole-possession records separate from students' educational records in keeping with state laws.
c. Recognizes the limits of sole-possession records and understands these records are a memory aid for the creator and in absence of privilege communication may be subpoenaed and may become educational records when they 1) are shared with others in verbal or written form, 2) include information other than professional opinion or personal observations and/or 3) are made accessible to others.
d. Establishes a reasonable timeline for purging sole-possession records or case notes. Suggested guidelines include shredding sole possession records when the student transitions to the next level, transfers to another school or graduates. Careful discretion and deliberation should be applied before destroying sole-possession records that may be needed by a court of law such as notes on child abuse, suicide, sexual harassment or violence.

A.9. Evaluation, Assessment and Interpretation

The professional school counselor:

a. Adheres to all professional standards regarding selecting, administering and interpreting assessment measures and only utilizes assessment measures that are within the scope of practice for school counselors.
b. Seeks specialized training regarding the use of electronically based testing programs in administering, scoring and interpreting that may differ from that required in more traditional assessments.
c. Considers confidentiality issues when utilizing evaluative or assessment instruments and electronically based programs.
d. Provides interpretation of the nature, purposes, results and potential impact of assessment/evaluation measures in language the student(s) can understand.
e. Monitors the use of assessment results and interpretations, and takes reasonable steps to prevent others from misusing the information.
f. Uses caution when utilizing assessment techniques, making evaluations and interpreting the performance of populations not represented in the norm group on which an instrument is standardized.
g. Assesses the effectiveness of his/her program in having an impact on students' academic, career and personal/social development through accountability measures especially examining efforts to close achievement, opportunity and attainment gaps.

A.10. Technology

The professional school counselor:

a. Promotes the benefits of and clarifies the limitations of various appropriate technological applications. The counselor promotes technological applications (1) that are appropriate for the student's individual needs, (2) that the student understands how to use and (3) for which follow-up counseling assistance is provided.
b. Advocates for equal access to technology for all students, especially those historically underserved.
c. Takes appropriate and reasonable measures for maintaining confidentiality of student information and educational records stored or transmitted over electronic media including although not limited to fax, electronic mail and instant messaging.
d. While working with students on a computer or similar technology, takes reasonable and appropriate measures to protect students from objectionable and/or harmful online material.
e. Who is engaged in the delivery of services involving technologies such as the telephone, videoconferencing and the Internet takes responsible steps to protect students and others from harm.

A.11. Student Peer Support Program

The professional school counselor:
Has unique responsibilities when working with student-assistance programs. The school counselor is responsible for the welfare of students participating in peer-to-peer programs under his/her direction.

B. RESPONSIBILITIES TO PARENTS/GUARDIANS

B.1. Parent Rights and Responsibilities

The professional school counselor:

a. Respects the rights and responsibilities of parents/guardians for their children and endeavors to establish, as appropriate, a collaborative relationship with parents/guardians to facilitate the student's maximum development.
b. Adheres to laws, local guidelines and ethical standards of practice when assisting parents/guardians experiencing family difficulties that interfere with the student's effectiveness and welfare.
c. Respects the confidentiality of parents/guardians.
d. Is sensitive to diversity among families and recognizes that all parents/guardians, custodial and noncustodial, are vested with certain rights and responsibilities for the welfare of their children by virtue of their role and according to law.

B.2. Parents/Guardians and Confidentiality

The professional school counselor:

a. Informs parents/guardians of the counselor's role with emphasis on the confidential nature of the counseling relationship between the counselor and student.
b. Recognizes that working with minors in a school setting may require counselors to collaborate with students' parents/guardians.
c. Provides parents/guardians with accurate, comprehensive and relevant information in an objective and caring manner, as is appropriate and consistent with ethical responsibilities to the student.
d. Makes reasonable efforts to honor the wishes of parents/guardians concerning information regarding the student, and in cases of divorce or separation exercises a good-faith effort to keep both parents informed with regard to critical information with the exception of a court order.

C. RESPONSIBILITIES TO COLLEAGUES AND PROFESSIONAL ASSOCIATES

C.I. Professional Relationships

The professional school counselor:

a. Establishes and maintains professional relationships with faculty, staff and administration to facilitate an optimum counseling program.
b. Treats colleagues with professional respect, courtesy and fairness. The qualifications, views and findings of colleagues are represented to accurately reflect the image of competent professionals.
c. Is aware of and utilizes related professionals, organizations and other resources to whom the student may be referred.

C.2. Sharing Information with Other Professionals

The professional school counselor:

a. Promotes awareness and adherence to appropriate guidelines regarding confidentiality, the distinction between public and private information and staff consultation.
b. Provides professional personnel with accurate, objective, concise and meaningful data necessary to adequately evaluate, counsel and assist the student.
c. If a student is receiving services from another counselor or other mental health professional, the counselor, with student and/or parent/guardian consent, will inform the other professional and develop clear agreements to avoid confusion and conflict for the student.
d. Is knowledgeable about release of information and parental rights in sharing information.

D. RESPONSIBILITIES TO THE SCHOOL AND COMMUNITY

D.1. Responsibilities to the School

The professional school counselor:

a. Supports and protects the educational program against any infringement not in students' best interest.
b. Informs appropriate officials in accordance with school policy of conditions that may be potentially disruptive or damaging to the school's mission, personnel and property while honoring the confidentiality between the student and counselor.
c. Is knowledgeable and supportive of the school's mission and connects his/ her program to the school's mission.
d. Delineates and promotes the counselor's role and function in meeting the needs of those served. Counselors will notify appropriate officials of conditions that may limit or curtail their effectiveness in providing programs and services.
e. Accepts employment only for positions for which he/she is qualified by education, training, supervised experience, state and national professional credentials and appropriate professional experience.
f. Advocates that administrators hire only qualified and competent individuals for professional counseling positions.
g. Assists in developing: (1) curricular and environmental conditions appropriate for the school and community, (2) educational procedures and programs to meet students' developmental needs and (3) a systematic evaluation process for comprehensive, developmental, standards-based school counseling programs, services and personnel. The counselor is guided by the findings of the evaluation data in planning programs and services.

D.2. Responsibility to the Community

The professional school counselor:

a. Collaborates with agencies, organizations and individuals in the community in the best interest of students and without regard to personal reward or remuneration.
b. Extends his/her influence and opportunity to deliver a comprehensive school counseling program to all students by collaborating with community resources for student success.

E. RESPONSIBILITIES TO SELF

E.1. Professional Competence

The professional school counselor:

a. Functions within the boundaries of individual professional competence and accepts responsibility for the consequences of his/her actions.

b. Monitors personal well-being and effectiveness and does not participate in any activity that may lead to inadequate professional services or harm to a student.

c. Strives through personal initiative to maintain professional competence including technological literacy and to keep abreast of professional information. Professional and personal growth are ongoing throughout the counselor's career.

E.2. Diversity

The professional school counselor:

a. Affirms the diversity of students, staff and families.

b. Expands and develops awareness of his/her own attitudes and beliefs affecting cultural values and biases and strives to attain cultural competence.

c. Possesses knowledge and understanding about how oppression, racism, discrimination and stereotyping affects her/him personally and professionally.

d. Acquires educational, consultation and training experiences to improve awareness, knowledge, skills and effectiveness in working with diverse populations: ethnic/racial status, age, economic status, special needs, ESL or ELL, immigration status, sexual orientation, gender, gender identity/expression, family type, religious/spiritual identity and appearance.

F. RESPONSIBILITIES TO THE PROFESSION

F.I. Professionalism

The professional school counselor:

a. Accepts the policies and procedures for handling ethical violations as a result of maintaining membership in the American School Counselor Association.

b. Conducts herself/himself in such a manner as to advance individual ethical practice and the profession.

c. Conducts appropriate research and report findings in a manner consistent with acceptable educational and psychological research practices. The counselor advocates for the protection of the individual student's identity when using data for research or program planning.

d. Adheres to ethical standards of the profession, other official policy statements, such as ASCA's position statements, role statement and the ASCA National Model, and relevant statutes established by federal, state and local governments, and when these are in conflict works responsibly for change.

e. Clearly distinguishes between statements and actions made as a private individual and those made as a representative of the school counseling profession.

f. Does not use his/her professional position to recruit or gain clients, consultees for his/her private practice or to seek and receive unjustified personal gains, unfair advantage, inappropriate relationships or unearned goods or services.

F.2. Contribution to the Profession

The professional school counselor:

a. Actively participates in local, state and national associations fostering the development and improvement of school counseling.
b. Contributes to the development of the profession through the sharing of skills, ideas and expertise with colleagues.
c. Provides support and mentoring to novice professionals.

G. MAINTENANCE OF STANDARDS

Ethical behavior among professional school counselors, association members and nonmembers, is expected at all times. When there exists serious doubt as to the ethical behavior of colleagues or if counselors are forced to work in situations or abide by policies that do not reflect the standards as outlined in these Ethical Standards for School Counselors, the counselor is obligated to take appropriate action to rectify the condition. The following procedure may serve as a guide:

1. The counselor should consult confidentially with a professional colleague to discuss the nature of a complaint to see if the professional colleague views the situation as an ethical violation.
2. When feasible, the counselor should directly approach the colleague whose behavior is in question to discuss the complaint and seek resolution.
3. If resolution is not forthcoming at the personal level, the counselor shall utilize the channels established within the school, school district, the state school counseling association and ASCA's Ethics Committee.
4. If the matter still remains unresolved, referral for review and appropriate action should be made to the Ethics Committees in the following sequence:
   - state school counselor association
   - American School Counselor Association
5. The ASCA Ethics Committee is responsible for:
   - educating and consulting with the membership regarding ethical standards
   - periodically reviewing and recommending changes in code
   - receiving and processing questions to clarify the application of such standards; Questions must be submitted in writing to the ASCA Ethics chair.
   - handling complaints of alleged violations of the ethical standards. At the national level, complaints should be submitted in writing to the ASCA Ethics Committee, c/o the Executive Director, American School Counselor Association, 1101 King St., Suite 625, Alexandria, VA 22314.

State Licensure Boards
and Requirements

Here is some basic information regarding licensure requirements by state as of 2010. For complete information, please visit the state licensing board Web site.

ALABAMA
Alabama Board of Examiners in Counseling
950 22nd St. North, Suite 670
Birmingham, AL 32255
www.abec.state.al.us

Title of License: Licensed Professional Counselor (LPC)
                            Associate Licensed Counselor (ALC)
Note: ALCs work under LPCs to attain hours for licensure.

Educational Requirements: Master's degree in counseling from a CACREP- or CORE-accredited program (or its equivalent) defined as 48 semester hours or 72 quarter hours.

Experiential Requirements: ALC is given when master's is verified. No experiential requirements. LPC: Three thousand hours of supervised experience in professional counseling with board approved supervision. An applicant may subtract 1,000 hours of the required professional experience for every 15 graduate semester hours (or 22.5 quarter hours) obtained beyond the master's degree from a regionally accredited college or university, provided that such hours are clearly related to the field of professional counseling. This formula can be used for up to 2,000 hours.

(Note: In the ACA book on state licensure numbers are written as: 2,000 not two thousand.)

Exam Required: NCE

ALASKA
AK Division of Occupational Licensing
Board of Professional Counselors
P.O. Box 110806
Juneau, AK 99811-0806
Eleanor.vinson@alaska.gov
www.dced.state.ak.us/occ/ppco.htm

Title of License: LPC

Educational Requirements: Master's degree in counseling from a regionally or nationally accredited institution approved by the board and consisting of at least 60 graduate semester hours.

Experiential Requirements: Three thousand post-master's supervised hours including 1,000 hours of direct client contact and 100 hours of face-to-face supervision over a 2-year period. The supervisor must be a licensed mental health professional.

Exam Required: NCE

ARIZONA
AZ Board of Behavioral Examiners
1400 W. Washington, Suite 350
Phoenix, AZ 85007
azbbhe@bbhe.state.az.us
www.azbbhe.state.az.us

Title of License: LPC
      Licensed Associate Counselor (LAC) practicing under a
       certified or licensed mental health professional.

Educational Requirements: Master's degree in counseling or a related field from a CACREP-accredited program or a program that includes a minimum of 60 semester hours.

Experiential Requirements: For LAC, no experiential requirements. LPC: Two years (3,200 hours required) post-master's supervised work experience in psychotherapy, including diagnosis and treatment. . One thousand hours of clinical supervision and 1,600 hours of direct client contact are required. (Note: Beginning July 1, 2006, an applicant must receive a minimum of 10 hours of clinical supervision obtained during direct observation or review of audiotapes or videotapes by the clinical supervisor while applicant is providing treatment and evaluation services to a client.)

Exam Required: NCE, NCMHCE, or CRCE

ARKANSAS
AR Board of Examiners
Counselors and Marriage-Family Therapist
P. O. Box 70
Magnolia, AR 71754
arboec@sbglobal.net
www.state.ar.us/abec

Title of License: LPC
       LAC

Educational Requirements: Graduate degree in counseling from a regionally accredited institution, with a minimum of 60 semester hours with a curriculum aligned to CACREP.

Experiential Requirements: For LAC, no experiential requirements. LPC: Three years of post-master's supervised experience. Supervision must be under a board-approved supervisor. One year of experience may be gained for each 30 semester hours earned beyond the master's degree (up to 2 years) provided the hours are clearly counseling in nature and acceptable to the board.

Exam Required: NCE and an oral exam.

CALIFORNIA
Licensure law just passed!
Pertinent Information: n/a
Name of License: Licensed Professional Clinical Counselor (LPCC)
Current Contact: California Coalition for Counselor Licensure (CCCL) for
    grandparenting and other information
info@caccl.org
www.caccl.org

January 1, 2010: The licensure law takes effect. The CA Board of Behavioral Sciences then has the responsibilities for developing the rules and regulations to implement the bill and it will accept LPCC applications.

January 1, 2011: Applications for grandparenting and reciprocity will be available through the CA Board of Behavioral Sciences. These requirements are now posted on CCCL's Web site under licensure requirements.

January 1, 2012: Applications for regular licensure will be available for those not eligible for grandparenting or reciprocity. These licensure requirements are now posted on CCCL's Web site under licensure requirements.

COLORADO
CO Department of Regulatory Agencies
Board of Licensed Professional Counselor Examiners
1560 Broadway, Suite 1340
Denver, CO 80202
Amos.martinez@state.co.us
www.dora.state.co.us/registrations

Title of License: LPC

Educational Requirements: Master's degree from a CACREP-accredited program (or equivalent) from a regionally accredited college/university with 48 semester hours.

Experiential Requirements: Two years/2,000 hours of post-master's practice under board-approved supervision. One hundred hours of supervision is required, 70 hours of which must be individual supervision.

Exam Required: NCE and CO Jurisprudence Exam (open book).

CONNECTICUT
CT Department of Public Health
Office of Practitioner Licensing and Certification
410 Capitol Ave., MS# 12APP
P. O. Box 340308
Hartford, CT 06134-0308
www.ct-clic.com

Title of License: LPC

Educational Requirements: Master's degree in counseling consisting of at least 42 semester hours and additional coursework totaling 60 graduate semester hours; doctoral degree with at least 60 graduate semester hours; or master's degree and 6th-year certificate totaling 60 graduate semester hours.

Experiential Requirements: Three thousand hours of post-master's supervised experience for a 1-year period. A minimum of 100 hours of direct supervision is required.

Exam Required: NCE or NCMHCE

DELAWARE
DE Board of Professional Counselors and Mental Health and
Chemical Dependency Professionals
Cannon Building
861 Silverlake Blvd.
Suite 203
Dover, DE 19904-2467
Customerservice.dpr@state.de.us
http://www.dpr.delaware.gov/boards/profcounselors/

Title of License: Licensed Professional Counselor of Mental Health (LPCMH)

Educational Requirements: Graduate degree, including a minimum of 48 semester hours. Must also be certified by NBCC as a CCMHC, or by the ACMHC, or other national mental health specialty certifying organizations approved by the board.

Experiential Requirements: Two years/3,200 hours full-time clinical experience within a 4-year period with at least 1,600 hours of professional direct supervision acceptable to the board.

Exam Required: NCE or NCMHCE

DISTRICT OF COLUMBIA
DC Department of Health
Board of Professional Counseling
717 14th St. NW, Suite 600
Washington, DC 20005
http://doh.dc.gov/doh

Title of License: LPC

Educational Requirements: Sixty graduate semester hours including a master's degree in counseling or a related field from an accredited institution.

Experiential Requirements: Must complete a total of 3,500 client-contact hours in no less than 2 years and no more than 5 years, including 200 hours of direct supervision (100 of the 200 can be group supervision). Also, for every 35 hours worked, the applicant shall have had 1-hour immediate supervision.

Exam Required: NCE

FLORIDA
FL Department of Health
Board of Clinical Social Work, Marriage & Family Therapy, and
   Mental Health Counseling
4052 Bald Cypress Way, BIN C-08
Tallahassee, FL 32399
www.doh.state.fl.us/mqa

Title of License: Licensed Mental Health Counselor (LMHC)
                   Provisional Mental Health Counselor: Counselor
                      provisionally licensed to provide mental health
                      counseling under supervision (valid for 24 months).
                   Registered Mental Health Counselor Intern: Person
                      completing the post-master's supervised experience
                      requirement.

Educational Requirements: Master's degree in mental health counseling or a related field from a CACREP-accredited program (or equivalent) that includes 60 semester hours and a supervised practicum, internship, or field experience.

Experiential Requirements: Two years supervised post-master's clinical experience. This includes 100 face-to-face hours of supervision, 50 hours of which can be group supervision.

Exam Required: NCMHCE

GEORGIA
GA Composite Board of Professional Counselors, Social Workers, and
  Marriage & Family Therapists
237 Coliseum Dr.
Macon, GA 31217
www.sos.state.ga.us/plb/counselors

Title of License: LPC
                    Associate Professional Counselor (APC): Applicant being
                    supervised for LPC.

Educational Requirements: Master's degree in a program that is primarily counseling in content from an institution accredited by a regional body recognized by
the Council on Postsecondary Education. Also, supervised practicum or internship consisting of at least 300 hours.

Experiential Requirements: Four years supervised, post-master's directed experience in a work setting acceptable to the board; or 3 years supervised, post-master's
directed experience in professional counseling in a work setting acceptable to the
board and a 1-year (300 hours) practicum or internship, which was part of the
graduate degree program. A minimum of 2 years supervision must be provided
by an LPC.

Exam Required: NCE

HAWAII
HI Department of Commerce and Consumer Affairs—Professional and
Vocational Licensing (PVL)
Mental Health Counselor Program
P. O. Box 3469
Honolulu, HI 96801
counselor@dcca.hawaii.gov
www.hawaii.gov/dcca/areas/pvl/programs/mental/

Title of License: LMHC

Educational Requirements: Master's or doctoral degree in counseling or an
allied field related to the practice of mental health counseling, with a minimum
of 48 semester hours (or 72 quarter hours) that includes coursework in core areas,
from an accredited institution; 2 academic terms of a supervised internship or
practicum in mental health counseling with 300 hours of supervised client contact (3 semester hours or 5 quarter hours should be earned each term).

Experiential Requirements: Three thousand post-master's direct counseling
work with 100 hours of face-to-face supervision within a 2-year period.

Exam Required: NCE

IDAHO
ID Bureau of Occupational Licenses
State Licensing Board of Professional Counselors and Marriage & Family Therapists
1109 Main Street, Suite 220
Boise, ID 83702
cou@ibol.idaho.gov
www.ibol.idaho.gov

Title of License: LPCC
LPC
Registered Counselor Intern (RCI): Graduate student under
supervision.

Educational Requirements: Graduate degree in a counseling field from an accredited college or university with 60 semester hours, including a 6-hour advanced practicum

Experiential Requirements: LPCC: Hold a valid LPC, 2,000 hours of supervised direct client experience accumulated in no less than a 2-year period, 1,000 hours of which must be under supervision of an LCPC. Minimum of 1-hour face-to-face, one-on-one supervision for every 30 hours of direct client contact.

LPC: 1,000 hours of supervised experience (400 hours direct client contact) with a minimum of 1 hour face-to-face supervision for every 20 hours of experience. Supervised practicum and/or internship taken at the graduate level may be used.

Exam Required: LPCC: NCMHCE
LPC: NCE

ILLINOIS
IL Division of Professional Regulation
Professional Counselor Licensing and Disciplinary Board
320 W. Washington St., 3rd Floor
Springfield, IL 62786
www.idfpr.com

Title of License: Licensed Clinical Professional Counselor (LCPC):
Holds license authorizing independent practice of
clinical professional counseling in private practice.
LPC: Holds license authorizing the practice of professional
counseling.

Educational Requirements: LCPC: A master's of doctoral degree in counseling or a related field from a regionally LCPC-accredited college/university; or hold a current CCMHC credential issued by NBCC (this meets requirements for licensure as an LCPC).

LPC: Master's degree in professional counseling (at least 48 semester credits) or related field from a regionally accredited college/university in a program approved by the IL Department of Professional Regulation.

Experiential Requirements: LCPC: Two years full-time satisfactory, supervised employment of experience working as a counselor in a professional capacity under the direction of a qualified supervisor, subsequent to degree.

If applicant holds a doctoral degree, 1 year must be subsequent to the degree and internships may count towards professional experience (1 year = maximum of 1,680 clock hours).

LPC: No experiential requirements.

INDIANA
IN Professional Licensing Agency
Social Worker, Marriage & Family Therapist, and Mental Health
    Counselor Board
402 W. Washington St., Rm. W072
Indianapolis, IN 46204
hpb5@hpb.in.gov
http://www.in.gov/pla/social.htm

Title of License: LMHC

Educational Requirements: Master's degree in an area related to mental health counseling from a CACREP- or CORE-accredited program, from a regionally accredited institution of higher learning to include a minimum of 60 graduate semester hours in counseling in 12 specified content areas.

Completion of a practicum (100 hours), internship (600 hours), and advanced internship (300 hours). One hundred hours of face-to-face supervision is required.

Experiential Requirements: Three thousand hours of postgraduate clinical experience for a 2-year period. One hundred hours of face-to-face supervision under an LMHC or equivalent supervisor is required.

Exam Required: NCMHCE

IOWA
IA Bureau of Professional Licensure
Board of Behavioral Science Examiners
Lucas State Office Building, 5th Floor
321 E. 12th St.
Des Moines, IA 50319
www.idph.state.ia.us/licensure/

Title of License: LMHC

Educational Requirements: Master's degree in counseling from a CACREP-accredited program (or equivalent), with at least 45 semester hours or 60 quarter hours. Degree must be from an accredited college/university; or hold a current CCMHC credential issues by NBCC.

Experiential Requirements: Minimum of 2 years of full-time, supervised work experience in mental health counseling following all graduate work with 1,000 hours of face-to-face mental health counseling. At least 100 of the 200 hours of required supervision must be individual supervision.

Exam Required: NCE, NCMHCE, or CRCE

KANSAS
KS Behavioral Sciences Regulatory Board
712 S. Kansas Ave.
Topeka, KS 66603
www.ksbsrb.org/

Title of License: LCPC

Educational Requirements: Master's degree in counseling from a CACREP-accredited program (or equivalent), with at least 45 semester hours or 60 quarter hours. Degree must be from an accredited college/university; or hold a current Certified Clinical Mental Health Counselor (CCMHC) credential issues by NBCC.

Experiential Requirements: Minimum of 2 years of full-time supervised work experience in mental health counseling following all graduate work, with 1,000 hours of face-to-face mental health counseling. At least 100 of the 200 hours of required supervision must be individual supervision.

Exam Required: NCE, NCMHCE, or CRCE

KENTUCKY
KY Board of Licensed Professional Counselors
P.O. Box 1360
Frankfort, KY 40602
http://lpc.ky.gov/

Title of License: LPCC
Licensed Professional Counselor Associate (LPCA):
Credential holder who has met all qualifications to engage in the practice of professional counseling under an approved clinical supervisor authorized by the board.

Educational Requirements: At least a master's degree in professional counseling or a related field from a regionally accredited institution with a minimum of 60 semester hours in 9 specified areas and a 400 hour practicum/internship.

Experiential Requirements: No experiential requirements for LPCA.

LPCC: Four thousand hours of post-master's experience under approved supervision, which includes 1,600 hours of direct counseling and 100 hours of individual, face-to-face clinical supervision. Applicants are encouraged to include 10 hours of direct counseling with individuals in a jail or correctional setting as part of the four thousand hours.

Exam Required: NCE

LOUISIANA
LA Department of Licensed Professional Counselors Board of Examiners
8361 Summa Ave.
Baton Rogue, LA 70809
lpcboard@eatel.net
www.lpcboard.org

Title of License: LPC

Note: Interns have 3 months to apply for licensure as an LPC after completing supervised experience.

Educational Requirements: Graduate degree, the substance of which is professional mental health counseling in content, from a regionally accredited institution, with 48 semester hours in specific coursework or completion of a CACREP-accredited counseling program. A supervised mental health counseling practicum and supervised internship of 400 hours.

Experiential Credentials: Three thousand hours to be completed in no less than 2 years and no more than 7 years. Hours to include 1,900–2,900 direct client contact in individual or group counseling. One thousand maximum hours of additional client contact, counseling-related activities, or education at the graduate level in the field of mental health. A minimum of 1,000 hours of face-to-face post-master's supervision by a board-approved supervisor. 500 hours of supervised experience may be gained for each 30 graduate semester hours beyond masters, but must have no less than 2,000 hours of supervised post-master's experience.

Exam Required: NCE

MAINE
ME Department of Professional & Financial Regulation Board of
    Counseling Professionals
35 State House Station
Augusta, ME 04333
Counsel.board@maine.gov
www.state.me.us/pfr/olr/

Title of License: LCPC

    LPC

    Conditional LCPC: A license granted to an applicant for licensure as an LCPC who has met all the requirements except for the supervised clinical experience.

    Conditional LPC: A license granted to an applicant for licensure as an LPC who has met all the requirements except for the supervised clinical experience.

Educational Requirements: LCPC/Conditional LCPC: Graduate program must include a minimum of 60 semester hours, and a practicum and internship consisting of at least 900 clock hours. In lieu of the practicum and internship, an applicant may provide documentation 1,000 hours of supervised clinical counseling. Program must be CACREP-accredited, or include specified coursework.

LPC/Conditional LPC: Master's degree or higher and a total of 60 semester hours of graduate study in counseling from a regionally accredited institution, including an internship consisting of 600 clock hours and a practicum. Program must be CACREP- or CORE-accredited, or include specified coursework.

Experiential Requirements: LCPC: Two years of experience after obtainment of a master's degree or higher, to include 3,000 hours of supervised clinical experience. Hours must include a minimum of 1,500 direct client contact and a minimum of 100 hours of individual supervision with an approved supervisor.

LPC: Two years of experience after obtainment of a master's degree of higher, to include 2,000 hours of supervised experience. Hours must include a minimum of 1,000 hours of direct counseling contact with individuals, couples, family, or groups and a minimum of 67 hours of individual supervision with an approved supervisor.

Exam Required: LCPC: NCMHCE,

    LPC/Conditional LCPC/Conditional LPC: NCE

MARYLAND
MD Department of Health & Mental Hygiene
Board of Professional Counselors and Therapists
4201 Patterson Ave., 3rd floor
Baltimore, MD 21215
www.dhmh.state.md.us/bopc

Title of License: LCPC

    Licensed Graduate Professional Counselor (LGPC): Title used while fulfilling the supervised clinical experience requirement.

Educational Requirements: (Same for both license tiers.)
Master's degree from an accredited educational institution in a professional counseling field with a minimum of 60 graduate credit hours in specific coursework, completion of an alcohol and drug counseling course, and supervised field experience. In addition to a degree, completion of 3 graduate semester hours in Diagnosis and Psychopathology and 3 graduate semester hours in Psychotherapy and Treatment of Mental and Emotional Disorders is required

Doctoral degree with a minimum of 90 graduate credit hours in counseling training approved by the board.

Experiential Requirements: No experiential requirements for LCPC. LGPC: Minimum of 3 years/3,000 hours of supervised clinical experience (2 years/2,000 hours must be post-master's). Fifteen hundred hours must be direct face-to-face client contact and 100 hours minimum of face-to-face clinical supervision. Supervision must be under a board-approved supervisor.

For those with a doctoral degree: Minimum of 2 years (1 year must be postdoctorate board-approved supervised experience). One thousand hours must be direct face-to-face client contact and 50 hours minimum of face-to-face clinical supervision. Supervision must be under a board-approved supervisor.

Exam Required: NCE and MD Professional Counselors and Therapists Act Exam

MASSACHUSETTS
MA Division of Professional Licensure
Board of Allied Mental Health and Human Services Professionals
230 Causeway St., Suite 500
Boston, MA 02114
www.mass.gov/reg/boards/mh

Title of License: LMHC

Educational Requirements: Minimum of 60 graduate credit hours in counseling or a related field from a regionally accredited institution of high education (48 hours are required for pre-7/98 grads). This includes a minimum of 48 semester credit hour master's degree in mental health counseling or a related field, including a practicum (100 hours), and internship (600 hours), and experience in each of the ten content areas as defined by the board; or hold a current Certified Clinical Mental Health Counselor (CCMHC) credential issues by NBCC.

Experiential Requirements: Minimum of 2 years/3,360 hours full-time, post-master's, supervised clinical experience after obtaining 60 graduate credit hours (48 hours for pre-7/98 grads). Hours must include 960 of direct client contact (250 hours may be group client contact), 130 total supervision hours required, 75 hours of which must be individual supervision. Supervision must include

1 hour of supervision for every 16 client contact hours. Note: These hours do not include the premaster's practicum and internship supervision requirements.

Exam Required: NCMHCE

MICHIGAN
MI Bureau of Health Professions
Board of Counseling
P.O. Box 30670
Lansing, MI 48909
www.michigan.gov/bhscr

Title of License: LPC
> Limited Licensed Professional Counselor (LLPC): A limited license is issued to those who have not yet completed the 3000 hour supervised counseling experience; valid for 1 year and may be renewed.

Educational Requirements: (Same for both licenses.)
Master's or doctoral degree in professional counseling, including a minimum of 48 semester hours from a program that reflects the CACREP curriculum. Internship consisting of 600 clock hours is also required.

Experiential Requirements: Minimum of 3,000 hours of post-degree counseling experience in not less than 2-year period to include a minimum 100 hours under immediate physical presence of the supervisor. Supervision must be under an LPC. For persons with 30 semester hours or 45 quarter hours beyond the master's degree, a minimum of 1 year/1,500 hours of postdegree supervised experience. To include a minimum of 50 hours under immediate physical presence of the supervisor. Supervision must be under a LPC.

Exam Required: NCE or CRCE

MINNESOTA
MN Board of Behavioral Health and Therapy
2829 University Ave. SE, Suite 120
Minneapolis, MN 55414
Bbht.board@state.mn.us
www.bbht.state.mn.us

Title of License: LPC

Educational Requirements: Master's degree in counseling that includes a minimum of 48 semester hours and a supervised field experience not fewer that 700 hours that is counseling in nature, from a regional accredited institution of CACREP accredited program. The degree must include specific coursework in 10 areas.

Experiential Requirements: Two thousand hours of postdegree supervised professional practice, or has submitted to the board a plan for supervision during the first 2,200 hours. Supervision must be under an LPC, Licensed Psychologist, or other qualified supervisor as determined by the board.

Exam Required: NCE

MISSISSIPPI
MS State Board of Examiners for Licensed Professional Counselors
419 East Broadway
Yazoo City, MS 39194
www.lpc.state.ms.us

Title of License: LPC

Educational Requirements: Master's degree or educational specialists degree in counselor education or a related program from a regionally or nationally accredited college/university, subject to board approval (60 semester hours or 90 quarter hours of graduate study in specified coursework required); or doctoral degree primarily in counseling, guidance, or related counseling field from a regionally or nationally accredited college/university program, subject to board approval (60 semester hours or 90 quarter hours of graduate study in specific coursework required).

Experiential Requirements: A minimum of 2 years/3,500 hours of supervised experience in a clinical setting. 1,167 hours must be directed counseling. 1,750 hours must be post-master's experience. Minimum of 100 hours of supervision (50 hours may be group supervision). Supervision must be under an LPC or other licensed mental health professional.

Exam Required: NCE

MISSOURI
MO Division of Professional Registration
State Committee for Professional Counselors
3605 Missouri Blvd.
P.O. Box 1335
Jefferson City, MO 65102-1335
profcounselor@pr.mo.gov
http://pr.mo.gov/counselors.asp

Title of License: LPC
            Provisional Licensed Professional Counselor (PLPC)/Counselor In-Training (CIT): CIT issued automatically when supervision is registered and approved and all other criteria are met.

Educational Requirements: At least a master's degree in counseling or another mental health discipline from a regionally accredited college or university, with at least 48 semester hours reflecting the CACREP or CORE curriculum, and a practicum consisting of 6 semester hours of direct counseling services.

Experiential Requirements: No experiential requirements for PLPC/CIT.

LPC: Three thousand hours of post-master's experience (full- or part-time) to be completed within 60 months. Twelve hundred hours must be direct client contact. A minimum of 24 months of continuous supervised experience required (at least 15 hours per week) with 1 hour a week of face-to-face individual supervision (no less than 48 hours per year). May substitute 30 graduate semester hours post-master's study for 1,500 of the 3,000 hours.

For those with doctorate or specialist degrees: a minimum of 1,500 hours (full- or part-time) required, to be completed within 36 months. Six hundred hours must be direct client contact. A minimum of 12 months of continuous supervised counseling experience (at least 15 hours per week). Supervision must be under an LPC, licensed psychologist, or licensed psychiatrist.

Exam Required: NCE

MONTANA
MT Department of Labor and Industry
Board of Social Work Examiners and Professional Counselors
301 S. Park 4th Fl.
P.O. Box 200513
Helena, MT 59620
dlibsdswp@state.mt.us
www.swpc.mt.gov

Title of License: LCPC

Educational Requirements: A 60 semester hours (or 90 quarter hour) counseling-in-nature graduate degree which contains a 6 semester hour advanced counseling practice from an accredited institution; or a minimum of 45 semester hours (or 67.5 quarter hours) counseling-in-nature degree, which contains 6 semester hours advance counseling practice, from an accredited institution, and, upon board approval, applicant must complete remaining hours to equal the total requirement of 60 semester hours.

Experiential Requirements: Three thousand hours of supervised experience, 1,500 hours of which must be direct client contact. Supervision must be under an LPC or licensed allied mental health professional.

Exam Required: NCE or NCMHCE and Montana LCPC Jurisprudence exam (included with application; open book).

NEBRASKA
NE Department of Regulation and Licensure
Board of Mental Health Practice
P.O. Box 94986
Lincoln, NE 68509
www.hhs.state.ne.us/crl/mhcs/mental/mentalhealth.htm

Title of License: Licensed Mental Health Practitioner-Certified Professional
Counselor (LMHP-CPC) or Licensed Professional Counselor
(LPC). This additional appellation is available for LMP's who
have a graduate degree from a CACREP-accredited program
or a program with equivalent coursework.
Licensed Mental Health Practitioner (LMHP): An individual
who is qualified to engage in mental health practice or
offers or renders mental health practice services.
Provisional Licensed Mental Health Practitioner (PLMHP):
Required before completing the 3,000-hour experience
require ment; valid for 5 years.

Educational Requirements: Master's degree from an approved educational
program that is primarily therapeutic mental health in content, in a CACREP-
accredited program (or complete equivalent coursework), from a regionally
accredited institution. Completion of a practicum or internship with a minimum
of 300 clock hours of direct client contact under the supervision of a qualified
supervisor.

Experience Requirements: LMHP, LMHP/CRC-LPC: Three thousand hours of
post-master's supervised experience in mental health practice accumulated during the 5 years immediately preceding application for licensure. Must include
a minimum of 1 hour per week of face-to-face supervision with a qualified
supervisor. Hours to include 1,500 hours of direct client contact (not more that
1,500 hours of nondirect service)

Exam Required: NCE of NCMHCE

NEVADA
The Board of Examiners for Marriage and Family Therapists and Clinical
Professional Counselors
P.O. Box 370130
Las Vegas, NV 89134-0130
nvmftb@mftbd.nv.gov
http://www.marriage.state.nv.us/

Title of License: Licensed Clinical Professional Counselor (LCPC)
Licensed Clinical Counselor Intern (LCCI)

Educational Requirements: (Same for both licenses.)
Forty-eight semester hours or 72 quarter hours master's degree in counseling or a related field from an accredited institution.

Experiential Requirements: No experiential requirements for LCCI. LCPC: Twelve hundred clock hours. Five hundred hours direct client contact. Not to exceed three hundred group counseling hours.

LCCI: At least three hundred hours supervised by an LCPC or other board approved supervisor.

Exam Required: The National Marital and Family Therapy Examination (NMFTE)

NEW HAMPSHIRE
NH Board of Mental Health Practice
49 Donovan St.
Concord, NH 03301
mylnch@dhhs.state.nh.us
www.state.nh.us/mhpb

Title of License: LCMHC

Educational Requirements: Master's degree in counseling or psychology from a regionally accredited college/university, which consists of a minimum of 2 academic years of full-time graduate study related to mental health counseling and 60 graduate semester hours (program must meet board's approval).

Experiential Requirements: Two years of paid post-master's experience in a mental health setting that includes 3,000 hours of supervised clinical work in no less than 2 years and no more than 5 years. Each year shall not be less than 1,500 clock hours. One hundred hours of face-to-face supervision, provided by a state-licensed, board-approved, mental health professional is required.

Exam Required: NCMHCE

NEW JERSEY
NJ Board of Marriage & Family Therapy Examiners, Professional Counselor
   Examiners Committee
P.O. Box 45007
Newark, NJ 07101
www.state.nj.us/lps/ca/medical/familytherapy.htm

Title of Credential: LPC
                    Licensed Associate Counselor (LAC): An individual who
                       is practicing counseling under the direct supervision
                       of an LPC or a supervisor acceptable to the board.
                       The supervisor must have passed the NCE.

Educational Requirements: Minimum of 60 graduate semester hours, which includes a master's degree in counseling or a related field from a regionally accredited institution. (45 of 60 hours are to be from eight areas defined by the board)

Experiential Requirements: LPC: Three years/4,500 hours full-time supervised counseling experience in a professional counseling setting, 1 year of which may be obtained prior to the granting of the master's degree. One year/1,500 hours of the experience may be eliminated by substituting 30 graduate semester hours beyond the master's degree. In no case may an applicant have less than 1 year of post-master's supervised work experience.

LAC: No experiential requirements.

Exam Required: NCE

NEW MEXICO
NM Counseling and Therapy Practice Board
2550 Cerrillos Rd.
Santa Fe, NM 87505
counselingboard@state.nm.us
http://www.rld.state.nm.us/counseling/

Title of License: LPCC
                   LPC
                   LMHC: Individuals who are pursuing either the LPC or the LPCC license but still need to complete the supervised experience requirement.

Educational Requirements: LPCC: Master's degree in counseling or a related field from a regionally accredited institution that includes 60 graduate hours with at least 48 graduate hours in the mental health clinical core curriculum.

LPC: Master's or doctoral degree in counseling from a regionally accredited institution; or master's degree in a related field that includes a minimum of 33 semester hours and a 12 semester hour practicum totaling 42 hours in the mental health core curriculum from a regionally accredited institution.

Experiential Requirements: LPCC: Two years/3,000 hours of postgraduate clinical counseling, with a minimum of 100 hours of face-to-face supervision. Supervision must come from an LPCC or other licensed mental health professional. One thousand hours of clinical client contact may come from the applicant's internship/practicum.

LPC: One thousand hours of postgraduate supervised counseling experience, with a minimum of 100 hours of supervision.

Exam Required: LPCC: NCE, and NCMHCE

LPC: NCE

NEW YORK
NY State Education Department
State Board for Mental Health Practitioners
89 Washington Ave.
Albany, NY 12234-1000
mhpbd@mail.nysed.gov
www.op.nysed.gov/mhp.htm

Title of License: LMHC; Limited Permit: Applicants who have met requirements except experience and/or exam may apply for a 2-year permit to practice under supervision.

Educational Requirements: Master's degree in counseling that includes 60 semester hours and completion of specific coursework. (Note: Prior to January 1, 2010, 48 credit hours were required). Completion of a 1-year/600 clock hours of supervised internship or practicum in mental health counseling. Completion of coursework or training approved by the education department in the identification and reporting of child abuse.

Experiential Requirements: Completion of a minimum of 3,000 hours of post-master's supervised experience relevant to the practice of mental health counseling.

Exam Required: NCMHCE

NORTH CAROLINA
NC Board of Licensed Professional Counselors
P.O. Box 1369
Garner, NC 27529
ncblpc@mgmt4u.com
www.ncblpc.org

Title of License: LPC

Educational Requirements: Master's degree in counseling from a regionally accredited institution of higher education that includes 48 semester hours and a 300-hour practicum/internship; or a graduate degree in a related field supplemented with coursework the board determines to be equivalent.

Experimental Requirements: No less than 2 years of master's or post-master's counseling experience, or both, in a professional setting that includes a minimum of 2,000 hours of supervised professional practice, of which 100 hours must be face-to-face supervision by a board-approved supervisor.

Exam Required: NCE, ECCP, or CRCE

NORTH DAKOTA
ND Board of Counselor Examiners
2112 10th Ave. SE
Mandan, ND 58554
ndbce@btinet.net
http://www.ndbce.org/

Title of License: LPCC
> LPC: Full professional license after LAPC criteria are met and supervised experience has been completed.
> Licensed Associate Professional Counselor (LAPC): A 2-year license, which allows for completion of the supervised experience. A 2-year plan of supervision and passage of the NCE required.

Educational Requirements: LPCC: Master's degree in counseling, including 60 semester hours. A minimum of 15 contact hours in 3 coursework categories determined by the board must be included. Eight hundred hours of clinical training in supervised practicum and internship.

LPC/LAPC: Forty eight graduate semester hours in counseling or closely related field from an accredited college or university, including specific core counseling coursework within the master's degree.

Experiential Requirements: LPCC: Must hold the first level LPC credential. Two years/3,000 hours of supervision by an LPCC in a clinical setting. Experience to include 100 hours of face-to-face supervision (60 hours must be individual, face-to-face supervision) by a board-approved supervisor.

LPC: Four hundred hours of client contact during the 2-year LAPC supervisory period. Experience to include 100 hours of direct supervision (60 hours must be individual, face-to-face supervision) by a board-approved supervisor.

Exam Required: LPCC: NCMHCE and a videotaped clinical counseling session of at least 30 minutes.
LPC/LAPC: NCE

OHIO
OH Counselor, Social Worker, and Marriage & Family Therapist Board
77 S. High St., 16th Fl.
Columbus, OH 43215
Cswmft.info@cswb.state.oh.us
http://www.cswmft.ohio.gov

Title of License: Licensed Professional Clinical Counselor (LPCC)
>   LPC: Professional Counselor/Clinical Resident: Title used
>   while completing the 3,000 hours of supervised experience
>   required for the LPCC license.
>   Registered Counselor Trainee: Title used while enrolled in a
>   practicum or internship.

Educational Requirements: At least a master's degree in counseling, with 60 semester or 90 quarter hours, from an accredited institution. Ours must be in clinical content areas and course content must be similar to CACREP- or CORE-accredited programs. One hundred-hour practicum and 600-hour internship.

Experiential Requirements: LPCC: Must already possess the 1st level Professional Counselor (PC) credential. Two years/3,000 hours of post-master's clinical experience under the supervision of a PCC holding the supervision credential. The supervision must include the diagnosis and treatment of mental and emotional disorders 50% of the time.

LPC: No experiential requirements for LPC, PC/CR/RCT.

Exam Required: LPCC: NCMHCE
>   LPC: NCE

OKLAHOMA
Division of Professional Counselor Licensing
1000 N.E. 10th St.
Oklahoma City, OK 73117
nenaw@health.state.ok.us
http://www.ok.gov/health/Protective_Health/ Professional_Counselor_
   Licensing_Division/

Title of License: LPC
>   Licensed Professional Counselor Candidate: A person
>   whose application for licensure has been accepted and is
>   completing the supervised experience requirement.

Educational Requirements: Master's degree in counseling or a related mental health field with 60 semester hours (90 quarter hours) from a regionally accredited college or university. Coursework in 10 areas and a practicum required. The board will define what qualifies as counseling related.

Experiential Requirements: LPC: Three years/3,000 hours full-time post-application experience supervised by an approved LPC supervisor. For each 1,000 hours, 350 hours must be direct face-to-face contact. Face-to-face supervision must be 45 minutes for every 20 hours of supervision. Up to 2 years of required experience may be gained at a rate of 1 year for each 30 graduate semester hours beyond the master's degree. The applicant shall have no less than 1 year of supervised–time experience in counseling.

Licensed Professional Counselor Candidate: Note: No experiential requirements for LPCC. The LPCC is applied for after completion of a master's degree.

Exam Required: NCE and Oklahoma Legal & Ethical Responsibilities Exam

OREGON
OR Board of Licensed Professional Counselors and Therapists
3218 Pringle Rd., SE
Salem, OR 97301-6312
Lpc.lmft@state.or.us
www.oblpct.state.or.us

Title of License: LPC

Registered Intern: An applicant registered to obtain postdegree supervised work experience toward licensure.

Educational Requirements: Graduate degree, with 48 semester hours in a CACREP-accredited program or the equivalent from a regionally accredited institution. An internship/practicum consisting of 600 clock hours.

Experiential Requirements: Three years full-time supervised experience to include 2,400 client contact hours and 120 hours of supervision (60 of which must be individual supervision by an approved supervisor). Eight hundred client contact hours may be obtained during the clinical portion of the qualifying degree program.

Exam: NCE, CRCE, NCMHCE, or other exam as approved by the board and Oregon Law and Rules (open book).

PENNSYLVANIA
PA Bureau of Professional & Occupational Affairs
P.O. Box 2649
Harrisburg, PA 17105-2649
stsocialwork@state.pa.us
www.dos.state.pa.us/bpoa

Title of License: LPC

Educational Requirements: Master's degree in counseling or a closely related field (as approved by the board) from an accredited institution, including 60 semester hours or 90 quarter hours of graduate coursework (includes coursework in 9 core areas and a supervised practicum and internship).

Experiential Requirements: Three years/3,600 hours of supervised clinical experience after completing 48 graduate level credit hours. An applicant holding a doctoral degree in counseling: 2 years/2,400 hours of supervised clinical experience is required, 1 year/1,200 hours of which must be obtained postdegree.

Exam Required: Any one of the following: NCE, CRCE, ATCB, CBMT, PEPK, AAODA, EMAC

PUERTO RICO
PR Office of Regulation of Certification of Health Professions
Board of Examiners of Professional Counselors
P.O. Box 10200
San Juan, PR 00908
www.salud.gov.pr

Title of License: Professional Counselor (PC)
> Professional Counselor with Provisional License (PCPL):
> Person who is granted a temporary/provisional
> authorization by the board; valid for 3 years.
> Certified Mentor (CM): A licensed PC who has been certified by
> the board to supervise those who wish to obtain licensure.

Educational Requirements: Master's degree in counseling from an institution accredited by the Council of Higher Education of Puerto Rico. Specific coursework required in 8 out of 10 areas.

Experiential Requirements: Completion of a minimum of 500 hours of practice supervised by a CM. Upon approval of the exam required, the board shall issue a provisional license.

Exam Required: NCE

RHODE ISLAND
RI Department of Mental Health Counselors and Marriage & Family Therapists
3 Capitol Hill, Rm. 410
Providence, RI 02908
www.health.ri.gov/hsr/

Title of License: Certified Counselor in Mental Health

Educational Requirements: Hold a current Certified Clinical Mental Health Counselor (CCMHC) credential issues by NBCC; graduate degree specializing in counseling or therapy from a college/university accredited by the New England Association of Schools & Colleges or an equivalent regional accrediting agency; or master's degree or certificate in advanced graduate studies or a doctoral degree in mental health counseling or allied field from a recognized educational institution.

For all options: Completion of 60 semester hours (90 quarter hours) within the graduate counseling/therapy program and a minimum of 12 semester hours of a supervised practicum and 1 calendar year of a supervised internship consisting of 20 hours per week in counseling.

Experiential Requirements: Two years/2,000 hours of direct client contact post-master's experience and 100 hours of post-master's supervised casework spread over a 2-year period. Supervision must be under a board-approved supervisor.

Exam Required: NCMHCE

SOUTH CAROLINA
SC Department of Labor, Licensing and Regulation, Board of Examiners for the
 Licensure of Professional Counselors, Marriage & Family Therapists, and
 Psychoeducational Specialists
P.O. Box 11329
Columbia, SC 29211-1329
www.llr.state.sc.us/pol/counselors

Title of License: LPC
            Professional Counselor Intern (PCI): An applicant who has
            met the education and exam requirements, but not the
            2-year supervised experience requirements.

Educational Requirements: Master's degree in professional counseling or a
related discipline from a regionally accredited institution that includes at least
48 graduate hours. Completion of specified coursework in 10 specific academic
areas. One hundred and fifty hours of supervised counseling practicum.

Experiential Requirements: Two years full-time, post-master's experience with
2,000 hours of direct client contact. One hundred and fifty hours of clinical supervision provided be a board-approved LPC supervisor, 100 hours must be individual supervision. Must already possess the 1st-level Professional Counselor
Intern (PCI) credential. (PCI does not require supervision.)

Exam Required: NCE or NCMHCE

SOUTH DAKOTA
SD Department of Commerce & Regulations
Board of Counselor Examiners
P.O. Box 1822
Sioux Falls, SD 57101
Sdbce.msp@midconetwork.com
http://www.state.sd.us/dhs/boards/counselor

Title of License: Licensed Professional Counselor-Mental Health (LPC-MH)
            LPC

Educational Requirements: Graduation from a CACREP-accredited program
with an emphasis in mental health counseling (48 semester hours required for
LPC licensure; 60 semester hours or completion of all required coursework for
LPC-MH licensure); or master's degree in counseling or related program with
completion of specific coursework and a supervised 100 hour practicum and a
600 hour internship from an accredited college/university (48 semester hours
required for LPC licensure; 60 semester credits or completion of all required
coursework for LPC-MH licensure).

Experiential Requirements: LPC-MH: Must already possess the 1st-level LPC
credential. Two years post-master's direct client contact hours; 1,000 hours of

post-master's direct client contact earned under the LPC credential may be counted toward the 2,000 hour requirement.

LPC: Two thousand hours of full-time, post-master's supervised experience in counseling, with 800 hours of direct client contact and 100 hours of face-to-face supervision.

Exam Required: LPC-MH: NCMHCE
         LPC: NCE

TENNESSEE
TN Division of Regulatory Boards
Board of Professional Counselors and Marital & Family Therapists
Cordell Hull Blvd., 1st floor
425 5th Ave. North
Nashville, TN 37247-1010
http://health.state.tn.us/boards/pc mft&cpt/

Title of License: Licensed Professional Counselor-Mental Health Service
         Provider (LPC/MHSP)
         LPC

Educational Requirements: LPC/MHSP: In addition to, or as part of the graduate-degree completion of 9 graduate semester hours of coursework related to diagnosis, treatment, appraisal, and assessment of mental disorders.

LPC: Sixty graduate semester hours in professional counseling or a related field from an institution accredited by the Southern Association of Colleges & Schools or CACREP which includes a master's degree in professional counseling and a supervised 500 hour practicum or internship, 300 hours of which must be completed in a clinical setting.

Experiential Requirements: Two years post-master's inexperience, including 1,000 hours of direct clinical experience (not less than 10 hours per week) and 50 hours of supervision as defined by the board.

Exam Required: LPC/MHSP: NCMHCE, NCE, and TN Jurisprudence Exam all required.

LPC: NCE and TN Jurisprudence Exam concerning TN Professional Counselors Statutes and Regulations (administered by NBCC).

TEXAS
TX Board of Examiners of Professional Counselors
1100 W. 49th St.
Austin, TX 78756
lpc@dshs.state.tx.us
www.dshs.state.tx.us/plc

Title of License: LPC
> Licensed Professional Counselor Intern (LPC-I): An applicant practicing under supervision; valid for 30 months.

Educational Requirements: Graduate degree from an accredited college/university in professional counseling or a related field consisting of 48 graduate semester hours. Completion of a 300-clock-hour practicum with at least 100 hours of direct client counseling.

Experiential Requirements: Thirty six months/3,000 hours of post-master's supervised experience, including 1,500 hours of face-to-face client time. Supervision must be provided by a board-approved professional counselor.

Exam Required: NCE and Texas Jurisprudence Exam

UTAH
UT Division of Occupational and Professional Licensing–Professional Counseling
P.O. Box 146741
Salt Lake City, UT 84114-6741
http://dopl.utah.gov/licensing/professional counseling.html

Title of License: LPC
> Certified Professional Counselor Intern: Credential required before starting the supervised experience requirement; valid for 3 years.

Educational Requirements: A master's or doctoral degree in mental health counseling from a CACREP-accredited program, including a minimum of 60 graduate semester hours of specific coursework. A minimum of 3 semester hours or 4.5 quarter hours of a practicum. A minimum of 6 semester hours or 9 quarter hours of an internship.

Experiential Requirements: Four thousand hours of post-master's supervised counseling experience, to be completed in no less than 2 years and no more than 4 years. One thousand hours must be in mental health therapy. One hundred hours face-to-face supervision required.

Exam Required: NCE, NCMHCE and the Utah Professional Counselor Law, Rules, and Ethics Exam.

VERMONT
VT Office of Professional Regulation
Board of Allied Mental Health Practitioners
Redstone Blvd.
26 Terrace St., Drawer 09
Montpelier, VT 05609-1106
clafaillc@sec.state.vt.us
http://vtprofessionals.org

Title of License: LCMHC

Educational Requirements: Master's degree or higher in counseling (minimum of 60 semester hours) from an accredited institution that includes a supervised practicum, internship, or field experience.

Experiential Requirements: Two years of post-master's experience including 3,000 hours of practice in mental health counseling and a minimum of 100 hours of face-to-face supervision. Supervision must be under a board-approved Licensed Mental Health Professional.

Exam Required: NCE and NCMHCE

VIRGINIA
VA Department of Health Professions
VA Board of Counseling
6603 W. Broad St., 5th fl.
Richmond, VA 23230
coun@dhp.virginia.gov
www.dhp.state.va.us/counseling

Title of License: LPC

Educational Requirements: Sixty semester hours or 90 quarter hours of graduate study in counseling, to include a graduate degree in counseling or a related field, from a CACREP or CORE curriculum. Completion of a supervised internship consisting of at least 600 hours.

Experiential Requirements: Four thousand hours of postgraduate supervised experience, of which 2,000 hours must be face-to-face client contact, with 200 hours of face-to-face supervision required (100 hours may be group counseling). Fifty percent of the 4,000 hours may be provided by a licensed mental health provider, whereas the remainder must come from an LPC. Graduate level internship hours may count toward the 4,000 hours depending on the program. Post-master's externship may count for up to 2,000 hours of required experience.

Exam Required: NCMHCE

WASHINGTON
WA Department of Health, Division of Health Profession Quality Assurance
Mental Health Counselor Program
P.O. Box 47865
Olympia, WA 98504-7865
Hqpa.csc@doh.wa.gov
http://www.doh.wa.gov/hsqa/Professions/MentalHealth/default.htm

Title of License: LMHC

> Registered Counselor (RC): Any individual may advertise
> themselves as a "Registered Counselor" after filling out
> the appropriate paperwork and completing a 4-hour HIV/
> AIDS training course. No minimum education, experience,
> or examination passage is required. Registered Counselors
> may practice independently and be paid directly by clients,
> but they cannot bill third-party health insurance.

Educational Requirements: Master's or doctorate degree in mental health counseling or related field from a regionally accredited college or university; a supervised counseling practicum or internship; 4 hours of HIV/AIDS education and training; or hold the National Board for Certified Counselors (NBCC) credential or the Certified Clinical Mental Health Counselor (CCMHC) credential.

Experiential Requirements: Three years of full-time counseling; or 3,000 hours postgraduate supervised experience, including 1,200 hours of direct client contact and 100 hours of immediate supervision by a board approved supervisor.

Exam Required: NCE or NCMHCE

WEST VIRGINIA
WV Board of Examiners in Counseling
P.O. Box 129
Ona, WV 25545
counselingboard@msn.com
www.wvbec.org

Title of License: LPC

Educational Requirements: Master's or doctorate degree from an accredited counseling program (CACREP or other accrediting body), or a closely related field as determined by the board.

Experiential Requirements: Two years/2,400 hours of professional supervised experience. One year must be postgraduate experience. A board-approved professional must provide supervision.

Exam Required: NCE or CRCE

WISCONSIN
WI Department of Regulation & Licensing Examining Board of Marriage &
Family Therapists, Social Workers, and Professional Counselors
P.O. Box 8935
Madison, WI 53708
http://www.drl.state.wi.us/profession.asp?profid=43&locid=0

Title of License: LPC

> Professional Counselor Trainee (PCT): An applicant who has completed all requirements for licensure except the supervised experience; valid for 24 months.

Note: LPCs are only allowed to practice psychotherapy in areas where they are qualified by education, training, and experience. Qualifications for practicing psychotherapy include passage of the NCMHCE, 180 contact hours of post-graduate training in psychotherapy modalities, and an affidavit by a supervisor qualified to practice psychotherapy that the experience requirements were met and client contact included DSM diagnosis and treatment.

Educational Requirements: Master's degree in counseling or equivalent program approved by the board, including a minimum of 42 semester hours.

Experiential Requirements: A minimum of 3,000 hours of post-master's supervised experience, including 1,000 hours of face-to-face client contact in not less than 2 years. Supervision must include 1 hour per week of face-to-face supervision and must be provided by a board-approved mental health professional.

Exam Required: NCE or CRCE and Wisconsin Jurisprudence Exam (open book).

WYOMING

WY Mental Health Professions Licensing Board
2020 Carey Ave., Suite 201
Cheyenne, WY 82002
vskora@state.wy.us
http://plboards.state.wy.us/mentalhealth/index.asp

Title of License: LPC

> Provisional Licensed Professional Counselor (PLPC): An applicant who has received a master's degree, but has not passed the NCE or completed the supervised experience requirement; valid for 36 months.

Educational Requirements: Master's degree (48 semester hours or 72 quarter hours) in counseling from a CACREP- or CORE-accredited program or a regionally accredited college or university.

Experiential Requirements: Three thousand hours (1,500 must be post-master's) supervised clinical experience, including 100 hours of face-to-face supervision. Supervision must be provided by a licensed mental health professional.

Exam Required: NCE

*Acronyms in the list of state licensure requirements refer to the following:

CACREP   Council for the Accreditation of Counseling and Related Educational Programs (an organizational affiliate organization of ACA that provides professional counselor-training accreditation)

CCMHC   Certified Clinical Mental Health Counselor (an NBCC professional counseling specialty title; not a required credential)

CORE   Council on Rehabilitation Education (an independent rehabilitation counselor-training accreditation board)

CRC   Certified Rehabilitation Counselor (a CRCC professional counseling specialty title; not a required credential)

CRCC   Commission on Rehabilitation Counselor Certification (an independent, nongovernmental rehabilitation counselor-credentialing board)

CRCE   Certified Rehabilitation Counselor Examination (administered by CRCC for the certification of rehabilitation counselors; also administered by some states for their own licensure process as an alternative to their clinically oriented exam)

NBCC   National Board for Certified Counselors (an independent, nongovernmental professional counselor-credentialing board and an organizational affiliate of ACA)

NCMHCE   National Clinical Mental Health Counselor Examination (administered by NBCC for the certification of mental health counselors; also administered by some states for their own licensure process)

**Exam acronyms listed because of a number of different examinations:

AAODA   Advanced Alcohol and Other Drug Abuse Counselor Examination (administered by the International Certification and Reciprocity Consortium/Alcohol and Other Drug Abuse, Inc.)

ATCB   Art Therapy Credentials Board Certification Examination

CRCE   Certified Rehabilitation Counselor Examination

CBMT   Certification Board for Music Therapists Examination

EMAC   Examination for Master Addiction Counselors (administered by NBCC)

NCE   National Counselor Examination

PEPK   Practice Examination of Psychological Knowledge (administered by the North American Association of Master in Psychology)

Practicum and Internship Contract

Old State University
Mental Health Counseling Program
Practicum and Internship Contract

This agreement is made on _____ by and between _____

                          (Date)   (Practicum/Internship Site)

and the Old State University Mental Health Counseling Program. The agreement will be effective for a period from:

_____ to _____ for 100/300* semester clock hours for _____

                                                                      (Name of Student)

Purpose

The purpose of this agreement is to provide a qualified graduate student with a practicum/internship experience in the field of counseling.

The University Program agrees:

To assign a university faculty liaison to facilitate communication between university and site;

To provide weekly classroom supervision and instruction for the practicum/internship student through EDU 679, EDU 685/686/687;

---

* Practicum requires a minimum of 100 clock hours. Internship requires 300 clock hours. For practicum, 40 of the 100 hours must be direct contact hours. For internship students, 120 of the 300 hours must be in direct service. Direct service is defined as: individual, group, couples or family counseling, cocounseling, clinical intakes, phone crisis counseling, team counseling and observation through a two-way mirror, running psychoeducational groups, and so forth.

To provide to the site, prior to placement of the student, the following information: profile of the student named above and an academic calendar that shall include dates for periods during which student will be excused from field supervision;

To notify the student that he or she must adhere to the administrative policies, rules, standards, schedules, and practices of the site;

That the faculty liaison shall be available for consultation with both site supervisors and students and shall be immediately contacted should any problem or change in relation to student, site, or university occur; and;

That the university supervisor (or practicum/internship instructor) is responsible for the assignment of a fieldwork grade. Grades are the S/U type.

The Practicum/Internship Site agrees:

To assign a practicum/internship supervisor who has appropriate credentials, time, and interest for training the practicum/internship student;

The clinical site must provide weekly supervision for 1 hour per week;

To provide opportunities for the student to engage in a variety of counseling activities under supervision and for evaluating the student's performance (suggested counseling experience included in the "Practicum/Internship Activities" section);

To provide the student with adequate work space, telephone, office supplies, and staff to conduct professional activities;

To provide supervisory contact that involves some examination of student work using audiovisual tapes, observation, and/or live supervision;

To provide written evaluation of student based on criteria established by the university program; and

To not involve students in any form of billing for professional services.

Within the specified time frame, _____ will be the primary on-site practicum/internship site supervisor. The training activities (checked below) will be provided for the student in sufficient amounts to allow an adequate evaluation of the student's level of competence in each activity.

_____ will be the faculty liaison/supervisor with whom the student and practicum/internship site supervisor will communicate regarding progress, problems, performance evaluations, and grading.

Practicum/Internship Activities

This list below is a list of possible clinical activities for the practicum/internship student. It is not necessary that field sites have the student counselor complete all or even most of these. Check all areas that seem to apply. Additional areas of responsibility may be added in the future.

1. **Individual Counseling/Psychotherapy**   _____
   Personal/Social Nature   _____
   Occupational/Educational Nature   _____

2. **Group Counseling/Psychotherapy**   _____
   Coleading   _____
   Leading   _____

3. **Intake Interviewing**   _____

4. **Couples or Family Counseling**   _____
   Leading   _____
   Coleading   _____

5. **Testing and Assessment**   _____
   Administration & Interpretation   _____

6. **Report Writing**   _____
   Record Keeping   _____
   Treatment Plans   _____

7. **Consultation**   _____
   Referrals   _____
   Team Consultation & Case Staffing   _____

8. **Community/Psychoeducational Activities**   _____
   Family Conferences   _____
   Community/Campus Outreach   _____
   In-Service Presentations   _____

9. **Career Counseling**   _____

10. **Other (please specify):**
    _____
    _____
    _____

Type of supervision student will receive: Individual _____   Group _____
(Needs formal 1 hour of supervision per week)

Clinical Site Supervisor: _____   Date _____

Student: _____   Date _____

Faculty Liaison: _____   Date _____

Field Supervision:

As per the Council for Accreditation of Counseling and Related Educational Programs' (CACREP) guidelines, on-site supervisors must hold a minimum of a master's degree earned in counseling or a closely related field. Closely related fields include Clinical Social Work, Counseling or Clinical Psychology, Marriage & Family Therapy, Psychiatric Nursing, and Psychiatry. On-site supervisors must have a minimum of 2-year post-master's degree experience and must be licensed in their field (LMHC, LCSW, LP, etc.)

On-site supervisors also provide individual or group supervision for 1 hour each week the practicum/internship student accrues hours. The on-site supervisor submits a written evaluation of the student's performance at the end of each semester (see Student Evaluation form in this manual). On-site supervisors also sign off on student's time logs.

Evaluation of Student Practicum/Intern's Performance:

At the conclusion of each semester, the field supervisor will complete an evaluation of the student practicum/internship student. The evaluation form can be copied from the NU MHC manual. The site supervisor should return the evaluation to:

Coordinator, Mental Health Counseling Program
College of Education
Old State University, NY 14190
712-285-8327
ssegdoh@oldstate.edu

Concerns regarding the student intern:

The Site Supervisor:

If the field supervisor has concerns regarding the student's abilities to meet the goals and objectives of the agency, the supervisor has the following options:

The field supervisor apprises the university supervisor of the concern.

The field supervisor discusses the concern with the student.

If resolution does not occur, the field supervisor should notify the university supervisor.

The university supervisor will schedule an appointment with the field supervisor and the student to facilitate the resolution.

If no resolution occurs, the field supervisor may terminate the placement.

For the student, in the event the placement is terminated, the student must find another placement and repeat the practicum or internship.

The University Supervisor:

If the university supervisor has a concern regarding the student's performance:

The university supervisor will inform the student that the field supervisor will be notified.

The university supervisor will seek feedback regarding the student's performance at the site.

If the concern cannot be resolved, the university supervisor will decide if the student will be placed in another setting.

If the student will receive an unsatisfactory grade he or she will inform the student and the field supervisor that the student will need to repeat the class.

If the student does not pass the classroom or the on-site portion of the practicum/internship, the student will need to repeat the class.

Because of the nature of student practicum/internships, either the clinical site or the counseling program reserve the right to dissolve this contract should concerns arise.

Note: The agency hosting the placement, the graduate program representative, and the practicum/internship student should all keep a copy of this agreement.

References

American Academy of Experts in Traumatic Stress. (2010). *Identifying students "at-risk" for violent behavior: A checklist of "early warning signs."* Retrieved May 12, 2010, from http://www.aaets.org/article108.htm

American Counseling Association. (2005). *ACA code of ethics.* Alexandria, VA: American Counseling Association.

American Counseling Association. (2010). *Licensure requirements for professional counselors.* Alexandria, VA: American Counseling Association.

American Institute of Stress. (2010). *Effects of stress.* Retrieved June 15, 2010, from http://www.stress.org/ topics-effects.htm.

American Psychiatric Association. (2000). *The Diagnostic and statistical manual of mental disorders* (text revision). Washington, DC: American Psychiatric Association. Author.

American School Counselor Association. (2003). *Position statement: Child abuse/neglect prevention: The professional school counselor and child abuse and neglect prevention.* Retrieved May 16, 2010, from http://asca2.timberlakepublishing.com//files/PS_ChildAbuse.pdf.

Anderson, J. R., & Barret, R. L. (Eds.). (2001). *Ethics in HIV-related psychotherapy: Clinical decision making in complex cases.* Washington, DC: American Psychological Association.

Appelbaum, P. S. (1985). Tarasoff and the clinician: Problems in fulfilling the duty to protect. *American Journal of Psychiatry, 142*(4), 425–429.

Arredondo, P., Toporek, M. S., Brown, S., Jones, J., Locke, D. C., Sanchez, J., et al. (1996). *Operationalization of the multicultural counseling competencies.* Alexandria, VA: Association of Multicultural Counseling and Development.

Association for Specialists in Group Work. (1998). *Principles for diversity-competent group workers.* Alexandria, VA: Author.

Baird, B. N. (2005). *The internship, practicum, and field placement handbook: A guide for the helping professions* (4th ed.). Upper Saddle River, NJ: Pearson/Prentice Hall.

Baird, B. N., Carey, A., & Giakovmis, H. (1992). *Personal experience in psychotherapy: Differences in therapists' cognitions.* Paper presented at the Western Psychological Association, Portland, OR.

Baird, K. A., & Rupert, P. A. (1987). Clinical management of confidentiality: A survey of psychologists in seven states. *Professional Psychology: Research and Practice, 18,* 347–352.

Beck, A. T., Steer, R. A., & Brown, G. K. (1996). *Manual for Beck Depression Inventory-II.* San Antonio, TX: The Psychological Corporation.

Beck, A. T., & Weishaar, M. (2008). Cognitive therapy. In R. J. Corsini & D. Wedding (Eds.), *Current psychotherapies,* (8th ed., pp. 263–294). Belmont, CA: Thomson Brooks/Cole.

Beck, A. T., Wright, F. D., Newman, C. F., & Liese, B. S. (1992). *Cognitive therapy of substance abuse.* New York: Guilford.

Benjamin, A. (1987). *The helping interview.* Boston: Houghton-Mifflin.

Benshoff, J. M. (1993). Peer supervision in counselor training. *Clinical Supervisor, 11,* 89–102.

Blanchard, K., Edington, D. W., & Blanchard, M. (1986). *The one minute manager gets fit.* New York: Quill.

Bolles, R. N. (2009). *What color is your parachute?: A practical manual for job-hunters and career-changers.* Berkeley, CA: Ten Speed Press.

Borders, L. D. (1991). A systematic approach to peer group supervision. *Journal of Counseling & Development, 69,* 248–252.

Borum, R., Bartel, P. A., & Forth, A. (2002). *SAVRY: Structured assessment of violence risk in youth.* Lutz, FL: Psychological Assessment Resources.

Borys, D. S. (1988). *Dual relationships between therapist and client: A national survey of clinicians' attitudes and practices.* Unpublished doctoral dissertation, University of California Los Angeles.

Boylan, J. C., & Scott, J. (2009). *Practicum and internship: Textbook and resource guide for counseling and psychotherapy*, (4th ed.). New York: Routledge.

Bradley, R. W., & Cox, J. A. (2001). Counseling: Evolution of the profession. In D. C. Locke, J. E. Myers, & E. L. Herr (Eds.), *The handbook of counseling* (pp. 27–41). Thousand Oaks, CA: Sage.

Bureau of Labor Statistics. (2010). *The occupational outlook handbook* (2010–2011 ed.). Washington DC: Department of Labor.

Bureau of Labor Statistics. (n.d.). *The occupational outlook handbook* (2010–2011 ed.). Washington DC: Department of Labor.

Cameron, S., & turtle-song, i. (2002). Learning to write case notes using the SOAP format. *Journal of Counseling & Development, 80*, 286–292.

Capacchione, L. (2000). *Visioning: Ten steps to designing the life of your dreams*. New York: Tarcher/Putnam.

Captain, C. (2006). Is your patient a suicide risk? *Nursing, 36*(8), 43–47.

Capuzzi, D. (2009). *Suicide prevention in the schools: Guidelines for middle and high school settings* (2nd ed.). Alexandria, VA: American Counseling Association.

Capuzzi, D., & Gross, D. R. (2008). *Youth at risk: A prevention resource for counselors, teachers, and parents* (5th ed.). Alexandria, VA: American Counseling Association.

Cashwell, C. S. (2010, May). Maturation of a profession, in CACREP perspective of *Counseling Today, 52/11*, 58.

Conte, H. R., & Karasu, T. B. (1990). Malpractice in psychotherapy: An overview. *American Journal of Psychotherapy, 44*, 232–246.

Corey, G. (2009). *Theory and practice of counseling and psychotherapy* (8th ed.). Belmont, CA: Thomson Brooks/Cole.

Corey, G., Corey, M., & Callanan, P. (2007). *Issues and ethics in the helping professions* (7th ed.). Pacific Grove, CA: Brooks/Cole.

Cormier, L. S., & Cormier, W. H. (1998). *Fundamental skills and cognitive behavioral interventions* (4th ed.). Pacific Grove, CA: Brooks/Cole.

Cormier, L. S., & Hackney, H. (2008). *Counseling strategies and interventions* (7th ed.). Boston: Pearson/Allyn & Bacon.

Cormier, S., & Cormier, B. (1998). *Interviewing strategies for helpers: Fundamental skills and cognitive behavioral interventions* (4th ed.). Pacific Grove, CA: Brooks/Cole.

Cottone, R. R., & Tarvydas, V. M. (2003). *Ethical and professional issues in counseling* (2nd ed.). Upper Saddle River, NJ: Merrill/Prentice Hall.

Council for Accreditation of Counseling and Related Educational Programs. (2008). *CACREP guidelines*. Alexandria, VA: Counseling on the Accreditation of Counseling and Related Educational Programs.

Council for Accreditation of Counseling and Related Educational Programs. (2009). CACREP accreditation standards. Retrieved from www.cacrep.org/2009standards.html

Covey, S. R. (1996). *The seven habits of highly effective people*. New York: Simon & Schuster.

Cox, W. M., & Klinger, E. (Eds.). (2004). *The handbook of motivational counseling: Concepts, approaches, & assessment*. West Sussex, England: John Wiley & Sons, Inc.

Davis, M., Eshelman, E. R., & McKay, M. (2008). *The relaxation and stress management workbook* (6th ed.). Oakland, CA: New Harbinger.

De Shazer, S., & Berg, I. (1988). Doing therapy: A post-structural revision. *Journal of Marital and Family Therapy, 18*, 71–81.

DeBecker, G. (1997). *The gift of fear: Survival signs that protect us from violence*. Boston: Little Brown.

Dixon, D. N., & Glover, J. A. (1984). *Counseling: A problem-solving approach*. New York: John Wiley & Sons.

Eggland, E. T. (1988). Charting: How and why to document your care daily and fully. *Nursing, 18*(11), 76–84.

Ellis, A. (2001). *Overcoming destructive beliefs, feelings, and behaviors*. Amherst, NY: Prometheus Books.

Garcia, J., Salo, M., & Hamilton, W. M. (1995). Report of the ACA Ethics Committee: 1994–1995. *Journal of Counseling & Development, 72*, 221–224.

Ginter, E. J., & Glauser, A. (2001). Effective use of the DSM from a developmental wellness perspective. In E. R. Welfal & R. E. Ingersoll (Eds.), *The mental health desk reference* (pp. 69–77). New York: John Wiley & Sons, Inc.

Gladding, S. T. (1990). Coming full cycle: Reentry after the group. *Journal for Specialists in Group Work, 15,* 130–131.

Gladding, S. T. (2009). *Counseling: A comprehensive profession* (6th ed.). Upper Saddle River, NJ: Merrill/Prentice Hall.

Glasser, W. H. (2004). *Warning: Psychiatry can be hazardous to your health.* Alexandria, VA: American Counseling Association.

Glosoff, H. L., Herlihy, B., & Spence, E. B. (2000). Privileged communication in the counselor-client relationship. *Journal of Counseling & Development, 78*(4), 454–462.

Goldstein, A. P. (1971). *Psychotherapeutic attraction.* New York: Pergamon Press.

Goodyear, R. K. (1981). Termination as a loss experience for the counselor. *Personnel and Guidance Journal, 59,* 347–350.

Granello, D. H., & Granello, P. F. (2007). *Suicide: An Essential guide for helping professionals and educators.* New York: Pearson/Allyn & Bacon.

Gustafson, K. E., & McNamara, J. R. (1987). Confidentiality with minor clients: Issues and guidelines for therapists. *Professional Psychology: Research and Practice, 18,* 503–508.

Guy, J. D. (1987). *The personal life of the psychotherapist.* New York: John Wiley & Sons, Inc.

Haller, R. M., & Deluty, R. H. (1990). Characteristics of psychiatric inpatients who assault staff severely. *Journal of Nervous and Mental Disease, 178*(8), 536–537.

Handelsman, M. M. (2001). Accurate and effective informed consent. In E. R. Welfel & R. E. Ingersoll (Eds.), *The mental health desk reference* (pp. 453–458). New York: John Wiley & Sons, Inc.

Harding, A, Gray, L., & Neal, M. (1993). Confidentiality limits with clients who have HIV: A review of ethical and legal guidelines and professional policies. *Journal of Counseling & Development, 71*(1) 297–305.

Hart, J., Berndt, R., & Caramazza, A. (1985). Category specific naming deficit following cerebral infractions. *Nature, 316,* 339–340.

Helms, J. E., & Cook, D. A. (1999). *Using race and culture in counseling and psychotherapy: Theory and process.* Boston: Allyn & Bacon.

Herlihy, B., & Corey, G. (1997). Codes of ethics as catalysts for improving practice. In B. Herlihy & G. Corey (Eds.), *Ethics in therapy* (pp. 37–56). New York: Hatherleigh.

Herlihy, B., & Corey, G. (2006). *Boundary issues in counseling: Multiple roles and responsibilities* (2nd ed.). Alexandria, VA: American Counseling Association.

Hodges, S. (2009, March). Counseling in the twenty-first century: Challenges and opportunities. *Counseling Today, 51*(9), 44–47.

Hodges, S., & Connelly, A. R. (2010). *A job search manual for counselors and counselor educators: How to navigate and promote your counseling career.* Alexandria, VA: American Counseling Association.

Hood, A. B., & Johnson, R. W. (2007). *Assessment in counseling: A guide to the use of psychological assessment procedures.* Alexandria, VA: American Counseling Association.

Housman, L. M, & Stake, J. E. (1999). The current state of sexual ethics training in clinical psychology: Issues of quantity, quality, and effectiveness. *Professional Psychology: Research and Practice, 30*(3), 302–311.

Ingersoll, R. E. (1998). Refining dimensions of spiritual wellness: A cross-traditional approach. *Counseling and Values, 42,* 156–165.

Ivey, A. E., & Ivey, M. B. (2007). *Intentional interviewing and counseling: Facilitating development in a multicultural society* (6th ed.). Belmont, CA: Thomson Brooks/Cole.

Jaffee v. Redmond et al. 1996 WL 314841 (U.S. June 13, 1996).

Johnson, W. B., Ralph, J., & Johnson, S. J. (2005). Managing multiple roles in embedded environments: The case of aircraft carrier psychology. *Professional Psychology: Research and Practice, 36,* 73–81.

Juhnke, G. (1996). The Adapted SAD PERSONS: A suicide assessment scale designed for use with children. *Elementary School Guidance & Counseling, 30,* 252–258.

Kadushin, A. (1985). *Supervision in social work* (2nd ed.). New York: Columbia University Press.

Kinney, J. A. (1995). *Violence at work: How to make your company safer for employees and customers.* Englewood Cliffs, NJ: Prentice Hall.

Kiselica, M. S. (1999). Confronting my own ethnocentrism and racism: A process of pain and growth. *Journal of Counseling & Development, 77,* 14–17.

Kraus, K., Kleist, D., & Cashwell, D. (2009, September). Professional identity: ACES, CACREP, NBCC share concerns. *Counseling Today 52/*, p. 60, NBCC perspective.

Kubler-Ross, E. (1969). *On death and dying*. New York: Macmillan Publishing, Co.

Lamb, D., & Catanzaro, S. (1998). Sexual and nonsexual boundary violations involving psychologists, clients, supervisees, and students: Implications for professional practice. *Professional Psychology: Research and Practice, 29*(5), 498–503.

Lazarus, A. A., & Zur, O. (Eds.). (2002). *Dual relationships and psychotherapy*. New York: Springer.

Lee, C. C. (2001). Culturally responsive school counselors and programs: Addressing the needs of all students. *Professional School Counseling, 4*, 257–261.

Lee, C. C. (Ed.). (2003). *Multicultural issues in counseling: New approaches to diversity* (3rd ed.). Alexandria, VA: American Counseling Association.

Lee, C. C. (Ed.). (2006). *Counseling for social justice*. Alexandria, VA: American Counseling Association.

Linde, L. (2010, May). From the president: Counseling is. . . . *Counseling Today, 52/11*, p. 5, 37.

Madden, R. G. (1998). *Legal issues in social work, counseling, and mental health*. Thousand Oaks, CA: Sage.

Mahoney, M. J. (1997). Psychotherapists' personal problems and self-care patterns. *Professional Psychology: Research and Practice, 28*, 14–16.

Maholick, L. T., & Turner, D. W. (1979). Termination: The difficult farewell. *American Journal of Psychotherapy, 33*, 583–591.

May, R. (1981). *Freedom and destiny*. New York: Norton

McClarren, G. M. (1987). The psychiatric duty to warn: Walking a tightrope of uncertainty. *University of Cincinnati Law Review, 56*, 269–293.

McGlothen, J. M., Rainey, S., & Kindsvatter, A. (2005). Suicidal clients and supervisees: A model for considering supervisor roles. *Counselor Education and Supervision, 45*, 135–146.

McIntosh, P. (1998). White privilege, color, and crime: A personal account. In C. R. Mann & M. S. Zatz (Eds.), *Images of color, images of crime* (pp. 207–216). Los Angeles: Roxbury.

Miller, D. J., & Thelan, M. H. (1986). Knowledge and beliefs about confidentiality in psychotherapy. *Professional Psychology: Research and Practice, 17*, 15–19.

Miller, S. D., Hubble, M. A., & Duncan, B. L. (1996). *Handbook of solution-focused brief therapy*. San Francisco: Jossey-Bass.

Miller, W. R., & Rollnick, S. (2002). *Motivational interviewing: Preparing people for change* (2nd ed.). New York: Guilford Press.

Mitchell, R. W. (2007). *Documentation in counseling records: An overview of ethical, legal, and clinical issues* (3rd ed.). Alexandria, VA: American Counseling Association.

Moore, K. (2010, February 3). Residents demand answers after S. Hadley bullying death. *The Boston Globe*, B3.

Myers, J. E., & Sweeney, T. J. (Eds.). (2005). *Counseling for wellness: Theory, research, and practice*. Alexandria, VA: American Counseling Association.

Myers, J. E., Sweeney, T. J., & Witmer, J. M. (2000). The Wheel of Wellness counseling for wellness: A holistic model for treatment planning. *Journal of Counseling & Development, 78*(3), 251–266.

National Board for Certified Counselors. (2009). *About us*. Retrieved June 2, 2010, from http://www.nbcc.org/

Neukrug, E., Milliken, T., & Walden, S. (2001). Ethical complaints made against credentialed counselors: An updated survey of state licensing boards. *Counselor Education and Supervision, 41*, 57–70.

Norcross, J. C., Strausser, D. J., & Faltus, F. J. (1988). The therapist's therapist. *American Journal of Psychotherapy, 42*, 53–66.

O'Hanlon, W. H. (1994). The third wave: The promise of narrative. *The Family Therapy Networker, 18*(6), 19–26, 28–29.

Okun, B. F., & Kantrowitz, R. E. (2008). *Effective helping: Interviewing and counseling techniques* (7th ed.). Belmont, CA: Thomson Brooks/Cole.

Patterson, W. M., Dohn, H. H., Bird, J., & Patterson, G. A. (1983). Evaluation of suicidal patients: The SAD PERSON scale. *Psychosomatics, 24*(4), 343–349.

Pedersen, P. B. (1994). *A handbook for developing multicultural awareness* (2nd ed.). Alexandria, VA: American Counseling Association.

Pedersen, P. B., Draguns, J. G., Lonner, W. J., & Trimble, J. E. (Eds.). (2002). *Counseling across cultures* (5th ed.). Thousand Oaks, CA: Sage.

Perls, F. S. (1969). *Gestalt therapy verbatim.* Lafayette, CA: Real People Press.

Pietrofesa, J. J., Hoffman, A., & Splete, H. H. (1984). *Counseling: An introduction* (2nd ed.). Boston: Houghton Mifflin.

Polanski, P. J., & Hinkle, J. S. (2000). The mental status examination: Its use by professional counselors. *Journal of Counseling & Development, 78,* 357–364.

Pope, K. S., & Tabachnick, B. G. (1994). Therapists as patients: A national survey of psychologists' experiences, problems, and beliefs. *Professional Psychology: Research and Practice, 25,* 247–258.

Pope, K. S., Tabachnick, B. G., & Keith-Spiegel, P. (1987). Good and poor practices in psychotherapy: National survey of beliefs of psychologists. *Professional Psychology: Research and Practice, 19,* 547–552.

Pope, K. S., & Vasquez, M. J. T. (1998). *Ethics in psychotherapy and counseling: A practical guide for psychologists* (2nd ed.). San Francisco: Jossey-Bass.

Prosser, W. L., Wade, J. W., & Schwartz, V. E. (1988). *Cases and materials on torts* (8th ed.). Westbury, NY: The Foundation Press.

Reeser, L. C., & Wertkin, P. A.(2001). Safety training in a social work education: A national survey. *Journal of Teaching in Social Work, 21,* 95–114.

Remley, T. P., & Herlihy, B. (2007). *Ethical, legal and professional issues in counseling* (2nd ed.). Upper Saddle River, NJ: Pearson.

Ridley, C. R. (2005). *Overcoming unintentional racism in counseling and therapy.* Thousand Oaks, CA: Sage.

Rogers, C. R. (1942). *Counseling and psychotherapy.* Boston: Houghton-Mifflin.

Rogers, C. R. (1951). *Client centered therapy.* New York: Houghton-Mifflin.

Rokeach, M. (1979). *Understanding human values: Individual and societal.* New York: Simon & Schuster.

Romans, J. S. C., Hays, J. R., & White, T. K. (1996). Stalking and related behaviors experienced by counseling center staff members from current or former clients. *Professional Psychology: Research and Practice, 27,* 595–599.

Saltzman, M., & D'Andrea, M. (2001). Assessing the impact of a prejudice prevention project. *Journal of Counseling & Development, 79,* 341–346.

Schwartz, R. C., & Feisthamel, K. P. (2009). Disproportionate diagnosis of mental disorders among African American versus European American clients: Implications for counseling, theory, research, and practice. *Journal of Counseling & Development, 87,* 295–301.

Seligman, L. A. (2004). *Diagnosis and treatment planning in counseling* (3rd ed.). New York: Kluwer.

Seligman, M. E. P. (1998). *Learned optimism* (2nd ed.). New York: Pocket Books.

Sodowsky, G. R., Taffe, R. C., Gutkin, T. B., & Wise, S. (1994). Development of the Multicultural Counseling Inventory (MCI): A self-report measure of multicultural competencies. *Journal of Counseling Psychology, 41,* 137–148.

Sommers-Flanagan, R. S., & Sommers-Flanagan, J. S. (1999). *Clinical interviewing* (2nd ed.). New York: John Wiley & Sons.

St. Germaine, J. (1993). Dual relationships: What's wrong with them? *American Counselor, 2,* 25–30.

Sudders, M. (2010, January 27). Kerrigan family faced dilemma with their adult son. *Boston Globe,* B6.

Sue, D. W. (1996). Ethical issues in multicultural counseling. In B. Herlihy & G. Corey (Eds.), *ACA ethical standards casebook* (5th ed., pp. 193–197). Alexandria, VA: American Counseling Association.

Sue, D. W., & Sue, D. (1998). *Counseling the culturally different: Theory and practice* (3rd ed.). New York: John Wiley & Sons, Inc.

Sue, D. W., Arredondo, P., & McDavis, R. J. (1992). Multicultural counseling competencies and standards: A call to the profession. *Journal of Multicultural Counseling & Development, 20,* 64–88.

Tarasoff v. The Regents of the University of California, 13 Cal. 3d 177, 529 P.2d. 533 (1976).

Thackery, M., & Bobbit, R. G. (1990). Patient aggression against clinical and nonclinical staff in a VA medical center. *Hospital and Community Psychiatry, 41,* 195–197.

Thapar v. Zezulka, 994 S. W. 2nd 635 (Tex. 1999).

Tomm, K. (1993, January/February). The ethics of dual relationships. *The California Therapist,* 7–19.

Tully, C. T., Kropf, N. P., & Price, J. L. (1993). Is the field a hard hat area? A study of violence in field placements. *Journal of Social Work Education, 29,* 191–199.

Tunnecliffe, M. (2007). *A life in crisis: 27 lessons from acute trauma counseling work.* Palmyra, Western Australia: Bayside.

Van der Kolk, B. (1994). The body keeps score. *Harvard Review of Psychiatry, 1*(5), 253–265.

Wampold, B. E. (2001). *The great psychotherapy debate: Models, methods, and findings.* Mahwah, NJ: Lawrence Erlbaum Associates.

Ward, D. E. (1984). Termination of individual counseling: Concepts and strategies. *Journal of Counseling and Development, 63,* 21–25.

Wehrly, B. (1991). Preparing multicultural counselors. *Counseling and Human Development, 24*(3), 1–24.

Weinhold, B. K., & Weinhold, J. B. (2009). *Conflict resolution: The partnership way,* (2nd ed.). Denver, CO: Love Publishing Co.

Weinrach, S. G. (1989). Guidelines for clients of private practitioners: Committing the structure to print. *Journal of Counseling & Development, 67,* 299–300.

Welfel, E. R. (2006). *Ethics in counseling and psychotherapy: Standards, research, and Emerging issues* (3rd ed.). Pacific Grove, CA: Thomson Brooks/Cole.

Welfel, E. R. (2010). *Ethics in counseling and psychotherapy: Standards, research, and emerging issues* (4th ed.). Belmont, CA: Brooks/Cole-Cengage.

Welfel, E. R., & Patterson, L. E. (2005). *The counseling process: A multitheoretical integrated approach* (6th ed.). Belmont, CA: Thomson Brooks/Cole.

Wheeler, A. M., & Bertram, B. (2008). *The Counselor and the law: A guide to legal and ethical practice.* Alexandria, VA: American Counseling Association.

Whitman, R. M., Armao, B. B., & Dent, O. B. (1976). Assault on the therapist. *American Journal of Psychiatry, 133,* 424–429.

Wilbur, M. P., Roberts-Wilbur, J., Morris, J. R., Betz, R. L., & Hart, G. M. (1991). Structured group supervision: Theory into practice. *Journal for Specialists in Group Work, 16,* 91–100.

Williams, A. (1995). *Visual and active supervision: Roles, focus, technique.* New York: W. W. Norton.

Witmer, J. M., & Granello, P. F. (2005). Wellness in counselor education and supervision. In J. E. Myers & T. J. Sweeney (Eds.), *Counseling for wellness: Theory, research, and practice.* Alexandria, VA: American Counseling Association.

Wrenn, G. (1962). *The counselor in a changing world.* Washington, DC: American Personnel and Guidance Association.

Yalom, I., & Leszcz, M. (2005). *The theory and practice of group psychotherapy* (5th ed.). New York: Basic Books.

Index

Note: An *f* following a page number indicates a figure, a *t* indicates a table.